Waving the Gentlemen's business goodbye

European University Studies
Europäische Hochschulschriften
Publications Universitaires Européennes

Series II
Law

Reihe II Série II
Rechtswissenschaft
Droit

Vol./Bd. 2305

PETER LANG
Frankfurt am Main · Berlin · Bern · New York · Paris · Wien

Christine Stammel

Waving the Gentlemen's business goodbye

From global deals to global disputes in the London reinsurance market

PETER LANG
Europäischer Verlag der Wissenschaften

Die Deutsche Bibliothek - CIP-Einheitsaufnahme

Stammel, Christine:

Waving the gentlemen's business goodbye : from global deals to global disputes in the London reinsurance market / Christine Stammel. - Frankfurt am Main ; Berlin ; Bern ; New York ; Paris ; Wien : Lang, 1998

(European university studies : Ser. 2, Law ; Vol. 2305)
Zugl.: Bremen, Univ., Diss., 1997
ISBN 3-631-32585-1

D 46
ISSN 0531-7312
ISBN 3-631-32585-1
US-ISBN 0-8204-3537-6

Printed in Germany 1 2 4 5 6 7

Contents

Acknowledgements

Several people have kindly contributed to the development of this project, which is a co-operation between the *Zentrum für Europäische Rechtspolitik (ZERP)*, University of Bremen and the *Centre for Socio-Legal Studies*, University of Oxford. Firstly, I would like to thank everyone at the Centre for Socio-Legal Studies, where I spent most of the time researching for this study, for their support and the use of the facilities there. Secondly, I wish to thank my supervisor Prof. Dr. Volkmar Gessner for admitting me into the research team for cross-border legal interaction. Many London law firms have been so kind as to give me some of their valuable time for an interview. Regrettably, a statement of confidentiality prevents the author from naming the participants involved in the study. However, I shall at this point take the opportunity to thank everyone for his or her time and co-operation. This thesis could not have been written without the information and support received. The German Volkswagen Foundation awarded a major research grant within its program 'Law and Behaviour' to the Zentrum für Europäische Rechtspolitik at the University of Bremen. This grant has provided the indispensable financial basis for this project.

1. Introduction

1.1 General

The opening up of borders and the internationalisation of industrial and commercial activities have had the effect of intensifying international trade and of enabling persons and goods to move freely within new geographic areas. As goods cross an increasing number of borders, there is a increase in the number of the situations in which products may cause injury or damage to consumers in countries other than the one in which the products were manufactured. The intensification of trade has, therefore, quite naturally been accompanied by an increased need for insurance, as the enterprises engaging in international trade see an ever-increasing growth in their risk exposure, both to their trading partners and to the consumers for whom their products are intended. Insurance companies must essentially cope with this new situation and prepare themselves in particular for the eventuality of being held liable in other countries under foreign law on grounds different to those which they are used to seeing adopted in their home countries. They must therefore give themselves the means to accompany their policyholders at all stages of their business, in order to assist them as effectively as possible in the difficulties they will surely encounter.

Insurers are not the only ones who have to adapt to this situation. Reinsurers too, must be capable of coping with the new aspects of international trade if they intend, as in the past, *„to follow the fortune of the insurer"*.[1] The reinsurer functions as a back-up for the insurer. He takes the whole risk, or a portion of it from the insurer and the latter is thus able to reduce the amount of his prospective loss. The legal bond between insurer and reinsurer is the reinsurance agreement or contract. The discussion of international disputes and the solution of cross-border legal conflicts in the context of reinsurance disputes is therefore conducted as one aspect of the globalisation discussion.

Globalisation has become a widely used term within the media business, as well as within financial and intellectual circles, underlying the widespread perception that modern communication technology has made the world a smaller

1 Christian Boukart, „Autonomy of choice for dispute resolution", Paper and Talk presented at the BILA London Colloquium on International Insurance and Reinsurance Arbitration, 22nd July 1996, London

place. A scientific definition was offered by McGrew in which globalisation refers to the multiplicity of links and interconnections that transcend the nation-states (and by implication the societies) which make up the modern world system.[2] It defines a process through which events, decisions, and activities in one part of the world can come to have significant consequences for individuals and communities in quite distant parts of the globe. Nowadays, goods, capital, people, knowledge, images, communications, crime and culture flow readily aross territorial boundaries. Transnational networks, social movements and relationships are extensive in virtually all areas of human activity. Consequently, it may be argued that territorial boundaries are increasingly insignificant since social activity and relations no longer stop at those boundaries.

However, what may be true for social activities and economical transactions may not apply to the law and to the resulting rights. The function of the law in the globalisation process has been made subject to research only recently. Whereas scientists of other disciplines such as politics or sociology have already accumulated knowledge on the globalization process, e.g. its influence on cultural identity[3] and on environmental issues[4], legal sociology has tackled this issue only recently. Nevertheless, legal sociological views might fruitfully complement what has so far been produced in other disciplines, as legal sociological approaches point to structural elements without which neither intercultural communication nor economic exchange can be effectively realised.[5]

Exploring the means by which cross-border conflicts are resolved and examining the effectiveness of law in cross-border conflicts can contribute to the discussion of globalisation. The assumption that the enforcement of legal claims becomes more difficult if those claims have to be enforced across boundaries, can now be supported by empirical evidence. These particular difficulties have been described in empirical studies for the commercial[6] and private[7] sector. The

---

2 Anthony McGrew, „A Global Society ?“ in: *Modernity and its Futures*, Cambridge, 1992, 61-102 (65)

3 Stuart Hall, „The Question of Cultural Identity“ in: *Modernity and its Futures*, Cambridge, 1992, 273-325

4 Steven Yearley, „Enviromental Challenges“ in: *Modernity and its Futures*, Cambridge, 1992, 117-166

5 Volkmar Gessner, „The Globalization of Legal Certainty“ in: Volkmar Gessner, Ali Cem Budak (eds.) *Cross-border legal interactions*, Empirical Studies on the Globalisation of Law, Forthcoming

6 Ali Cem Budak, „The Infrastructure of cross-border debt collection: Examples in Turkey and Germany“ in: Volkmar Gessner, Ali Cem Budak (Eds.), *Cross-border legal interactions,*Empirical Studies on the Globalisation of Law, Forthcoming

first study comes to the conclusion that even if parties prudently procure securities before granting various types of credit, they have to follow cumbersome, costly and inefficient ways of collecting their claims. The results of this particular study indicate that the „infrastructure of cross-border debt collection" is provided, if not pre-dominantly, to a considerable extent by autonomously created structures which successfully substitute the national state-based enforcement mechanisms.[8] Budak suggests that alternative methods should be developed to further the globalisation of commercial relations and to achieve speedy legal results. The role of national states in cross-border, as well as in the domestic enforcement of debts, must be reduced in the future – or at least be extended – to supervising and controlling privatised debt collection, instead of enforcing the law itself. The second study, which deals with children's maintenance claims, acknowledges that the assistance of the courts is not relied upon in obtaining and enforcing cross-border maintenance titles. In her study, Grotheer[9] explains that private support agencies, such as the German Institute for Guardianship, are set up to help creditors enforce such claims and obtain their money.

The effectiveness of national courts in the resolution of cross-border disputes was, until quite recently, not subject to a systematic empirical approach. One particular publication takes a step in this direction by looking at the role of national courts in cross-border legal interaction.[10] In examining the effectiveness of national courts in dealing with cross-border cases, this study supports the conclusion that national courts may be ineffective and may even increase transaction costs in international matters. They may be inexperienced, inadequately organised for this type of case or even biased against foreign parties. They may or may not take into consideration foreign elements of the cases, just as they may or may not understand other legal systems and legal cultures. There is also the possibility that they are unfamiliar with the impressive number of uniform and international legal conventions .

With reference to the respective courts, von Freyhold[11] for the New York District Court, comes to the conclusion that conflicts are, more often than not,

---

7 Kirsten Grotheer, „Structures of the enforcement of cross-border maintainance claims of children" in: Volkmar Gessner Ali Cem Budak (Eds.) *Cross-border legal interactions*, Empirical Studies on the Globalisation of Law, Forthcoming

8 Ali Cem Budak, ibid, 34/35

9 Kirsten Grotheer, ibid

10 Volkmar Gessner (Ed.), *Foreign Courts: Civil Litigation in Foreign Legal Cultures*, Aldershot: Dartmouth, 1996

11 Hanno von Freyhold, „Cross-border Legal Interaction in New York Courts" , in: Volkmar Gessner (Ed.), *Foreign Courts: Civil Litigation in Foreign Legal Cultures*, 42-148 (143)

simply resolved by abandonment of the perceived right. Such a reaction may even be anticipated in the risk calculation in advance of the international interaction by calculating different prices, taking out insurance or by adopting an attitude to the transaction which is somewhat similar to an expectation of a lottery, rather than a calculated assumption of success. This suggests that companies litigating in foreign jurisdictions take it as given that they may not be able to succeed despite having a justified claim, at least in the New York courts where this study has been conducted.

Regarding the use of statutes regulating international matters, the conclusion can be drawn that it seems- despite scholarly approaches to Conflicts of Laws, comity and international treaties providing for recognition of foreign court proceedings and judgments- unlikely that a claim involving a foreign party will be brought to and positively concluded in court. As far as judgments are concerned, it appears that in cases where the plaintiff was successful, these judgments will in practice be enforceable only against assets in New York itself.[12] Results of studies on the Continent[13] show a differentiated brighter picture of what national courts are able to achieve with respect to the resolution of cross-border disputes. In his study of 'International Cases in German first instance Courts', Gessner states that although in terms of the internationalisation of legal thinking, globalisation has simply not reached German civil procedure ... international cases are taken to German courts and these courts are managing them quite effectively in terms of time outcome. German courts therefore play a role in global legal interaction, handling and deciding cases according to German rules and procedures.

He continues to point out that taking into account the astonishing number of foreign plaintiffs who voluntarily use the German jurisdiction, this may be exactly what both parties in conflict want. Assuming the rationality of the parties and their legal counsel in choosing their forum one must conclude that the German forum is considered adequate for certain kinds of cases, namely those where there is little at stake and low in legal complexity, and for cases where cultural differences between parties are considered unimportant. All other cases – and this may be the great majority – are resolved elsewhere, either in foreign fora where a more adequate law than the German law is applied or in fora with a more global reputation or by arbitration and non-judicial procedures developed for specific branches, conflict areas and groups of persons. These abovementioned studies provide evidence that national courts and infrastructure alone

12 Hanno von Freyhold, ibid, (144)

13 Volkmar Gessner, „International Cases in German First Instance Courts", in: Gessner/Budak (Eds.) *Foreign Courts: Civil litigation in Foreign legal cultures,* 149-207 Vittorio Olgiatti, „Cross-border Litigotiation in Italy", ibid, 209-247

are either unable or have only limited capability to handle cross-border legal disputes. It comes therefore as no surprise that in cases were global players with the possibility to sustain world-wide communication, try to circumvent the traditional structures of dispute resolution in their cross-border legal conflicts. Areas of global financial transactions have become involved in and subject to the development of „third cultures“, outside of and transcending nation-state based legal cultures and barriers. In the particular case of cross-border payments this has been proven by an empirical study. [14] Frick[15] describes in his essay the resolution of cross-border money transfers by banks. The banks have created their own internal system to process such payments on behalf of their customers. Conflicts or legal disputing in the usual way, i.e. going to the courts does not occur. Grounded on a basic understanding of business rules and justice, other more informal ways are used to structure those international relations.

Such behaviour patterns shared and learned by men of different societies in the process of relating their societies have been described as „third culture“[16]. With reference to legal relations, „third legal culture“ represents autonomous structures which have developed international legal relations to bridge legal-cultural differences in the resolution of cross-border conflicts. A "third culture" may be created by major economical players who participate in global legal exchanges. One of the basic assumptions on a "third legal culture" is that most of its exchanges remain outside the system of national courts and even outside national legal systems. The reasons for those „third cultures“ may be manifold. On the one hand, repeat players tend not to destroy the mutual trust for business by disputing formally. On the other hand, courts are not deemed to be the appropriate forum for resolving the disputes of global players because of the peculiarities they involve.

Among the areas that have globally developed a particular autonomy from interference by governments and court is the insurance business. Four main aspects of insurance, namely actual acceptance of the risk, premiums, conditions, and loss recovery all involve intricate legal questions as well as significant commercial questions. However, when it comes to large sums, international transactions and special areas of insurance, e.g., the reinsurance business, con-

14 Klaus Frick, „The Infrastructure of cross-border payments“ in: *Cross- border legal interactions*, Empirical Studies on the Globalisation of Law, Forthcoming

15 Klaus Frick, ibid.

16 John Useem, et. al. (1963), Men in the Middle of Third Culture: The Role of American and Non-Western People in Cross-Cultural Administration, Human Organisation 22; 169-179, cited in: Volkmar Gessner and Angelika Schade, „Conflicts of Culture in Cross- border Legal Relations: The Conception of a Research Topic in Sociology of Law“, in: *Theory, Culture & Society,* Vol. 7, (1990), (253- 277) 259

flicts and court decisions seemed to be rare, at least between the reinsurers and their clients, the ceding offices. Historically, a reinsurance contract has been viewed to be a „gentlemen's agreement". In this „gentlemen's agreement" the participants relied upon the good faith and integrity of one another without contesting the degree to which the technical elements of their contracts had been adhered to or satisfied.[17] The reinsurer usually looked upon his relationship with his reinsured on a long-term basis. On this long term basis, he would remain as a participant and share the reinsured's risk year after year after year. He knew that if the reinsured made money, he would do so as well; conversely, the years in which the reinsured suffered losses, he would equitably and contractually share the burden with his reinsured. Considering the continuing relationship between the parties, the reinsurer would come to know, respect, and rely upon the underwriting and claims handling expertise of the reinsured's personnel. The reinsured, on the other hand, was aware of the long-term relationship surrounding the reinsurance contract. He did not wish to jeopardise the additional financial capacity made available to him by the existence of the reinsurance protection. Therefore he would generally seek to protect his reinsurer's interests to the same extent that he would protect his own.

Until approximately 15 years ago, the reinsurance industry seemed to be a typical example for a „third legal culture" in the sense that disputes did not come to public attention. This may be either because disputes did not occur or because those disputes were solved within the reinsurance industry. Until this time the reinsurance industry seemed to follow the above described pattern to bypass traditional state provided and judicially controlled means of dispute resolution. Today, of course, we live in more litigious times and this is no more evident than in the context of reinsurance. In general, the volume of reinsurance transactions has increased to a significant extent on a world-wide basis. Reinsurance relationships have become temporary in nature. Those reinsured shop around for cheaper forms of reinsurance. The younger reinsurance companies agree to provide such protection in order to accumulate the investment income from the newly acquired premiums and underlying losses and claims have escalated to enormous proportions.[18]

For a long period, legislators, in many parts of the world, avoided the problems arising from writing insurance policies across state boundaries, both as to the rights of the buyers of such insurance and the enforceability of contracts

17 Thomas R. Cherry, „Reinsurance in the United States – Legal and Practical Aspects", DYP Course documentation, London 1991, 4

18 Thomas R. Cherry, ibid

against the issuers thereof.[19] Reinsurance, a sector which is, by its very nature, is atypical to other daily commercial activities, as well as international in scope, has therefore tended to escape the legislators' attention – other than as a possible source of revenue. The experience of recent years could show that legal problems are of considerably greater importance. Fundamental changes concerning the course of business and results in the reinsurance market since the end of the 80's have resulted in a reassessment of the relationship between reinsurer and cedant.[20] Ten or fifteen years ago, reinsurers paid even the most dubious claims of cedants out of goodwill. Reinsurers nowadays take increasingly critical views on claims managing. Additionally, intermediaries, such as brokers, have to reassess their roles. This applies to their position in paving the way towards reinsurance contracts and collaboration in closing the deals.

These changes have not gone by without having influenced the conflict avoidance and resolution mechanism systems in reinsurance, dominated by major international actors who participate in global legal exchange. The reinsurers and their clients belong to this category. One attribute of the group of social players gives the study additional significance in the sense that reinsurance disputes have traditionally been international but only since comparatively recently have entered the courts. The study elaborates the legal structures of reinsurance and looks at how the actions of the participants shape its legal development and dispute behaviour.

1.2 Cross-border legal interaction and "third cultures"

For the purpose of this study *cross-border legal interaction* shall refer to legal interaction of private parties being residents of different states or conducting business in different countries or having to fulfil duties resulting from their relationships in places other than where this obligation arose. These interactions must contain a foreign element. Foreign element means any contact with some system of law other than national. The term „international" dispute may also apply when the parties of a dispute are non-nationals[21]. The question arises, how cross-border legal interactions are co-ordinated in the first place, and how they

19 C.E. Golding, *The Law and Practice of Reinsurance*, 5th ed., Witherby & Co. Ltd., London, 1987, 16

20 Davies Arnold Cooper Reports, *Back to the Basics – Reinsurance Retro- Chic*, London: January 1994

21 Dicey and Morris, *Conflict of Laws*, 12 ed., Vol. I, Sweet & Maxwell, London, 1993, 3

are dcalt with when the relationship between the parties ends. The focus here is on commercial cross-border interactions.

With regard to the law itself, Private International Law (Conflict of Laws), internationally unified law and in EEC countries, legislation resulting from harmonisation within the European Community (e.g. Treaties of Rome) govern cross-border legal relations. The expression „Private International Law“ was coined by Story in 1834 and is used in most civil law countries.[22] The chief criticism directed against its use is its tendency to confuse private international law with law of nations or public international law. There are two obvious differences between the two. The latter primarily governs the relations between sovereign states. It may perhaps be regarded as the common law of mankind in an early state of development. The former is designed to regulate private disputes, notwithstanding that one of the parties may be a sovereign state. Despite this criticism „Private International Law“ is generally accepted and applied for disputes of private nature in cross-border contexts.

According to Kegel, the unification of Private International Law is based on the comparison of the same, because one has to know the laws which one intends to unify.[23] But the unification of law is not a science, it is a reform. In this reform, movements of codification which started in the 18th century are completed with the crossing of state boundaries in the 20th century. However, a world-wide Private International Law is far from reach. The contrasts between „Continental Law“ (the law on the European continent influenced by Roman law), „civil law“ on the one hand and the Anglo-American law on the other are too great. As far as material Private Law and therefore an identical decision on all cases cannot be achieved, there must be at least an attempt to come to a coherent set of rules regarding International Private Law and an identical decision on all cases in accordance with these laws.

Two possible ways exist to ameliorate the lack of unanimity among the various systems of private international law.[24] The first is to ensure the unification of the internal laws of the various countries on as many legal topics as possible by international conventions. If one pays attention to the fundamental differences in principle that distinguish one legal system from another, especially in the common law systems as opposed to their civil law counterparts, it is obvious that this form of unification holds out no great prospect of success. Nevertheless, a few departments of law where this unity is imperative and possible have made a cer-

---

22 Cheshire and North's, *Private International Law*, 12th edition, Butterworths, London, 1992, 12

23 Gerhard Kegel, *Internationales Privatrecht*, München, Beck, 1987, 43

24 Cheshire and North's, *Private International Law*, 12th edition, 1992, 9;10

tain amount of progress. An important example of unification is the Warsaw Convention of 1929 as amended at The Hague 1955. The Guadalajara Convention, 1961,[25] supplemented the Warsaw Convention. It made the international carriage of persons or goods by aircraft for reward subject to uniform rules regarding both jurisdiction and the applicable law. It states that any agreement by the parties purporting to alter the rules on these matters shall be null and void. Worth mentioning is also the Berne Convention of 1886, amended several times, at which an international union for the protection of the rights of authors over their literary and artistic works was formed. The Council of the League of Nations entrusted to the Institute for the Unification of Private Laws – UNIDROIT. UNIDROIT had the task to indicate the lines along which further unification might be attained. An important result of its labours, in conjunction with those of the Hague Conference, was the establishment of a convention at The Hague in 1964, establishing a uniform set of rules on international sales of goods and also on the formation of contracts for such sales. The United Kingdom accepted the convention and the rules contained. They were incorporated in the Uniform Laws on International Sales Act 1967. If their provisions apply, they exclude the rules of private international law. There is now a successor to the 1964 Convention, the United Nations Convention on Contracts for the International Sale of Goods (1980). It was prepared under the auspices of another body concerned with the unification of law, the United Nations Committee on International Trade Law – UNCITRAL.[26]

The second method by which the inconvenience that results from conflicting national rules may be diminished, is to unify those rules of private international law. This aims at ensuring that a case containing a foreign element shall result in the same decision irrespective of the country of its trial.[27] In 1951 a charter was drafted designed to place the Hague Conference on a lasting footing, by the establishment of a permanent bureau. The chief functions of this bureau are to examine and prepare proposals for the unification of private international law. It keeps in touch with the Council of Europe and with governmental and non-governmental organisations, such as the International Law Association. In addition to the conventions mentioned above many similar arrangements have been made between individual countries. An example is the bilateral conventions on civil procedure, concluded by the United Kingdom with a large number of foreign states. An example of a limited multilateral convention is that concluded in

25 This was part of the law of the United Kingdom by the Carriage by Air (Supplementary Provisions) Act 1962.

26 For a detailed description on treaties for the unification of law see: Gerhard Kegel, *Internationales Privatrecht,* München, Beck 1987, 43-77

27 Cheshire and North's, Private International Law, 12th edition, 1992, London, 11

1969[28] between the Benelux states – Belgium, the Netherlands and Luxembourg. This convention unifies the rules of private international law on the more important matters, such as capacity and status, succession to property on death and essential validity of contracts.[29]

Finally, the European Community creates uniform Community law and also tries to assist in unifying private international law between the Member States.[30] The Convention on contractual obligations was agreed in 1980. There are also directives and regulations containing private international law provisions. The Civil Jurisdiction and Judgments Act 1982 implementing the Convention in Britain is now in force. It governs jurisdiction, the recognition and the enforcement of foreign judgments between Member States of the European Community. An even broader area has been created with the implementation of the 1988 Lugano Convention, extending a similar regime to include also the EFTA countries.

The practical use of those conventions and regulations is often challenged by scholars and practitioners.[31] Although much effort is put into drafting regulations handling the conflicts of law, it may emerge that Private International Law contributes little to solving the dilemma of insecurity of international contracts.[32] This view, shared by practitioners, has also received feed back in literature[33]but the insights into the shortcomings of Private International Law are not new. The reason for the unsatisfactory application of Private International Law may on the one hand be attributed to cultural differences.[34] These cultural differences may become evident by the conditions under which conflicts probably arise or by attitudes and strategies adopted towards conflict.[35] On the other hand, routine and prejudice may be responsible for the fact that the conventions and regulations do not result in the practical use they are aimed at when drafted and probably rati-

28 Replacing a convention of 1951

29 Cheshire and North's, Private International Law, 12th edition, 1992, London, 12

30 Cheshire and North's, Private International Law, 12th edition, 1992, London, 12

31 For a comprehensive overview see: Rene David, *The International Unification of Private Law, International Encyclopedia of Comparative Law*, Volume II, Chapter 5

32 Volkmar Gessner, The Institutional Framework of Cross-border Interaction, in: Volkmar Gessner (Ed.), *Foreign Courts: Civil Litigation in Foreign Legal Cultures*, Aldershot: Dartmouth, 1996

33 Gerhard Kegel, *The Crisis of Conflict of Laws*, Recueil des Cours, Hague Academy of International Law, Vol. 11 (1964), 93

34 Volkmar Gessner and Angelika Schade, „Conflicts of Culture in Cross- border Legal Relations: The Conception of a Research Topic in Sociology of Law", in: *Theory, Culture & Society,* Vol. 7, (1990), 253- 277 (253)

35 Gessner u. Schade, ibid, 258; 259

fied. Routine and prejudice are the reasons which David points out as being obstacles to unification in the first place.[36] These reasons may also account for the lacking application of the unified law. It seems plausible, as David describes, that the spirit of routine in the legal professions prevents the application of law in the sense that arguments are suppressed, which give the case the „foreign element". The same may apply to judges, who may be reluctant to apply collision norms even where required. It may also occur that there be two solutions, adopted in different places, which are equally good in practice. In this case, unification, while desirable, could imply one party sacrificing its procedures without receiving a better answer to the problem.[37]

The reasons for which the creation of unification or the application of unification fail cannot be generalised. But there are findings as to how singular fields of international legal contacts, such as international trade, try to cope with the consequences of a lacking unification of the law. In the late 1920s, there were hints at a development, which Großmann-Doerth described as a developing autonomous or self-created order in world trade.[38] Observations in this direction were later pursued by Schmitthoff. He observed a general trend of commercial law everywhere to move away from the restriction of national law to a universal, international conception of the law of international trade. From these observations, he concluded (1963) [39] that the area of conflict between laws is reduced as the area of the autonomous law of international trade is enlarged. These autonomous rules consist of customs and usage inherent in a specific field of business. Bärmann (1977) supports Schmitthoff's observation. He also maintains a tendency to acknowledge autonomous customs and usage in international trade.[40] He refers to the Hague Convention on the Purchase of Goods[41]. This Convention refers explicitly to commercial practice. Article 9 Paragraph 2 and 3 of the Convention read:

„In the event of conflict with the present law, usage shall prevail unless otherwise agreed by the parties. Where expressions, provisions or forms of contract

---

36 Rene David, *The International Unification of Private Law, International Encyclopedia of Comparative Law*, Volume II, Chapter 5, 5-55

37 David, ibid, 5-56

38 Hans Großmann-Doerth, Der Jurist und das autonome Recht des Welthandels, in: *Juristische Wochenzeitschrift*, 1929, 3447-3449 (3448)

39 Clive M. Schmitthoff, *International Trade Law and Private International Law*, in: Festschrift für Hans Dölle, Vol. II, Internationales Recht, Kollisionsrecht und Internationales Zivilprozessrecht, Tübingen, 1963, 257 – 272 (270)

40 Johannes Bärmann, „Ist Internationales Handelsrecht kodifizierbar ?" in: *International Law and Economic Order*, Essays in Honour of F. Mann, München,1977, 548 – 573

41 Haager Kaufrechtsabkommen vom 1.7.1964 (BGBl.1973 II 885)

commonly used in commercial practise and employed, they shall be interpreted according to the meaning unusually given to them in trade concern."

But even if this retreat to usage may seem a solution, there may also exist reservations about the deviation and rivalry of customs, trade usage and commercial practice with national or international statutory law. Regarding this rivalry, Bärmann concludes that this may, in his opinion, lead to a dilemma of contradictions between the two. The dilemma is even more serious since international trade has only arbitration at its disposal. When it comes to effecting and executing the awards, arbitration itself has to rely on the national jurisdictions. He suggests that it would probably be desirable to give international trade law a universal legislatory framework. However at the same time he points out the limits such attempts of universal legislation face. He maintains, that a uniform international trade law created by states, will encounter the same difficulties as the application of Conflicts of Laws. The regulation of cross-border legal interaction generally finds itself in an area of tension. There is, on the one hand the necessity for a minimum level of legal certainty, but for a degree of essential flexibility on the other. Most authors acknowledge and welcome the application of autonomous rules in the sense of customary usage under pragmatic and utility aspects. However, there is also criticism against their application and a call for the strict application of statutory rules. Bonell (1978) shares this approach[42]. He structures his comments on the autonomous law of international trade according to the criticism which autonomous regulations encounter. From a public policy perspective he supports a transnational approach. He maintains that the application of national or international legislatory rules contrary to the alleged autonomous rules of trade[43] could prevent the international business community from moulding or conducting their business dealings completely independent of government encroachment and control.

The scholarly discussion in literature on cross-border legal interaction has so far shared the focus on the regulations and unification aspect. This discussion lays the foundation for the theoretical norm oriented discussion on the statutory structure of cross-border legal interaction. However there is a new approach that looks at the private ordering of cross-border transactions from a different perspective, which is not norm oriented. Schmidtchen develops the idea of an in-

42 Michael J. Bonell, „Das autonome Recht des Welthandels – rechtsdogmatische und rechtspolitische Aspekte",in: *Rabels Zeitschrift für ausländisches und internationales Privatrecht (RabelZ) 1978* (42) 485-506

43 On the transnational approach see: Eugen Langen, „Vom IPR zum Transnationalen Handelsrecht", in: *Neue Juristische Wochenzeitschrift*, 1969, 358 – 360, Eugen Langen, Transnationales Handelsrecht", in: *Neue Juristische Wochenzeitschrift*, 1969, 2229 – 2233

terdisciplinary research approach in his essay. He maintains that private international trade has taken place under the difficult circumstances of territoriality of law and problems of enforcing the law (legal uncertainty). In his opinion, this is not so much owing to the law of conflict or the regulative influence of co-operating state governments (international constitutional policy). It is the merit of spontaneous forces that have resulted in an almost complete self-regulation of this area of economic life, based upon private initiative *(spontaneous entrepreneurial co-operation)*.[44] These spontaneous forces shape dispute behaviour and are geared by motives which can be assessed as rational and economically countable factors. One such factor may be the probability of re-encountering a business partner, especially in the case of repeat players. In promoting this theory, Schmidtchen falls back on thoughts developed earlier. Macauly[45] (1976) stated, that the use of extra-legal strategies for settling disputes is based on the need to maintain long-term relationships.

Indeed – despite lacking unification or its application, disputes or conflicts must be resolved – especially in trade, even across boundaries. If national courts do not seem the right instruments, other ways must be found to solve such conflicts pragmatically. One way of emerging dispute resolution institutions being state controlled for global players in international transactions is to turn to arbitration. Arbitration seems a venue where autonomous legal rules are being applied.[46] Böckstiegel (1977)[47] maintains that in world trade, international arbitration increasingly replaces national jurisdiction as a decision maker in international trade disputes. At the same time Böckstiegel points in the right direction, that scientific interest and research into arbitration cannot do without the unwritten rules of practice. This applies even more to international arbitration. In international arbitration only little codification exists and the awards are subject to confidentiality. Whilst it is generally true that arbitration provides a more commercial and pragmatic solution to a legal problem, a complete release from the statutory law and judicial control in most jurisdictions is not accepted. This at least applies to the English legal system that is subject to this study. In cases where arbitration is subject to judicial control, rules being applied which are not

---

44 Dieter Schmidtchen, „Territorialität der Rechts, Internationales Privatrecht und die privatautonome Regelung internationaler Sachverhalte", in: *Rabels Zeitschrift für ausländisches und internationales Privatrecht,* 59 (1995), 57-138 (111)

45 Stewart Macauly in: Lawrence M. Friedman and Stewart Macauly, *Law and the Behavioral Sciences*, 2nd. ed., Madison, Wisconsin, 1976, 160

46 Aleksander Goldstajn, *The New Law Merchant Reconsidered,* in: Festschrift für C. Schmitthoff, München, 1973, 171-185 (171)

47 Karl-Heinz Böckstiegel, „Die neue Schiedsgerichtsordnung der Internationalen Handelskammer" in: *Neue Juristische Wochenzeitschrift* 1977, 463-469 (463)

statutory but which are linked more to commercial equity, will be reviewed by the courts if the award is challenged by one party. So in the end, international trade needs the assistance of the courts also in arbitration to effect arbitration awards and enforce them. Since the problem was recognised, the relevant arbitration acts have been altered towards a more lenient view of judicial control. Still, the basic feature of judicial control remains. Arbitration as an area where autonomous legal rules are applied will only work, if the parties submit themselves to the arbitration agreement with the intention of sticking to the final award. Because this intention is necessary, arbitration is often used in long term commercial relationships where the parties have on-going dealings with one another. However, findings of the study presented show, that this dispute resolution mechanism can often not be sustained, even in areas where arbitration was traditionally found and the economic climate changed drastically for the worse. Consequently, if the alleged traditional means of co-ordination of cross-border legal interaction are not sufficiently categorised to include the ways conflicts are handled on this level, the question arises as to whether a wider categorisation of structures should be used when looking at cross-border legal interaction. The discussion of cross-border legal interaction usually leaves out the behavioural pattern of the actors, although this behaviour may contribute more to the chosen mechanisms in cross-border conflict resolution than statutes and regulations. This study suggests that a model containing different structures attempts to cope with the problem of cross-border legal interaction, whereby the behaviour of the actors involved must be regarded as essential.

Gessner (1995) suggests the formulation of three – not necessarily exclusive – assumptions on how cross-border legal interactions may be co-ordinated.[48] These assumptions are explicitly tailored to the problem of order in world society. This may seem a very broad scope. But it is suggested that this pattern shall be suitably transferred to the co-ordination of cross-border legal interactions of an even smaller community comprising world society – the international business community.

In this model cross-border legal interactions are

(1) structured by state regulations and international conventions,

(2) structured by semi-autonomous institutions and regulations,

(3) in the main unstructured resulting in anomic situations.

The second level of semi-autonomous activities can be equated to „third legal culture“. One may speak of a „third legal culture“ if actors are able to, and make

48 Volkmar Gessner, „The Institutional Framework of Cross-Border Interaction“, in: Volkmar Gessner (Ed.), *Foreign Courts: Civil Litigation in Foreign Legal Cultures*, Aldershot: Dartmouth, 1996, 15-41 (19)

the most of the opportunity to arrange their legal affairs outside of and transposing nation state based legal culture and barriers, according to their special needs and with a high degree of compatibility. Such a third legal culture can start at an early stage of a legal relationship. Freedom of contract is granted by nearly all legal orders, so the arrangement of individual contract shall not be regarded as an explicit example of a third legal culture. More interesting appears to be the behaviour with regard to conflict behaviour and dispute resolution. Conflict avoidance, in the sense of not making use of any state provided or at least legislatory designed conflict resolution mechanism, clearly falls within the scope of this definition. One form of such an autonomous legal behaviour or third legal culture is when business is carried out according to its own rules (*'lex mercatoria'*).

According to Goldstajn the *lex mercatoria* or law merchant is a body of customary law consisting of the business practise and customs of international executives.[49] Again the application of *lex mercatoria* is often connected to arbitration in the sense that a set of autonomous rules are applied.[50] Apart from simple usage or trade custom there are caveats to lex mercatoria that are elaborated below. One could also define legal decision making as something which goes beyond the nation state based legal cultures, i.e. which is practised by the actors in a way not catered for. This would include the handling of conflict resolution mechanisms (Arbitration, Litigation, Alternative Dispute Resolution) in a way not designed for by its creators. This, for example, may be the case where legal disputes are used to delay payment. Dispute resolution mechanisms provided by states were in the first place not set up taking into account economical considerations and tactics, but as means of resolving disputes. Aspects of evolution of the law – assuming this is a state privilege – can also be affected by the autonomous and unsystematic use of conflict resolution mechanisms. It may occur that a group of global players favour arbitration for a long time. As long as there are no appeals against arbitration awards, the state's participation in developing the law by judicial power within a certain commercial area is minimised not to say entirely excluded.

As shown above, while problems in the development of international law have become part of the established canon of research in jurisprudence, hardly any attention has been paid to the behaviour patterns of the groups such law is

---

49 Aleksander Goldstajn, „The New Law Merchant", in: *Journal of Business Law,* 1961, London, pp. 12 et sequ. (12)

50 Ole Lando, „The Lex Mercatoria in International Commercial Arbitration", in: *International and Comparative Law Quaterly,*(34) 1985, 747-768

aimed at.[51] The above-mentioned studies looked at the Courts and their dealings with international matters in a broad scope, i.e. all kinds of plaintiffs and defendants and all kinds of claims. This study follows the above suggested approach of looking at a group of global players involved in cross-border legal interaction (international). It shall highlight the way conflicts are handled in the reinsurance industry which is in the London market. It reports on developments that the conflict resolution mechanisms have undergone. Furthermore, it is aimed at answering the question to what extent the conflict avoidance and resolution system in the London reinsurance market can support the theory of a third legal culture in the activities of global players in a special field of business.

---

51 Volkmar Gessner and Angelika Schade, „Conflicts of Culture in Cross- border Legal Relations: The Conception of a Research Topic in the Sociology of Law", in: *Theory, Culture & Society, Vol. 7,* (1990), 253-277 (253)

2. Material and methodology

2.1 Practice of reinsurance in legal literature

Well-established literature on the legal aspects of reinsurance exists both in the United Kingdom and Germany.[52] However, the sources of reinsurance law are foremost governed by the contractual relationship between the parties of a reinsurance contract. Additionally, a high share of dispute resolution happens in the privacy of arbitration. Both circumstances make it difficult to make any qualified statement as to how conflict avoidance and resolution in reinsurance works. As Pfeiffer states, the sources of reinsurance law do not literally flow in the dark, however do they generate from sources not openly accessible. Such sources are reinsurance contracts, which are guarded as business secrets. Other sources derive from arbitration awards and from market practice which is difficult to understand for outsiders and from a customary law highly influenced by reinsurance practice as well as equity as an element of the Common Law in general .[53]

Probably for these reasons, literature remains silent regarding what the reality of reinsurance law and dispute resolution in reinsurance on a day to day basis entails. Legal literature on reinsurance focuses on the "how it is supposed to work" aspect, namely describing the legal statutory framework and setting in which legal actions in reinsurance take place. Socio-legal literature does not seem to exist[54] either. The few books and published review articles which are

---

52 C. E. Golding, *The Law and Practice of Reinsurance*, 5th ed., Chapter 2, London: Witherby & Co. Ltd., 1987; J. S. Butler and R. Merkin, *Reinsurance Law*, London: Kluwer, 1986; Klaus Gerathewohl (Ed.), *Rückversicherung Grundlagen und Praxis*, Vol. I, Chapter 7, Karlsruhe: Verlag Versicherungswirtschaft e. V., 1976, 403 – 599; Andrea Schulte, *Rückversicherung in Deutschland und England: Unterschiede in Recht und Praxis*, Chapter 4, Karlsruhe: Verlag Versicherungswirtschaft e. V., 1990

53 Christoph Pfeiffer, *Einführung in die Rückversicherung*, 4th ed., Wiesbaden: Gabler, 1994, 1.4.1

54 For the general shortcomings of socio-legal research in the world of big business and its reasons see Volkmar Gessner, "Global Approach in the Sociology of Law – Problems and Challenges", in: *Journal of Law and Society*, Volume 22, Number 1, March 1995, 85-96

available focus on practical aspects for insiders.[55] The recent dynamic increase of disputes has generated a lot of case law and many non-published decisions. Reinsurance professionals at all levels (underwriting, legal, claims managing) must know of these legal developments. They have to take them into account in their daily business. Therefore the demand for confidential written information and documentation is well recognised by professional organisers of seminars such as Hawksmere, DYP, Euroforum and others. High calibre speakers, mostly top reinsurance solicitors and barristers, speak at those seminars about reinsurance law matters. Written material is circulated and the audience is supplied with legal advice, e. g. *'how to avoid expensive mistakes and unnecessary payments'*.

Such material gathered from seminars proved to be excellent material, especially in illustrating the tactical deliberations reinsurance disputes and litigation require. A considerably high share of the existing literature stems from reinsurance companies or entities close to them. This applies to the UK and Germany alike.[56] The high amount of arbitration in reinsurance disputes has promoted the development of literature by insiders to a certain degree, due to the fact that arbitration proceedings and arbitration awards are confidential. Standard works containing an assessment of conflict behaviour are significantly outdated. The development in the London Reinsurance Market in particular has been particularly dynamic in recent years with respect to dispute resolution. As a result, articles in the reinsurance press, briefings and brochures of law firms were essentially the most appropriate and up to date sources of information.

However these sources do not actually try to detect the underlying pattern of the development. Therefore, literature which claims to assess where the legal development in reinsurance is heading in the sense of a prognosis, does not seem to exist. The small insight available into the system has led some authors to make statements as to the character of reinsurance law and disputes coming from a theoretical approach. This refers to the "lex mercatoria" discussion. Kappus

---

55 J. S. Butler, *Reinsurance Practice and the Law*, London: Lloyd's of London Press Ltd, 1993, looseleaf, Service issue No. 7, 1 September 1996; C.E. Golding, *The Law and Practice of Reinsurance*, 5th ed., London: Witherby & Co. Ltd, 1987

56 The authors are frequently managers or employees of reinsurance companies. A good example for the phenomenon of reinsurance literature from insiders for insiders is Butler, Reinsurance practice and the Law. The book is edited by Barlow, Lyde and Gilbert (BLG), the London law firm with the biggest reinsurance division in the City. It carries the name of John Butler, previous in house counsel of Mercantile & General, the leading British reinsurance company and now counsel with BLG. Klaus Gerathewohl, editor of "Rückversicherung – Grundlagen und Praxis", the German standard work on reinsurance, was board member of Munich Re, which held top positions amongst world reinsurers in 1990 regarding the net insurance premium.

(1990) and Reichert-Facilides (1988) argue that the reinsurance law and disputes are a qualified example for *"lex mercatoria"*.[57] This work shall try to assess the value of the lex mercatoria discussion in the context of reinsurance. The limited access to information on reinsurance disputes however may not alone be the reason for such limited interest in reinsurance disputes on a broader level. The findings of this study suggest that the legal behaviour of global players with a strong self interest protection potential, has not yet attracted socio-legal curiosity. Thoughts of consumer protection might have been driving forces for socio-legal analysis with regards to primary insurance on broader terms. As long as insurance conflicts and legal battles relate to consumers, it appears that there is an incentive to study the legal behaviour of the primary insurers towards their clients, e.g. with respect to claims handling.[58] But legal interaction on an equal footing between actors with business experience may appear less attractive for socio-legal research. This is probably because there might be the feeling that both actors are able to protect their interests and do not need any interference from outside. Large firms and international organisations have hardly ever been the objects of empirical analysis in the sociology of law. But they cannot be neglected if global developments are to be observed and explained.[59] The actors themselves contribute to the fact that no undesired attention, neither on their business activities nor on their legal disputes with another, is received. This applies to banks and insurance companies alike. With respect to the business activities of reinsurance, Gerathewohl (1987) states that until two decades ago reinsurance was a service industry which lived its life largely unrecognised by the public, more or less hidden behind the backs of its insurance clients. [60]

This has changed to the extent that reinsurance in a country like the United States, is held responsible by the public in a quite unprecedented way, for lack of cover in certain classes of liability insurance. Reinsurance was rather shy about presenting its case to the public, even to the insurance public. In the London re-

---

57 Andreas Kappus, *"Lex mercatoria" in Europa und Wiener UN- Kaufrechtskonvention 1980*, Frankfurt: Lang, 1990, 182; Fritz Reichert- Facilides," Rechtsvereinheitlichung oder Rechtsvielfalt ?" in: Fritz Schwind (Ed.), *Europarecht, Internationale Privatrechtsvergleichung, Veröffentlichung der Kommission für Europarecht Nr. 6*, Wien 1988, (150-170) 155;162

58 Samantha J. Jones, *Compensating victims of mass accidents, A Socio- Legal Analysis*, Centre for Socio-Legal Studies and Pembroke College, University of Oxford, 1992

59 Volkmar Gessner, "Global Approaches in the Sociology of Law, Problems and Challenges", in: *Journal of Law and Society*, Volume 22, Number 1, March 1995, 85-96 (86)

60 Klaus Gerathewohl, "The International Reinsurance Markets Today – Developments and Perspectives", in: *Versicherungswirtschaft* 14/1987, 901-910 (901)

insurance market, public attention was first attracted when the Names litigation[61] started. Large corporate reinsurance companies did however also begin to seek legal assistance from the judiciary. As far as the continental reinsurance market is concerned, reinsurance has managed to stay out of the public interest. This, nevertheless, offers no proof that legal battles do not take place in this area.

2.2 Research on dispute behaviour in the reinsurance market

2.2.1 General

The special of role of financial institutions with regard to their dispute resolution is often stressed. Weise (1989) notes that banks and insurance companies are in a special position regarding their conflict resolution. He maintains that appearances can be deceiving. In other words, it could be a mistake to think that in international banking and insurance business there is no reason for commercial disputes. Internal measures have, however, been taken to resolve such disputes where access is limited for outsiders.[62] Gessner (1995) states, with regard to the conflict behaviour of global players, that although they are, economically speaking, by far the most important actors, they are inclined to put their legal claims aside and work on a basis of mutual trust and economic dependence.[63] The chosen or created conflict avoidance and resolution system sees to it, that the attention of a broader audience is not attracted. Due to the high share of arbitration, this also applies to reinsurance and probably to an even higher degree than in banking and insurance. Neither in the UK nor in Germany is the reinsurance industry subject to legislators' interest regarding extensive statutory regulation that may govern the contractual relationship of the parties of a reinsurance contract. Aspects of state-control are negligible compared to the amount of regulations that are to be observed by the banking and primary insurance industry concerning their customer relations.[64] This work attempts to present a con-

---

61 The Names litigation is a collective for claims of 'Names' brought against their underwriting agents for negligent underwriting, a type of litigation which has become prominent and publicly reported in recent years.

62 Paul-Frank Weise, *Materielles Recht vor der internationalen Handelsschiedsgerichtsbarkeit*, Frankfurt: Lang, 1989, 51-52

63 Volkmar Gessner, "Global Approaches in the Sociology of Law, Problems and Challenges", in: *Journal of Law and Society*, Volume 22, 1995, No. 1, 85-96 (86)

64 For an overview of the regulatory framework of primary insurance in the UK see: Ulrich Hübner, *Rechtliche Rahmenbedingungen des Wettbewerbs in der Versicherungswirtschaft*, Baden-Baden: Nomos, 1988, 23 – 78. For regulatory details in reinsurance in the UK see: Andrea Schulte, *Rückversicherung in Deutschland und*

flict resolution pattern. Further it aims to describe under which economical and legal circumstances such an alleged "internal" or autonomous system comes into existence, under which conditions it can be sustained and under which conditions it is to break up.

If one refers to the model which illustrates the degree of autonomy, a three step model can be developed:

Non-autonomous structured state-provided dispute resolution mechanisms through Courts according to national law and international conventions: Conflict resolution which is only minimally geared by the parties involved but still subject to tactics.

Semi-autonomous dispute resolution mechanisms: Arbitration as state provided dispute resolution mechanism is subject to limited judicial control. Arbitration is probably more lenient towards 'market practice' and other merchant customs *(lex mercatoria)* due to the application of honourable engagement clauses.

Autonomous dispute resolution mechanisms: Private ordering of international transactions, conflict avoidance, negotiations, settlements prior to proceedings.

As far as reinsurance disputes are concerned, the main principle in the reinsurance industry used to be conflict avoidance. This conflict avoidance attitude became less apparent in as much as the reinsurance industry took measures to standardise contract wordings or created other instruments which pointed towards standardisation. On the contrary, it must be stated that attempts towards standardisation – may they concern contract wording or only part of the wording, e. g. a standardised arbitration clause – were of limited success.[65] It was more a question of readiness to pay on the reinsurer's side, which was the prevailing attitude until 10 to 15 years ago. Negotiations should take place if a dispute arose. Until recently it was unusual for the reinsurance market to resort to the adversial system to resolve its disputes.[66] However arbitration was deemed to be appropriate if a dispute could not be resolved by means of previous negotiations. Again, negotiations and – as a result – a settlement within arbitration pro-

---

England: Unterschiede in Recht und Praxis, Karlsruhe: Verlag Versicherungswirtschaft e. V., 1990, 103 – 127

65 For approaches of explanation for the reason of failure see: Klaus Gerathewohl, *Rückversicherung Grundlagen und Praxis*, Vol. I, Chapter 7, Karlsruhe: Verlag Versicherungswirtschaft e. V., 1976, 507 Andrea Schulte, *Rückversicherung in Deutschland und England: Unterschiede in Recht und Praxis*, Karlsruhe: Verlag Versicherungswirtschaft e. V., 1990, 136 – 141

66 J. S. Butler, *Reinsurance Practice and the Law*, London: Lloyd's of London Press Ltd., 1993, looseleaf, Service Issue No. 7, 1 September 1996, 25.1

ceedings was the favoured solution. In the London reinsurance market however, the court – the Commercial Court in particular – is having an important task in reinsurance disputes under certain circumstances.

Generally, the courts may become involved if the law recognises the dispute or claim as no fit subject for arbitration[67] or if the parties have no arbitration agreement. If an arbitration agreement does exist, it seems that there is no choice between arbitration and litigation anyway. According to the terms of the contract, the parties are bound to solve all disputes by arbitration. However there are possible ways to bypass arbitration. The parties can go to court directly, if one party can persuade the court that its issuing court proceedings is merely an attempt to collect a debt and there is no "dispute". It may further be that the defendant does not want to arbitrate either in which case the arbitration clause can be conveniently ignored.

One other procedure regarding reinsurance claims worth noting, is the possibility of third or additional parties joining the proceedings. An arbitration will only be between the parties who have agreed to arbitrate. If one party has not agreed to arbitrate, this party will not be involved in the arbitration. Normally separate arbitration will have to take place between the cedant and each reinsurer. However, before the court, necessary third parties or additional defendants may join the proceedings. For example, a cedant may sue in the alternative its reinsurer and its broker. He may sue the former for sums claimed under the contract. He may sue the latter in the alternative argument, that if the sums are not due under the contract, the broker has been negligent. Additionally, the defendant may join third parties from whom he may seek a contribution to or indemnify from any judgment against him. A major advantage of this right is that there is one hearing for one case. A party is not subjected to the additional costs arising from the duplication of cases nor the possibility of differing awards.[68]

The courts may further become involved if:

- a third party, which cannot be bound by the arbitration agreement, is involved as plaintiff or defendant, e. g. a broker,
- one of the parties being involved in arbitration appeals against an arbitration award,
- an interlocutory order is sought.

Also in the U. K the Courts give the following kind of assistance to arbitration:

---

67 Michael J. Mustill and Stewart C. Boyd, *The Law and Practice of Commercial Arbitration in England*, 2nd ed., London and Edinburgh: Butterworth, 1989, 149

68 Colin Croly and Clive O'Connel, The Case for the Commercial Court, in: *The Review*, March 1988, 40-42 (40)

1. They enforce the agreement to arbitrate indirectly, by refusing to allow a party to litigate a matter in court which he has agreed to resolve by arbitration.

2. They enforce an arbitration award directly, whether interim (e.g. an order for payment or account) or final.

3. They give interlocutory assistance in the conduct of the arbitration, for example,

(a) by appointing an arbitrator if the contractual procedure for doing so fails,

(b) by making and enforcing interim orders for the preservation of the subject matter of the arbitration,

(c) by compelling the attendance of a witness.

(d) by removing an arbitrator, remitting a matter to him for misconduct, for example, if he has failed to disclose some prior connections with a party; or if he has accepted a bribe; or if he has received evidence from one party without the knowledge of the other.[69]

Movements in the London reinsurance market have brought changes to the handling of legal issues, ranging from the drafting of contracts to the dispute resolution culture.[70] The primary focus of this paper will be to catch the "winds of changes" and to convey the developments to the reader.

2.2.2 Empirical research

To the best of the author's knowledge no one ever seems to have undertaken any empirical socio-legal research on conflict behaviour in a field which is of such economic importance. It can be said that without the existence of reinsurance the primary insurance industry and its capacity would be limited. The existence of reinsurance is therefore a prerequisite of a highly technological industry.[71] The role of reinsurance is outstanding in terms of function as well as sheer size. It sets the framework to allow insurance to exist in the first place. Reinsurance companies take on risks of private individuals, enterprises and institutions. It is so to speak the „wholesaler“ in the insurance industry. It deals with world wide risks – be it the shooting of the moon rocket Arraign or a Californian earthquake.

---

69 Ronald Bernstein, „Arbitration and the Courts“, in: *The Journal of the Chartered Institute of Arbitrators*, February 1993, Vol. 59, No.1, 4

70 Even insider books mention the "lack of attitude" in resolving a dispute compared to previous times. See: J. S. Butler, *Reinsurance Pratice and the Law*, London: Lloyd's of London Press Ltd, 1993, looseleaf, Service issue No. 7, 1 September 1996, 25.5.1

71 Horst K. Jannott, "Rückversicherung – einige praktische Aspekte der Arbeit im Ausland", in: *Versicherungswirtschaft* 7/1982, 376-386 (376)

To this end, it is necessary that reinsurance orients itself globally because otherwise a spread of risk is not possible. One insurance enterprise could go bankrupt as a result of one major disaster. It can also pose a serious economic threat if numerous smaller claims accumulate. The economic importance of reinsurance is reflected impressively by the premiums earned in the business. In the list of the top players based on 1994 figures[72], Münchener Rück earned $9,97 billion net premium resulting from its reinsurance business. Second in line was Schweizer Rück with $8,23 billion profit, followed by the US enterprises Employers Re and General Re making profits of $5,98 billion and $5,5 billion respectively. A process of concentration characterises the highly competitive market of reinsurance recently. From 1984 to 1994 alone the market share of the ten biggest reinsurers in the world increased from 22 % to 39 %. After a period of high losses, which directly related to the increase in legal disputes, 100 reinsurers ceased business.

2.2.3 Research design

Given the privacy of the system and the limited number of players[73] in the London reinsurance market, insight into the conflict avoidance and resolution system in reinsurance can only spring from certain sources. One source might be to collect the available legal and practical literature and to look at the decisions and the awards (if published). This might be a useful approach to assess the focus of legal problems in reinsurance disputes.[74] A more global approach to pinpoint the characteristics of the system as a whole and its strengths and weaknesses would be to interview various experts of reinsurance disputes. These experts are primarily solicitors. They accompany negotiations, litigation and arbitration proceedings and are legal advisers. They are in contact with the parties involved and the institutions that are deemed to resolve the conflicts. Further experts are barristers, claims managers of reinsurance companies, brokers, arbitrators, expert witnesses and judges. A file and a judgment analysis were also part of the research design.

---

72 Handelsblatt v. 15.8.1996, 4

73 Since the London reinsurance market does not consist of very many professional reinsurers, but primarily of underwriters who write both direct and reinsurance, the term „limited number“ of actors refers to the parties of a reinsurance contract which have to meet the obligations of reinsurance premium and reinsurance cover.

74 see: Geoffrey M. Hall, *Reinsurance Law Casebook*, Business & Maritime Publications Ltd, 1989

2.2.4 *Interviews*

The number of law-firms being involved in reinsurance in the London market is limited, approximately 35 „City law firms", i.e. London based offices of solicitors, which are involved in work worth mentioning relating to reinsurance law. This includes the leaders in the field, as well as those firms that are only occasionally concerned with reinsurance disputes. This fact has been taken into account during the attempt to obtain a realistic picture of the situation by talking to more than one lawyer of a firm with a significant workload in reinsurance files. Besides contentious work, the City law firms provide a whole range of reinsurance work that is non-contentious such as, *inter alia*, assistance with inspections and investigation, interpretation and drafting of wording, setting up arrangement schemes, commutation, coverage issues and document management. This work contains the results of interviews carried out during the period of January to March 1995 with solicitors of City law firms involved in reinsurance disputes and reinsurance law work. With the help of lawyers' directories, the practitioners involved in reinsurance disputes in London were selected and asked for their co-operation in answering a questionnaire[75] , and in giving a free format interview. In the case of consent to co-operate in the study, the questionnaire was mailed with the confirmation of the interview appointment. It must be stressed that the response and the received co-operation were generously given by most law firms. Therefore it was possible to cover most of the relevant firms. Twenty-nine interviews were conducted with lawyers and often more than one practitioner participated.

The focus of the research was especially on the development and the evaluation of change in conflict resolution in reinsurance during the last 10 to 15 years. The lawyers were therefore asked to indicate the length of their professional experience. This was necessary to find out to what extend the interview partners relied on information stemming from their personal working experience. The average was 12 years professional experience. The data can claim to be exhaustive regarding the topics covered in the questionnaire and the free format interview. Only interviews with the full range of information were included in the data base. Therefore the reader will have 31 lawyers as a basis for the data collected. Where considered appropriate this paper will refer to information obtained during pre-test interviews with brokers, reinsurance consultants and leading employees of reinsurance companies conducted within the same time period . In January and February 1996 follow up interviews were conducted with solicitors who took a special interest in the continuation of the study. Chambers known for

75 Please find the questionnaire in Appendix I

their work in reinsurance were also approached for co-operation. This resulted in approximately 12 free format interviews during January and February 1996. Again, during this time interviews with arbitrators, brokers, expert witnesses and two Commercial Court judges ruling on reinsurance cases were conducted.

2.2.5 File analysis at the Commercial Court

In order to underpin the structure of court proceedings in reinsurance disputes in the London market, the intention was to conduct a random file analysis of one particular year, 1993, at the Commercial Court. The underlying idea in doing so was to extrapolate the share of reinsurance cases in which foreign parties were involved and to collect random information on the course of proceedings. Information was modelled on a scheme used in cross-border legal interactions in New York Courts[76] such as:

- where parties originate from
- how service was effected
- difficulties due to the involvement of foreign parties, duration of proceedings, translation of documents
- application of foreign law
- how was the applicable law determined (jurisdiction, conflict of laws, agreement)
- reference to market practice, law merchant (lex mercatoria) or reinsurance usage
- were any actions taken abroad?
- have expert witnesses been heard?
- was there a discovery?
- questions of law or questions of fact prevailing
- case ended by judgment, judgment by default, summary, settlement[77]

---

76 Hanno v. Freyhold, „Cross-border legal interactions in New York Courts“ in: Volkmar Gessner (Ed.), *Foreign Courts: Civil Litigation in Foreign Legal Cultures*, Aldershot: Dartmouth, 1996, 42-148 (56)

77 According to information obtained by the Court Service Business Management Unit, 95 % of all writs issued never lead to a full trial. To shed light on the expectations of parties in reinsurance disputes, it would have been interesting to see if the share of reinsurance disputes ending with a verdict outnumbers this average. The expectation was that the share of writs issued in reinsurance cases leading to a full trial would lie above the average. This was substantiated on the assumption that the chances for settlement prior to court proceedings would be investigated more carefully.

– did the case arise from arbitration, e.g. an arbitration award
– duration of proceedings from filing of writ to decision.

Accordingly an application for research at the Commercial Court was filed and sent to the Lord Chancellors Department on 9th of November 1995. The front pages of writs are in folders that are open to inspection for a fee. These folders however do not contain the statement of claim, nor do they contain orders made in the case. If a case could be identified as dealing with a reinsurance dispute, e.g. if a party's name contained „reinsurance company xyz", one has to ask for the full writ at a counter to identify the claim. Access to files, however, would not be given due to confidentiality of the parties. I inspected the folders at the Commercial Court containing the aforementioned writs from 1.1.1993 until 18.6.1996 (1050 writs of 2276 writs issued at the Commercial Court in 1993). It became clear that it was not possible to reveal reinsurance cases on a reliable basis by looking at the abbreviated writs for the above-mentioned reasons. Even where reinsurance cases were identified, access to the files was not granted. I then tried to obtain access to four reinsurance files by obtaining privileged permission for access from the Lord Chancellor's Department. The application was rejected on the grounds of confidentiality of the parties.

2.2.6 Judgment analysis of Commercial Court decision in reinsurance

The purpose of the judgment analysis was two-fold at the starting point of the thesis. Firstly, it was hoped to gain an insight into how the Commercial Court deals with reinsurance cases that involved parties coming from different countries. Secondly it was hoped to make visible, if and how market practice, the evidence of expert witnesses and law merchants *(lex mercatoria)* flow into the Commercial Courts' decision making process. Additionally if the database provided decisions regarding arbitration, this information would be taken into account. This could be in the form of appeals against arbitration awards or judges making statements relating to arbitration. Where necessary, the analysis will also refer to decisions made by the Court of Appeal or the House of Lords. The judgment analysis was conducted within the LEXIS legal database. LEXIS online service provides different „libraries". The judgment analysis presented has been conducted within the English General Library (ENGGEN). The English General Library provides access to English case and statutory materials including unreported cases, transcripts or unreported cases, Public and General Acts of Wales, Rules, Regulations, Orders of England and Wales as published in the statutory Instruments series, and English taxation materials. *Reported cases* were introduced in January 1945 (or when the series of reports started publication) reported in one or more series of law reports. Relevant sources for reinsurance matters are the Law Times Report (LT) and the Lloyd's Law Reports (Lloyd's Rep). *Unreported cases* are available in transcripts since January 1980 on the LEXIS service. Main relevant sources to reinsurance are all House of Lords cases, all Court of Appeal (Civil Division Cases), selected Queen's Bench Commercial Cases and transcripts of English Cases (High Court of Justice) reported or summarised in different journals, e. g. „The Times" et cetera.

Up until January 4th 1996, LEXIS contained 405 cases under the keyword „reinsurance". A cut was made in 1980. This was because from then onwards, also *unreported cases* were available. Cases from 1980 onwards were therefore subjected to the judgment analysis presented. However, the cases looked for were only those relating to „real" reinsurance disputes in the sense of the thesis, i. e. where the insured, the primary insurance and reinsurer or intermediaries to a reinsurance contract were involved. Within this scope, also cases where foreign parties were involved had to be identified. Hence some cases had to be excluded. Firstly the cases relating to employment, tax and company matters were excluded. Those cases were identified by the court they were dealt by, i. e. the Employment Tribunal, London VAT Tribunal and Chancery Division (Companies Court). Also cases relating to criminal activities, indicated by R.v. (Regina versus) and dealt by the Criminal Court were excluded. The research focused on the London reinsurance market and the question as to how the Commercial Court deals with those disputes. Therefore also foreign courts judgments, such those of US or Canadian Courts, which were occasionally cited in ENGGEN were excluded. With reference to identifying the origin of the parties, a LEXIS research may well encounter difficulties involved in a file analysis where information on the origin of the parties is frequently not found. If the fact then that one party is foreign is not important to the conclusion of the case, it may not be mentioned at all that a foreign party is involved, in which case there is no indicator apart from the name.

Dealing with companies however, the name and the way it is registered often indicates the origin of the party. If mentioned, this is a reliable factor to identify a foreign party. Some of the cases were therefore self-evident. Where the origin of parties was not indicated by Names and the way they were registered, the facts of the cases were considered. Sometimes already the KWIC (key word in context) outline of LEXIS gave sufficient information to identify if foreign parties were involved. On 04.06.1996 under the keyword „reinsurance", LEXIS provided 405 „uncleared" cases, 55 before 1980. Regarding the abovementioned overall goal of the study, a search within LEXIS under keywords was conducted. After several trial runs it became apparent that a joint key word search possible under LEXIS was the most likely to bring results. The search was conducted under the keywords *reinsurance and .... (second key word).*

A search relating to the question of involvement of foreign parties was run under keywords such as *reinsurance and jurisdiction, reinsurance and forum non-convenience, reinsurance and conflicts of laws.* Also conventions were included into the search such as *Rome Convention, Brussels Convention and Lugano Convention.* With reference to the question of market practice and the evidence given by expert witnesses, a search under these keywords was conducted. Also *law merchant* and *lex mercatoria* were used as keywords jointly with reinsurance. Since it was difficult to obtain first hand information on arbitration proceedings because of their private and confidential nature and the fact that arbitration awards are not published, I tried to gain information from court decisions. Key words such as *reinsurance and arbitration awards, reinsurance and appeal against arbitration awards*, as well as *reinsurance and honourable engagement clause* were subjected to analysis. Additionally the „x-tree pro", a search program, was used. On 04.01.1996 all cases containing the key word *„reinsurance"* were downloaded from LEXIS onto disk and hard disk. A key word search was conducted relating to aspects of foreign law, foreign parties etc. in the manner outlined above using LEXIS.

2.2.7 Data evaluation and presentation

In order to evaluate the data from the lawyers' completed questionnaires, the computer program „access" was used. This way figures given could be processed to produce a graph and the answers to each question could also be seen in the form of a table. This made the comparison easier. For the free format interviews, notes were taken during the interviews and then protocols were written immediately after the interviews. The data from the judgment analysis was processed as described above. The relevant decisions and text paragraphs were studied. Both the evaluation and subsequent presentation of the data are strictly topic oriented. If arbitration, for example, is the topic, all data collected: interviews, decisions, articles, etc. were examined and compiled to a survey on the topic concerned. The data presentation is not meant to deliver any statistical information. This procedure was chosen to allow comparisons to be made between the comments of the interviewees and the results of the literature research.

3. The London Reinsurance Market

3.1 Reinsurance Business and Forms

This study is not aimed explaining the basic principles of reinsurance law, nor the economical and technical proceedings of reinsurance at length. However, it is considered necessary for an understanding of the legal conflicts which may occur that a brief introduction to the reinsurance market, its participants and its legal framework in the UK shall be given.

Reinsurance is a method whereby an original insurer distributes its risks by giving the whole or some portion of it to another insurer, with the aim of reducing the amount of his possible loss.[78] Reinsurance is an independent branch of the insurance industry. The so called *Spartentrennungsprinzip*[79] does not apply for reinsurance in the UK as a consequence of which a reinsurance company theoretically can reinsure all categories of risks. The reinsurance contract is an indemnity contract.[80] The purpose of reinsurance could be said to be covered under the headings "capacity, stabilisation, confidence, catastrophe protection and spread of risks".[81] Reinsurance can provide indemnity for the primary insurer's written business which is constantly threatened by the risks of coincidence, change and error. Accidental change of damage charts may occur. Catastrophes may cause damage which are above average especially if the primary insurer is held liable for contracts that are concerned by one event (accumulation of damages). Fluctuation in currency values may affect prices and salaries. As a consequence, deviations of the course of damage development may occur. New technical developments can make the starting point for calculation invalid. Wrong calculations for insurance premiums may occur due to the false interpretation of statistics.[82]

78 C. E. Golding, *The Law and Practice of Reinsurance*, 5th ed., London: Witherby & Co. Ltd., 1987, 17
79 Separation of field principle
80 Christoph Pfeiffer, *Einführung in die Rückversicherung,* 4th ed., Wiesbaden: Gabler, 1994, 1.3.1
81 G. C. A. Dickson and J.T. Steele, *Introduction to Insurance*, 2nd ed., London: Pitman, 1984, 178 subs.
82 Christoph Pfeiffer, *Einführung in die Rückversicherung,* 4th ed., Wiesbaden: Gabler, 1.2.2.

As the direct insurers can reinsure part of certain risks they can therefore accept more of the original risk and increase their capacity. From the current perspective of the primary insurer reinsurance mainly serves the purpose of increasing capacity.[83] The result is growth within the insurance market as a whole and added prestige to the individual insurer. Just as the insured has no knowledge of when a claim will occur or what it will cost, similarly the direct insurer also lacks such knowledge. The reinsurance company has far more experience in handling losses, and statistical techniques can assist in the prediction of handling losses. Reinsurance helps the direct insurer to stabilise his loss levels by removing some of the uncertainty. In order to help remove uncertainty factors on the part of the primary insurers, professional reinsurers collect information on damage prevention, help to increase the knowledge on risk evaluation and co-operate in damage prevention.[84]

One of the advantages of insurance is to give confidence to the insured.[85] The same applies for reinsurance regarding the insurer. An example of this is found where an insurer wishes to offer insurance in an area in which it has no previous dealings. With limited experience in the new area the insurer may be rather hesitant. The existence of reinsurance, however, removes many of the uncertainties and may make the insurer more confident. If the worst possible state of affairs combine to produce losses of catastrophic proportions, the financial resources of a direct insurer would be seriously strained. Reinsurance is deemed to act as a cushion to protect insurers against this eventuality. Insurance is a mechanism by which the impact of losses is spread. The direct insurer may not want a concentration of liability in any one type of business, any one class of risk, any one geographical area or in any other classification. By organising reinsurance facilities correctly it can spread the potential impact of future losses.

For centuries there was only one method of reinsurance, the facultative reinsurance of a single risk. When reinsurance grew during the 19th century, numerous new forms were developed. Nowadays, in the daily reinsurance practice, there are two methods of classifying the forms which reinsurance may take, and each of these methods has the same two broad sub-divisions.[86] A reinsurance contract can be described as having been arranged in advance for use as and

---

83 Christoph Pfeiffer, *Einführung in die Rückversicherung,* 4th ed., Wiesbaden: Gabler, 1994, 1.2.1

84 Horst K. Jannott, "Rückversicherung – Einige Aspekte der Arbeit im Ausland", in: *Versicherungswirtschaft* 7/1982, 376-386 (376)

85 G. C. A. Dickson and J. T. Steele, *Introduction to Insurance*, 2nd. ed., London: Pitman, 1984, 178 subs.

86 G. C. A. Dickson and J.T. Steele, *Introduction to Insurance*, 2nd. ed., London: Pitman, 1984, 181 subs.

when required. This is known as a treaty contract. Under a *treaty contract* the reinsurer agrees to accept in advance a certain class of risk for reinsurance in a portfolio that the ceding office will cede to him during the course of business. An example would be a motor policy or a household policy portfolio. As the treaty contract concerns risks from future insurance contracts of the primary insurer, both parties – the reinsurer and the primary insurer (ceding office) agree upon risks that they do not yet know about in detail.[87] Accordingly under a treaty contract, the primary insurer has the obligation to cede all risk that falls under this contract to the reinsurer and the reinsurer is not entitled to turn down this offer. Compared to a facultative reinsurance contract, which requires separate negotiation of the individual risk that shall be ceded, the ceding of the risk takes place more or less automatically under a treaty contract.

Under a treaty reinsurance contract, the ceding office has a duty to cede all risks that are described under the contract more specifically to the reinsurer. This may be for example all direct written fire business in Germany, the written French transport policies or all machinery risks of an English ceding office. Here it goes without saying, that the reinsurer accepting a share, may not be able to give an assessment of the risk in each single case. For pragmatic reasons the right to write business must be left rather to the ceding office within its own discretion. This discretion includes the setting of the premium price, taking administrative measures involved in the reinsurance policy and dealing with damages as he thinks to be in the interest of all parties.[88]

In all decisions the ceding office has to protect the reinsurer's interest as well as it's own. If it acts negligently or even deliberately against the reinsurer's interest, the reinsurer may not be held liable under the reinsurance contract. The primary insurance has the right to lead the deal, the reinsurer must follow. The obligation to follow is limited by the scope of what the ceding office may agree upon with the insured. This is within the mentioned boundaries. Payments for damages out of good will may also be made by the ceding office to the insured. According to world-wide reinsurance practice this will constitute a binding obligation for the reinsurance to follow. This obligation however is limited to the extent that the damage of the concerned risk is subject matter to the insurance policy and therefore falls under the reinsurance treaty. Especially with those payments the ceding office is obliged to avoid misuse and acting against good faith. For settlement and discounts the same applies.

---

87 Andrea Schulte, *Rückversicherung in Deutschland und England: Unterschiede in Recht und Praxis,* Karlsruhe: Verlag Versicherungswirtschaft e. V. 1990, 20

88 Christoph Pfeiffer, *Einführung in die Rückversicherung,* 4th ed., Wiesbaden: Gabler 1994, 1.3.1

If the reinsurance contract contains a risk that has been individually negotiated between reinsurer and insurer as the risk arises, this contract is described as a *facultative contract*. An example is the reinsuring of an aviation risk or an oil rig platform. Facultative reinsurance gives a high degree of control to a reinsurer regarding the quality of its risk. This control is not available under the treaty method.[89] The facultative reinsurance contract corresponds to both parties' desire to negotiate performance and price in advance for each deal, individually and according to the reinsurance premium. It is down to the primary insurer to decide if he wants to reinsure the individual risk and he reinsurer can decide if he wants to accept the offer or not. A facultative reinsurance offer from the ceding office shall contain all relevant information of the risk which enables the reinsurance company to assess it.[90] This information shall include:

- name and address of the insured
- proportional or non-proportional risk
- type/ country/ place of risk
- insured interest
- conditions/ covered risks (including all exceptions and clauses deviating from standard terms)
- total insurance sum
- insurance premium
- reinsurance premium and other costs
- terms of contract
- damage prevention measures
- statistical data on damages in the last five years (if obtainable)
- information regarding other existing reinsurance contracts
- percentage excess of the ceding offices.

This list of information serves only as an example, it is not final. Other specific information may be needed according to the specific risk that is reinsured. Often only a short time span lies between the offer and the commencement of the facultative reinsurance contract. Therefore, it is of utmost importance that the ceding office supplies the reinsurer with the necessary information to save time consuming requests which may cause delay and endanger the receipt of the reinsurance cover.

After the reinsurer has assessed the offer, he will inform the ceding office which share he is willing to take over. This will usually happen by telephone,

89 C. E. Golding, *The Law and Practice of Reinsurance*, 5th ed., London: Witherby & Co. Ltd., 1987, 21

90 Christoph Pfeiffer, *Einführung in die Rückversicherung*, 4th. ed., Wiesbaden: Gabler, 1994, 1.3.1

telex, fax or by sending a signed copy of the offer showing the accepted share. The conditions of such a facultative reinsurance are theoretically confirmed later in a written note and signed by both parties. The reality of business, however, shows that the written detailed contract that should be signed is often omitted. This leaves the parties without written evidence if they want to refer to facts that are not laid down in the contract.

In facultative reinsurance the reinsurer may as well reject the offer of the ceding office to take on reinsurance cover. The rejection will be transmitted by phone, telex or fax. It will probably include the reasons why the offer is not accepted. It might also be that the reinsurance company Names conditions under which it will accept. These conditions may significantly deviate from the original offer. Facultative reinsurance expires after the term of the contract. Usually the ceding office seeks prolongation of the facultative reinsurance contract premature to expiry. It will inform the reinsurer of alterations in the original contract and the statistical chart or course of business. The reinsurer may reject the offer to extend the contract.

Regarding the need for information, a facultative reinsurance business very much resembles the direct business between primary insurance and its insured individuals or companies. The larger professional reinsurance companies have set up departments for the facultative business. Experts work in these departments ,which are divided into different fields or classes of risks. These experts are able to give a quick and fair assessment of the risk. The task of the facultative reinsurer is not purely restricted to provide capacity. He is also required to counsel and support the ceding office in estimating the risk, in drafting the terms of a contract and in determining damage prevention measures, which may well include a joint on-site inspection of the risk. In practice, facultative reinsurance cover will be offered mostly by reinsurers with which the ceding office already has treaty business dealings. It is of great importance to the primary insurer that it does not have to fear competition from the professional reinsurer when giving away detailed information about risks.

Considering the distribution of the single types of contracts, a reverse trend can be observed. In earlier years treaty reinsurance contracts did seem to supersede facultative contracts.[91] This was attributed to the alleged labour intensive costs because of individual negotiations of the single risks and connected possible delays in obtaining reinsurance cover. But despite time and cost aspects,

---

91 M. Grossmann, *Rückversicherung – eine Einführung*, Bern, Frankfurt a. M., 1977, 83

there are prospects for a resurgence in the popularity of facultative reinsurance.[92] On the one hand, this is because on-going technological development has led to a significant increase in both insurance cover and the insurance premium. Risks have also become more difficult and complicated to assess as a result of this development. Facultative reinsurance today extends into many fields, however with varying priorities. In industrial fire insurance a permanent increase of sums insured occurred. Jointly, an increase of estimated highest damage and considerable exclusions of liability in fire production interruption insurance force the ceding offices to demand facultative reinsurance cover.

In transport insurance facultative reinsurance has a broad scope of application, especially insurance objects with high sums insured, such as:

- coverage (kasko) insurance for fleet or single ships of big shipping companies
- in construction risk insurance of new – or reconstruction of big and/or expensive ships
- the insurance of oil-rigs or technical machinery used at sea
- in the insurance of goods with highest lines (maxima)
- in exhibition insurance especially art exhibitions with extremely high sums insured
- in the insurance of valuables like in transport of securities, precious metal, precious stones and/ or cash.

In aviation, the demand for facultative reinsurance cover results mainly from space travel projects and from big aircraft fleets with high sums insured for coverage insurance (kasko – Selbstschaden). Additionally, the extraordinary high sums insured for liability damage contribute to the demand for facultative reinsurance. In technical insurance branches, large-scale projects require facultative reinsurance cover despite strong intensive primary risk distribution by co-insurers and treaty reinsurance. Technical insurance concerns energy projects, such as power stations and nuclear power stations. Large scale industry projects and the machinery involved also belong to this category. Large construction projects such as tunnels or dams and cover for computer technology are also types of technical insurance. A consumer friendly legislation in recent years led to increasing demand for higher liability insurance. The sums insured have risen accordingly to hundreds of millions of dollars. Facultative reinsurance contracts are increasingly made for liability cover and for difficult risks that are exempt

---

92 Christoph Pfeiffer, *Einführung in die Rückversicherung,* 4th. ed., Wiesbaden: Gabler, 1994, 2.2.1.
J. S. Butler, *Reinsurance Practice and the Law,* London: Lloyd's of London Press, 1993, looseleaf, Service Issue No. 7, 1 September 1996, 5.2.1

from treaty insurance contracts. Product liability risks, especially if the products are exported to the US, belong to thc set of risks that are exempt from treaty reinsurance.

A third form of reinsurance is the facultative-obligatory treaty, which allows the reinsured an option if to use the treaty.[93] The reinsurer, however, must accept the offer of the cedant. Treaty reinsurance is commonly found where the reinsured already subscribes to the reinsurance programme but where the reinsurer is willing to provide the cedant with additional capacity on selected risks. This is generally achieved by the treaty being written as a first or an additional surplus like contract. This gives the cedant automatic reinsurance facilities to when the capacity of any quota share or surplus contract taking priority is exhausted. An essential element of this reinsurance treaty relationship again is trust, as the reinsured obtains automatic attachment on any risk he chooses to cede.

Treaty and facultative contracts may occur in a proportional or non-proportional form. In the proportional form of reinsurance the amount retained and the amount ceded will represent certain proportions of the cover accepted by the ceding office. The premium received by the ceding offices will be shared in these proportions.[94] When a client puts in a claim to the ceding office, the claim payment will be shared by the ceding office and the reinsurers in the same proportions. This is irrespective of the size of the claim.[95] A common form of a proportional treaty is the quota share contract. Under this contract an agreed proportion of all original risks within the portfolio or claim of business covered is ceded on „identical" terms and conditions to reinsurers.[96] The principle between the quota share interest is that a reinsurer participates in the reinsured's original business on almost the same terms as the reinsured. This excludes profit commissions and reinsurance overriders deducted by the reinsured before cession.

Another form of proportional treaty is the surplus contract. The surplus reinsurance contract does not cover the whole primary risk, but only a part of the sum insured exceeding the so called „retention" determined by the cedant to the reinsurance agreement.[97] The retention may vary from risk to risk. If the parties make a reinsurance contract on an obligatory basis, reinsurance cover will only begin after the sum of retention has been fixed by the cedant. The sum exceeding

---

93 J. S. Butler, *Reinsurance Practice and the Law*, London: Lloyd's of London Press, 1993, looseleaf, Service Issue No. 7, 1 September 1996, 5.3.2.1 subs.

94 G.C.A. Dickson and J.T. Steele, *Introduction to Insurance*, 2nd. ed., London: Pitman Publishing, 1984, 182 subs.

95 C. A. Dickson and J. R. Steele, *Introduction to Insurance*, 2nd ed., 181 subs.

96 J. S. Butler, *Reinsurance Practice and the Law*, ibid, 5.3.3.1

97 Andrea Schulte, *Rückversicherung in Deutschland und England: Unterschiede in Recht und Praxis*, Karlsruhe: Verlag Versicherungswirtschaft 1990, 22

the retention is called „surplus". It represents – with reference to its amount – a multiple of the retention. This surplus is split into layers – so called „lines". Each reinsurer can determine how many lines he is going to take on until the whole sum insured is covered.

The advantage of the quota share contract lies in the ease of administrative with which the cessions can be processed. The retention does not have to be negotiated for each contract. The disadvantage lies in the fact that the cedant – irrespective of the sum insured – must always reinsure a certain percentage of the risk. In a surplus treaty however, the cedant may fix the retention at his discretion so that only a part or nothing is reinsured. Many of the reciprocal arrangements reached between European companies are effectively an exchange of quota share participants in each other's national business. These offer a simple pro rata share of the original premium and reinsurers enjoy (or suffer) the same spread of risk and experience with claims as the reinsured.[98]

In *non-proportional contracts* the ceding office and the reinsurers do not share each loss in fixed proportions, and may not share losses at all. A common form of these is that the ceding office underwrites its retention as a form of first loss insurance. It bears all losses up to a certain amount, and the reinsurers deals with the balance of any loss above this figure, usually with an upper limit. The reinsurer agrees to pay the reinsured a specified amount of losses in a portfolio. This amount exceeds an agreed excess point, in exchange for an adjustable premium. The adjustable premium is expressed either in percentage of a portfolio's premium income, or for example, as a factor of the loss ratio. Since the reinsurer assumes a share of only the larger losses (i.e. those exceeding the cedant's retention), he receives a correspondingly reduced share of premium to reflect the reduced loss frequency and severity.[99]

Historically, excess of loss reinsurance has been a low-cost mechanism. With this mechanism, those reinsured have caused a dispersal of large amounts of risk to a wider group of reinsurers. The mechanism applied wherever it was necessary to limit the exposure to loss from a large individual risk, or through an aggregation of losses from numerous risks emanating from a single event or loss. It became characteristic of the London retrocession market to accept similar inward business themselves. This led to a substantial and specialised section of the London market to exchange risks within the market, rather that with external reinsurers.[100] The stop-loss reinsurance contract also belongs to the category of non-proportional reinsurance. Here the amount of damage is the criterion on

98 J. S. Butler, *Reinsurance Practice and the Law*, ibid, 5.3.3.2
99 J. S. Butler, *Reinsurance Practice and the Law*, ibid, 5.3.5.1
100 J. S. Butler, *Reinsurance Practice and the Law*, ibid, 5.3.5.3

which the decision to reinsure or not is based. At the same time there is a parallel to the quota share because the criterion is not the damage occurring in one occurrence but the damage accumulating in one year. The damage must exceed a certain percentage, then reinsurance steps in. For the reinsurer involved an upper-limit liability applies.[101]

3.2 Development of the London Market

Reinsurance business in the UK is concentrated in the City of London. According to figures released by Lloyds Market Planning Department in 1991[102] the City accounted for 13 % of total reinsurance premium income making it the third largest supplier in reinsurance world-wide.[103] The entire London insurance market is the fourth biggest after the German market.[104] However the premium income is not the figure decisive in selecting the London market for this study. The significance of the London market lies in a characteristic that distinguishes it from other reinsurance markets which are superior in terms of premium income, e. g. the US.

No other reinsurance market maintains a comparable share of international business contacts and is especially noted for the high proportion of its business originating from abroad.[105] The role of London as an international centre of *insurance* has grown historically. Its origin was linked to a great extent to shipping and increasing world trade. Great Britain had a leading role as the biggest marine nation with a large merchant fleet. The vast scope of the British empire led to a steady increase in the international significance of the British insurance industry. Additionally another aspect which is still of importance today played an important role, namely the spread of the use of the English language world-wide.

However London's role as a *reinsurance* centre did not develop as smoothly as the insurance tradition may suggest. Before World War II most English insurance companies reinsured their risks with reinsurance companies on the Conti-

---

101 Andrea Schulte, *Rückversicherung in Deutschland und England: Unterschiede in Recht und Praxis,* Karlsruhe: Verlag Versicherungswirtschaft e. V., 1990, 23

102 1991 was the most recent year in which Lloyd's Market planning department provided figures.

103 Toby Shelley, "Maintaining the City's global role," in: The London Underwriting Centre, One year on, *A Lloyds List Special Supplement*, October 1994, 9-10

104 Horst K. Jannott, "Rückversicherung – Einige praktische Aspekte der Arbeit im Ausland", in: *Versicherungswirtschaft* 7/1982, 376-386 (382)

105 Horst K. Jannott, "Rückversicherung – Einige praktische Aspekte der Arbeit im Ausland", in: *Versicherungswirtschaft* 7/1982, 376-386 (382)

nent. This may come as a surprise if one considers the fact that reinsurance can be traced back to the 14th century. Reinsurance began with marine reinsurance, where England having a vast merchant fleet had to be involved. What is perhaps the earliest recorded example of a reinsurance contract was a marine reinsurance contract drawn up in 1370.[106] On a voyage from Cadiz to Sluys, the underwriter reinsured that part of the journey through the Mediterranean. Marine reinsurance also became common in England by served the purpose of securing the owner's ship and goods against the financial loss of sinking by backing up the cedant.

Increasingly the profit margins in reinsurance became of interest to parties who were not always honest in their intentions. Speculators became involved in the business.[107] People insured things in which they had not the slightest interest. In case of loss they could nevertheless enforce their claims if the policy was a so called „policy proof of interest" (ppi). The „policy" contained a kind of warranty to indemnify each person being party to the contract regardless of whether the person had an insurable interest or not. There were cases in which multiple contracts for the loss of one ship were signed. It was also the case that insurers took on risks and reinsured those risks for a premium lower than the premium for the primary insurance premium. („Prämiendifferenzgeschäfte") As a result of this abuse, marine insurance was declared illegal by the Marine Insurance Act (MIA) 1746.[108] An exception was made if the original insurer became insolvent or bankrupt or should die. Of course this exception could only enable a fresh insurance policy to be taken out by the insured, since the first insurance had become void. So the effect of the act was to forbid the practice of reinsurance but not to forbid insuring again in the circumstances mentioned. It is clear from early available records that reinsurance was generally practised throughout the eighteenth century and had become well established by the beginning of the nineteenth century. The prohibition of marine reinsurance put into force by the act of 1746 was not abolished until 1864. It appears nevertheless that cases of marine reinsurance were recorded in England during the intervening period, while the practice steadily developed abroad. Reinsurance not only developed in Continental Europe during this time, but also in the US. In the US the courts refused to acknowledge the English MIA as part of the accepted Common Law and there-

---

106 C. E. Golding, *The Law and Practice of Reinsurance,* 5th ed., London: Witherby & Co. Ltd., 1987, 2

107 Christoph Pfeiffer, *Einführung in die Rückversicherung,* 4th. ed., Wiesbaden: Gabler, 1.5.1.; Andrea Schulte, *Rückversicherung in Deutschland und in England: Unterschiede in Recht und Praxis,* Karlsruhe: Verlag für Versicherungswirtschaft, 6

108 C. E. Golding, *The Law and Practice of Reinsurance,* 5th ed., London: Witherby & Co. Ltd, 1987, 3

fore in the US reinsurance could strongly develop at quite an early stage.[109] Remarkably, American judges in the early 18th century fell back on French reinsurance norms and practice and therefore adopted French jurisdiction as source of law for the American reinsurance practice.

Despite the fact that the beginnings of reinsurance were not very favourable in England, London was able to catch up as a centre in spite of those obstacles. After abolition of the 1864 reinsurance prohibition no new legislation was passed to allow reinsurance. But since London was already an important primary insurance market where all the necessary communication was running, those facilities could easily be used to integrate reinsurance structures too. As such, London serves as a special assembly point for reinsurers coming from all countries. The London reinsurance market's character is to bring the parties together in one place. This distinguishes it from e.g. the Continent, where no comparable reinsurance business centre is to be found.[110]

3.3 Market participants

3.3.1 The reinsurer

For the reasons mentioned above, primary insurers seek to cede the risks or part of the risks they have written. Every kind of primary insurer – even motor or health insurers- seeks reinsurance cover. Reinsurance companies sell this reinsurance cover. A distinction must be made between two kinds of reinsurance companies. A professional reinsurance company conducts exclusively reinsurance business, i.e. such an enterprise does not carry out any primary insurance and subsequently has no direct dealings with the insured.[111] A professional reinsurance company is able to insure all categories of risks offered by the primary insurer – the ceding office. As already mentioned, the „separation of field" principle (*Spartentrennungsprinzip*) does not apply in reinsurance. It may also occur that primary insurance companies take on reinsurance business. Two categories

---

109 Christoph Pfeiffer, *Einführung in die Rückversicherung,* 4th. ed., Wiesbaden: Gabler, 1994, 1.5.1.

110 For the German insurance and reinsurance business it is significant, that the companies have offices all over the country in Munich, Hanover or Cologne, but not in one particular place which supersedes the other in importance. Andrea Schulte, *Rückversicherung in Deutschland und England: Unterschiede in Recht und Praxis,* Karlsruhe: Verlag Versicherungswirtschaft e. V., 1990, 206

111 Christoph Pfeiffer, *Einführung in die Rückversicherung*, 4th. ed., Wiesbaden: Gabler, 1994, 1.3.1

shall be distinguished according to the volume of business to illustrate this.[112] The majority of primary insurers take on reinsurance business on an occasional basis. They conduct reinsurance business on a reciprocity basis with other primary insurance companies to distribute a certain risk. Besides this type of insurer, there are primary insurers that appear systematically in the reinsurance market. At some stage they make a previously integrated reinsurance department independent, which then acts like a professional reinsurer in its own right.

3.3.2 Lloyds of London

Lloyds of London has been the traditional London insurance institution since the late seventeenth century. It is active in all insurance business segments and acts as primary insurer as well as reinsurer. Even during the 19th century Lloyds was able to profit from the prohibition of reinsurance as mentioned above by acting as a co-insurer during this time. It is no different to other insurance entities that simultaneously sell and seek reinsurance cover.[113] However, the special character of Lloyds derives from the fact that it is organised into so called "syndicates". A „syndicate" is an assembly consisting of "Names". These are underwriting members – private individuals, who are liable to pay for an underwritten risk, if a claim arises. Its involvement in reinsurance disputes – either in the role of a ceding office or as a reinsurance syndicate – reflects the importance of Lloyds for the London reinsurance market. The lawyers interviewed stated that Lloyds is involved in every second reinsurance file they open. This figure does not include the Names litigation.[114]

3.4 Reinsurance intermediaries

3.4.1 General

Insurance intermediaries[115] act as brokers or underwriting agents. As underwriting agents they are employees of the insurance company. As brokers they are

112 Christoph Pfeiffer, *Einführung in die Rückversicherung*, 4th ed., Wiesbaden: Gabler, 1994, 1.3.2

113 For further information on Lloyds: Anthony Brown, *Hazard Unlimited*, London: Lloyd's of London Press Ltd, 1987

114 The term „ Names litigation" refers to a collective for claims of "Names" brought against their underwriting agents for negligent underwriting, a type of litigation which has become very prominent and publicly reported in recent years.

115 The term „intermediary" has no legal definition. In this context it shall mean a third

self- employed. According to English law they then act on behalf of the insured in placing insurance.[116] Although he is an agent of the insured, the broker generally receives commission from the insurer.

3.4.2 The broker

Brokers attend to the vast majority of business originating exclusively from abroad. One may say that reinsurance placed in the London market is international and is mainly placed through brokers. The duties of reinsurance brokers are governed by the law of agency, the customs and practices of the London insurance market, the Insurance Brokers (Registration) Act 1977, and the rules and regulations that have been promulgated under this act.[117] Additionally a Code of Conduct applies which is pursuant to Section 10 of the Insurance Brokers (Registration) Act, and which was drawn up by the Insurance Brokers Registration Council („IBRC“), coming into effect on 21 November 1994. It replaced the previous Code of Conduct that had been in force since 1978.

Also in the relationship between the parties to a reinsurance contract and the brokers, a special relationship of trust used to be the basis for business. This becomes apparent if one considers that traditionally, reinsurance brokers did not enter into written agreements with their clients setting out the parties' respective duties and obligations.[118] When London market clients place business, they give instructions orally. Instructions from overseas reinsureds are either received directly or from locally based brokers, who are called „producing brokers“. The client expects not only that the reinsurance broker places the reinsurance contract at the most competitive rates and on the best terms, but also that the broker provides a comprehensive range of services to administer the contract.

The customer's spirit of trust should be rendered with loyalty and integrity by the broker. This is in accordance with one of the fundamental principles of the 1994 IBRC Code of Conduct. It requires that:

„if insurance brokers are placed in the position where interests or the interests of a third party to whom the insurance broker owes a duty conflict with the interest of the client, they should withdraw from the matter unless after full disclosure all relevant parties agree in writing that they should continue.“

---

person or entity who in some way assists in a particular reinsurance deal.

116 Edward H. Gumbel, "Neue Vertriebswege und das Beispiel des britischen Versicherungsmaklers", in: *Versicherungsrecht*, 1992, Heft 31, 1293 – 1300 (1293)

117 J.S. Butler, *Reinsurance Practice and the Law*, London: Lloyd's of London Press,1993, looseleaf, Service Issue No. 7, 1 September 1996, 2.2.1

118 J.S. Butler, *Reinsurance Practice and the Law*, ibid, 2.1.

The broker's main task is to place the reinsurance cover that the ceding office is seeking. He will present the reinsurer with the relevant information needed to assess the risk. He will then try to adjust the terms under which the risk can be placed between the ceding office and the reinsurer. He will talk to and mediate between the parties until an agreement can be reached or until it becomes obvious that the parties will not close the deal.

The broker will usually draft the "slip" as well as the wording of the policy that is to follow the slip. A slip is a paper that documents the reinsurance contract in short. The slip may vary slightly in form or content, depending upon the nature of the risk ceded, however it will contain the following elements:

- the identity of the reinsured
- the nature of the risk
- the duration of the reinsurance
- the limits of the indemnity and the reinsured's retention
- the premium.[119]

This brief form of contract is only preliminary however. The slip is subsequently replaced by a full contract wording. The full wording describes the content of the contract at length. Unfortunately it may happen and often has happened in the past, that a contract wording never comes into existence. This may lead to implications that shall be discussed below. The broker will also collect the premium from the ceding office and deduct his royalty from it before he passes the money on to the reinsurer. His task is furthermore to collect the claims arising under the reinsurance contract. He will sustain communication between reinsurer and ceding office. It may also occur that the brokers will act both as broker and underwriting agent, which may lead to implications that will also be discussed below.

3.4.3 Underwriting agencies

Underwriting agencies are authorised by the reinsurer to accept a reinsurance risk on his behalf. In reinsurance a direct relationship between the professional reinsurers present in the London market and their clients is kept within limits which seem modest compared to German standards.[120] One obvious way of establishing underwriting operations in new markets is for the insurer to set up

---

119 J. S. Butler, *Reinsurance Practice and the Law*, ibid, 8.1.1

120 Edward H. Gumbel, "Neue Vertriebswege und das Beispiel des britischen Versicherungsmaklers", in: *Versicherungsrecht*, 1992, Heft 31, 1293 – 1300 (1295)

branch offices or subsidiaries in those markets.[121] These methods require substantial investment before business can start. One solution to this problem which became very widespread, was the use of underwriting agents. They were able to provide local expertise and underwrite on behalf of insurers without the need for substantial capital investment.

The underwriting agreement is the contractual bond between the underwriting agent and his principal. It is an agreement that creates an agency and bestows on the agent authority to underwrite.[122] The agent is obliged to use reasonable care and skill in underwriting. In addition, each party will be entitled to rely on representations which are made by one party and relied on by the other. However, there will not, as a matter of law, be any implied assumption that the principal has little or no knowledge relevant to the underwriting. The same applies regarding the agent's access to all relevant information. This is despite the fact that such assumptions would, in most cases, reflect the true nature of the relationship. The necessary control by underwriters of underwriting agents has often in the past been absent from Underwriting Agency agreement.

The agent usually delegates authority under the Agency Agreement to undertake functions in addition to underwriting such as the investigation and payment of claims. However, the agent also has implied authority to perform whatever functions are necessary to enable him to carry out his duties properly. Such implied authority normally includes authority to collect premiums and handle claims. When one considers that underwriting is, by nature, an inexact science (if it can be properly described as a science at all) and that underwriters and their agents are often hundreds or thousands of miles away and the agents' earnings based upon premium income, then it is not difficult to see obvious conflicts of interests which may arise, and consequently, the enormous temptations which the agent may be led into.[123]

Although genuine fraud may be comparatively rare, it is difficult for a relationship of trust and good faith to be established where the agent has every interest in the volume of business and little or no interest in the ultimate profitability of the underwriting. Common factors arising in disputes concerning underwriting agencies are very often one or more of the following:

(a) underwriters moving into types of business of which they have little knowledge or experience;

---

121 John Hanson, „Reinsurance, Binding authorities, Brokers, Fronting companies & Premium Stripping“, Paper presented at the 2nd annual Reinsurance coverage dispute strategy Euroforum Seminar, 17th November 1995, The Merchant Centre, London, 1

122 John Hanson, ibid, 6;7

123 John Hanson, ibid, 2

(b) underwriters doing business in countries in which they have little experience;

(c) underwriters relying on promises made by brokers or underwriting agents;

(d) the broker acting both as broker and underwriting agent;

(e) regulatory obstacles preventing underwriters writing direct through the underwriting agent and fronting companies being interposed between underwriting agent and principal.

For these reasons and as experience has shown, contractual obligation such as the agency agreement may on occasions be worthless. Frequently, as a consequence when it comes to disputes resulting in litigation between the respective insurer and reinsurer, which has been created by the defaulting underwriting agents, the agent is ignored as a potential litigant, while the two principals resolve the dispute themselves.[124] Taking the starting point that underwriting agencies are instituted if the principal for some reason in not able to be geographically present in the marketplace concerned, defaulting agencies create cross-border litigation, where the key issue is the extent of the agent's authority to bind its reinsurer to reinsurance or retrocession contracts.

3.4.4 The broker as underwriting agent

When a broker acts as underwriting agent, the broker will have access to far more information about the risk than the underwriter on whose behalf the broker acts.[125] The broker, based on information available to him, will take underwriting decisions that bind the underwriter without the broker taking on any of the underwriting risk. The basis on which commission payable to the broker will normally be calculated, can create a strong commercial incentive to the broker to underwrite as large a volume of business as possible. This may occur without sufficient regard to the quality of the risks that are bound on behalf of the underwriter.

A broker acting as underwriting agent will typically receive brokerage from the insured, underwriting commission from the underwriters, and possibly overriding commission along with this. Commission may be calculated as part of the premium income. Commission paid to the broker may total as much of the gross premium paid by the insured. This leaves underwriters with only 60 % of gross

---

124 J. S. Butler, *Reinsurance Practice and the Law*, ibid., 3.2

125 John Hanson, „Reinsurance, Binding authorities, Brokers, Fronting companies & Premium Stripping, ibid, 8

premium income out of which to pay 100 % of claims must be paid. Without a duty of utmost good faith implied into the agency relationship, it should be the function of the Underwriting Agency Agreement to, as far as possible, set out the duties owed by each of the parties.

3.5 Reinsurance in the London market

All forms of reinsurance contracts are signed within the London market. However the London market is known most for its "excess of loss" reinsurance business.[126] These *excess of loss* contracts are a subdivision of non-proportional contracts and they may come in the form of excess of loss, catastrophe excess of loss or excess of loss ratio (stop loss ratio).[127] These forms of reinsurance cover have the following aspect in common: the ceding office and the reinsurers do not share each loss in fixed proportions, and may not share some losses at all. The ceding office will bear all losses up to a certain figure (a so called retention) and the reinsurer will deal with the balance of any loss above this figure.

The basis of LMX (London Market Excess of Loss) business is similar to that of standard excess of loss treaty reinsurance. It is intended to limit the exposure of the reinsured. The exposure may regard a single loss arising from a major individual risk, or come from an aggregation of losses on a number of policies triggered by a single event or occurrence. A „spiral“ developed rapidly during the 1980s in the London retrocession market. Many purchasers of reinsurance in that market began to accept such reinsurance from other participants in the same market who were exposed to the same original risks.[128]

It is obvious that this kind of business bears a high amount of risk for the reinsurer. The underwriting of excess of loss policies did indeed prove to bring trouble to reinsurance to an extent previously unknown. That is not say that Excess of Loss business cannot be profitably underwritten. The recent troubles arose primarily from the spiral, but generally from inadequately high rate levels. The resulting concentration of loss back into the hands of relatively few participants has clearly exaggerated the poor underwriting results recorded by many London companies and Lloyds syndicates in recent years.

---

126 Andrea Schulte, *Rückversicherung in Deutschland und England: Unterschiede in Recht und Praxis*, Karlsruhe: Verlag Versicherungswirtschaft e. V., 1990, 216

127 G.C.A. Dickson and J.T. Steele, *Introduction to Insurance*, 2nd ed., London: Pitman Publishing, 1984, 185-186

128 J. S. Butler, *Reinsurance Practice and the Law,* London: Lloyd's of London Press, looseleaf, 1993, Service Issue No. 7, 1 September 1996, 5.3.5.3

4. Potential Legal Conflicts

4.1 Reinsurance law

With regards to the legal framework, a distinction may be made between regulatory, contractual issues and regulations that apply for reinsurance intermediaries such as brokers. Since this paper shall examine the relationship of the reinsurance parties, it is not intended to deal with regulatory aspects and state control on reinsurance.[129]

4.1.1 General

A reinsurance transaction is an agreement made between two parties. In this agreement the reinsured or ceding company[130] and the reinsurer, agree that the reinsurer accepts a certain fixed share of the reinsured's risk upon terms as set out in the agreement.[131] The contract itself may relate to one particular reinsurance and be expressed in a reinsurance policy. It may also provide for the reinsurance of a number of risks and be expressed in the form of a treaty. In either case the reinsurance is defined by the terms of the contract and is subject to all its provisions and limitations. The „reinsured" (or „ceding company") is the original insurer who, having issued a policy to an insured to cover a certain risk, wishes to relieve itself of a part thereof. The „reinsurer" is the company who accepts that part of the risk that is reinsured. This gives an idea of the real nature of reinsurance. It cannot exist without there first being direct insurance, for the first party is the reinsured who has already insured a direct policy. Yet the insured

---

129 For an overview of the regulatory framework of reinsurance in Germany and the U.K. see: Andrea Schulte, *Rückversicherung in Deutschland und England: Unterschiede in Recht und Praxis*, Karlsruhe: Verlag Versicherungswirtschaft e. V. 1990, 103 – 127. On regulatory framework concerning brokers compare: Edward H. Gumbel, "Neue Vertriebswege und das Beispiel des britischen Versicherungsmaklers", in: *Versicherungsrecht*, 1992, Heft 31, 1293 – 1300

130 This is a term also often used, especially in relation to reinsurance on a proportional basis.

131 C. E. Golding, *The Law and Practice of Reinsurance*, Witherby & Co., London 5th ed., 1987, 7 subs.

under that direct policy has no interest in or rights regarding the reinsurance. It has no privity of contract in the transaction and can make no claim thereunder.[132] The common law doctrine of *privity of contract* establishes that only the parties to a contract can sue or be sued under it. It can neither confer rights nor impose liabilities on others. [133] The reinsurer is certainly liable concerning its share of any claim made by the insured. Its liability is limited to the insurer and to the insurer only, for the insurer alone is the other party to the contract. The insured may have an indirect interest in knowing that his insurer is supported by sound reinsurers, since that goes to increase his security. However he has not and cannot have direct interests in the reinsurance contract.

The consideration for the contract is the reinsurance premium paid by the reinsured to the reinsurer. *Consideration* is essential to the validity of any contract other than one made by deed. Without consideration an agreement which is not made by deed is not binding.[134] This may be a share of the original premium subject to a deduction, such as for commission or otherwise as may be agreed at the time the contract was made. The wording embodying the terms of the agreement under the contract is signed by the party charged. In the case of facultative reinsurance a policy would be issued and signed by the reinsurer.

A treaty wording, which contains reciprocal undertakings, is signed by or on behalf of each party thereto. As shown, reinsurance law very much concentrates on the contractual relationship of the parties.[135] In English law a special statute for reinsurance does not exist. The Marine Insurance Act 1906 is to be regarded as setting out the general legal position for marine and non-marine insurance and reinsurance. However the extent to which the Marine Insurance Act (MIA) of 1906 is applicable to reinsurance is under dispute.[136]

The relevant paragraphs of the Marine Insurance Act state the following:

17. A contract of marine insurance is a contract based upon utmost good faith, and if the utmost good faith is not observed by either party the contract may be avoided by the other party.

18.(1) Subject to the provisions of this section, the assured must disclose to the insurer before the contract is concluded, every material circumstance which

---

132 There may exist however certain exceptions, e. g. the „cut-through" clause.

133 Elizabeth A. Martin, *A Dictionary of Law*, 3d ed., Oxford University Press, Oxford 1994, 307

134 Elizabeth A. Martin, *A Dictionary of Law*, 3 ed., Oxford University Press, Oxford, 1994, 87

135 Christoph Pfeiffer, *Einführung in die Rückversicherung*, 4th ed., Wiesbaden: Gabler, 1994, 1.4.1

136 Andrea Schulte, *Rückversicherung in Deutschland und England: Unterschiede in Recht und Praxis*, Karlsruhe: Verlag Versicherungswirtschaft e. V., 1990, 73

is known to the assured, and the assured is deemed to know every circumstance which, in the ordinary course of business, ought to be known by him. If the assured fails to make such a disclosure the insurer may avoid the contract.

18.(2) Every circumstance is material which would influence the judgment of a prudent insurer in fixing the premium or determining whether he will take the risk.

18.(3) In the absence of enquiry the following circumstances need not be disclosed, namely ....

(b) any circumstance which is known or presumed to be known to the insurer. The insurer is presumed to know matters of common notoriety or knowledge and matters which an insurer in the ordinary course of his business, as such ought to know;

(c) any circumstance as to which information is waived by the insurer.

18.(4) Whether any particular circumstance which is not disclosed be material or not, is in each case a question of fact.

18.(6) The term „circumstance“ includes any communication made to, or information received by, the assured.

19. Subject to the provisions of the preceding section as to circumstances which need not be disclosed, where an insurance is effected for the assured by an agent, the agent must disclose to the insurer:

(a) every material circumstance which is known to himself, and an agent to insure is deemed to know every circumstance which in the ordinary course of business ought to be known by, or to have been communicated to, him; and

(b) every material circumstance which the assured is bound to disclose unless it comes to his knowledge too late to communicate to the agent.

20.(1) Every material representation made by the assured or his agent to the insurer during the negotiations for the contract, and before the contract is concluded, must be true. If it be untrue the insurer may avoid the contract.

20.(2) A representation is material which would influence the judgment of a prudent insurer in fixing the premium or determining whether he will take the risk.

20.(3) A representation may be either a representation of a matter of fact or of a matter of expectation or belief.

20.(4) A representation as to a matter of fact is true if it be substantially correct, that is to say if the difference between what is represented and what is actually correct would not be considered material by a prudent insurer.

20.(5) A representation as to a matter of expectation or belief is true if it is made in good faith ...

20.(7) Whether a particular representation is material or not, is in each case a question of fact.

Independent of statutory provisions the following inherent principles apply to insurance and reinsurance alike.[137]

(1) There must be an insurable interest.

(2) The contract is made in utmost good faith (*uberrima fidei*). It calls for the disclosure by the reinsured to the reinsurer of every material fact relating to the risk to be reinsured.

(3) The contract is one of indemnity.

(4) The subject matter of the contract must be in existence at the time the contract is made.

Insurable interest is vested in the reinsured and the fact that it has issued a policy and accepted liability to its original insured has been held to give it an insurable interest sufficient to enable it to reinsure. The point is, that although the reinsured has no actual legal interest in the property subject to the original insurance, it has assumed responsibility in regard to it. It has therefore put itself into a position, recognised by law, in which it would be harmed by its loss. Hence, its insurable interest must be circumscribed by the nature and scope of the liability which it has assumed, so that a company which has undertaken to insure property against (say) fire, would not thereby incur loss in the case of burglary, for that is a loss which was not object to the policy. It has been mentioned that reinsurance disputes do not always go to court but are also frequently dealt with privately through arbitration. Therefore, it is difficult to get an overview of which general legal problems reinsurance disputes focus on. For this reason, it was even more important to see which results the interviewees gave on the subject of general legal problems.

4.1.2 Misrepresentation and Non-Disclosure

A special field of legal attention in reinsurance disputes is the information presented to a prospective reinsurer. The principle of *utmost good faith* requires that the reinsured discloses every material circumstance. These are circumstances that might affect the reinsurer's judgment in determining whether or not he shall enter the contract or on what terms.[138] The duty of disclosure in reinsurance business is qualified by the important fact that it is transacted between parties

137 C. E. Golding, *The Law and Practice of Reinsurance,* 5th ed., London: Witherby & Co. Ltd., 1987, 8 subs.

138 J. S. Butler, *Reinsurance Practice and the Law*, London: Lloyd's of London Press Ltd, 1993, looseleaf, Service Issue No. 7, 1 September 1996, 24.4.1

who are equally expert in their business.[139] Therefore the imbalance concerning knowledge of the risk, that is the underlying justification for the obligation to fully disclose, is not so acute in the case of reinsurance.[140] There is still of course an imbalance in that the reinsurer will not know about many aspects of the reinsured's business. But, subject to any peculiarities attaching to that particular reinsured, the reinsurer should have a reasonable knowledge of the way in which the reinsured does its business. He may either, through his own direct writings or the underwriting of other reinsureds be familiar with the risks that he is being asked to reinsure against. This situation will sometimes lessen to a minor degree the duty imposed upon the reinsured. This may occur where the facts should be known by the intending reinsurers, or which the reinsured is fully entitled to assume that they already know. Subject to this qualification and provided that even this is fully justified by the circumstances, the duty of good faith is no less important. A fundamental rule of reinsurance is expressed as follows:

The foundation of reinsurance is

(1) full information, as far as is possessed by the reinsured, regarding the risk on which the reinsurance is requested.

(2) full information as to the amount retained by the reinsured on the identical property on which the reinsurance is requested.

The lawyers revealed information that every second case on average involves misrepresentation or non-disclosure. Misrepresentation means the making of a wrong statement with the intention of persuading someone to enter into a contract. It is a general contract law feature that a party having entered into a contract under those circumstances can seek to avoid the contract. Non-disclosure goes beyond the general duty not to deliver any false information to the other party. The remedy in these cases is avoidance, not damages.[141] The effect of the remedy of avoidance is generally speaking a reversal of account. The parties are restored to the position, *inter-se*, in which they would have been in if they had not entered into the contract. It is the policy that is avoided, not the claim. An insurer cannot say „I am not paying this claim because of non-disclosure." If he does, and he keeps the policy alive, he puts his right to avoid at risk.[142]

---

139 C.E. Golding, The Law and Practice of Reinsurance, 5th ed., Witherby & Co.Ltd., London, 1987, 9

140 Martin Bakes, „Misrepresentation, Non-disclosure and the legal length of Pinocchio' nose", Paper presented at the 2nd Euro-Forum Reinsurance Coverage Dispute Strategy, 17th November 1995, The Merchant Centre, London, 1-20 (18)

141 Martin Bakes, „Misrepresentation, Non-disclosure and the legal length of Pinocchio' nose", Paper presented at the 2nd Euro-Forum Reinsurance Coverage Dispute Strategy, 17th November 1995, The Merchant Centre, London, 1-20, (2,3)

142 West -v- National Motor and Accident Insurance Union Limited (1955) 1 Lloyd's

The remedy of avoidance has been criticised as being draconic.[143] It takes no fault into account . It does not matter for these purposes, whether the failure to disclose was deliberate, negligent or incorrect. It hits the insured very hard. It is seen as the insurer's remedy. Whilst the duty is owed by the insured to the insurer and by the insurer to the insured the case law is almost invariably concerned with insurers seeking to avoid a policy in circumstances where claims far outweigh the premium paid. Cases in which the insured seeks to recover the premium are very rare indeed. The frequency of misrepresentation and non-disclosure occurring however, may be attributed to the increasing complexity of the business of reinsurance in recent years. For many years the test of materiality was based upon the idea of the „prudent underwriter". Facts are *material* if their revelation to the prospect reinsurer is essential; otherwise the contract may be null and void.

The court's task, in deciding whether or not the defendant insurer can avoid the policy for non-disclosure, must be to determine based on fact whether by applying the standard of the judgment of a prudent insurer, the insurer in question would have been influenced in fixing the premium or determining whether to take the risk if he had been informed of the undisclosed circumstances before entering the contract. The effect of non-disclosure may be clear enough that the court will not require any further or only little additional evidence, to decide in favour of the insurer. In doubtful cases, on the other hand, the court may require evidence from the insurers themselves before being able to hold that the right to avoid the policy has been established. Subsequently, two prominent cases as to the information which has to be revealed to the reinsurer have been decided on by the courts: Container Transport International Inc. v. Oceanus Mutual Underwriting Association (Bermuda) Ltd[144] and Pan Atlantic Insurance Company Limited v. Pine Top Insurance Company Limited[145] in which case CTI v. Oceanus was partly overruled. In January 1984,the Court of Appeal held in the case of CTI v. Oceanus that the duty of disclosure in a marine insurance situation required disclosure of every fact which a prudent underwriter would wish to take into account whilst considering the proposed insurance, with a view to deciding whether to take it up and on what terms.[146] No evidence need be given as to what the actual underwriter would have done. It is not necessary to produce evidence to the effect that, had disclosure of the fact concerned been made, then a differ-

---

Rep. 207

143 Martin Bakes, ibid

144 (1984) 1 Lloyd's Rep 476

145 (1992) 1 Lloyd's Rep 101 (QB Com. Court), (1993) 1 Lloyd's Rep 496 (CA)

146 Gordon Cornish, "Some Recent Developments in English Reinsurance Law", in: *Zeitschrift für Versicherungswesen*, 21/86, 556 – 560 (558)

ent decision would have been reached. This is known as the "CTI test" on the interpretation of materiality of the wording of Section 18 (2) Marine Insurance Act 1906 under which the insurer may avoid a contract if material facts have not been disclosed to him. In the case of Pan Atlantic v. Pine Top, the court followed the ruling of the decision on CTI v. Oceanus and favoured the criterion that non-disclosed facts are generally qualified to alter the risk.[147] However, the Pan Atlantic decision contains a new element insofar as the insured now has to prove that the non-disclosed fact indeed has influenced him to underwrite the risk. The question arises to what extent the knowledge of facts ("material circumstances") may be assigned to intermediaries. This is a legal question of great relevance for the London market where brokers mainly close the deals. The legal position may be summarised as follows:[148]

An underwriter is entitled to avoid the policy if:

(a) any material fact has either been misrepresented or not disclosed, a fact being „material" if it would influence the judgment (in the sense of playing a part in the decision making process) of a prudent underwriter in determining whether to accept the risk and, if so, on what terms he will do so and

(b) the actual underwriter has been induced thereby to enter into the contract.

The element of inducement introduces the need for a causal connection between the non-disclosure/misrepresentation and the underwriting of the risk. It does not mean that it has to be the cause of the risk being underwritten. It is put to the „decisive influence" test in another guise although as has been pointed out by judges and commentators it that goes some way towards meeting the concerns of those who feel that the decisive influence test should be adopted. With reference to a prognosis of the legal development in this area, Bakes (1995) suggests that[149]

„in practice relatively few cases of non-disclosure/misrepresentation will be decided differently, e.g. have a different result, following the decision in Pan Atlantic, to the way in which they would have been decided before Pan Atlantic. I say this because within the confines of the duty of good faith few judges in my experience have said that they have been driven to decide a case in a particular

147 David Kendall, "Auswirkung der neuesten englischen Rechtsprechung zu den Versicherungsnehmern obliegenden vorvertraglichen Aufklärungspflichten", in: *Zeitschrift für Versicherungswesen*, 21/94, 581 – 588, (583)

148 Martin Bakes, „Misrepresentation, Non-disclosure and the legal length of Pinocchio' nose", Paper presented at the 2nd Euroforum Reinsurance Coverage Dispute Strategy, 17th November 1995, The Merchant Centre, London, 1-20(16)

149 Martin Bakes, „Misrepresentation, Non-disclosure and the legal length of Pinocchio' nose", Paper presented at the 2nd Euro-Forum Reinsurance Coverage Dispute Strategy, 17th November 1995, The Merchant Centre, London, 1-20,(16;17)

way because of the terms of the Court of Appeal judgments in CTI. I would suggest that the problem (if one perceives it as a problem) lies not with the decision in CTI but in the general duty of good faith and the duties enshrined in the Marine Insurance Act closely linked, of course, with the nature of the remedy, i. e. avoidance. In future the need for inducement may provide judges with another ground on which to find against an underwriter's case if the judge is hostile to the case. ... Inducement will however allow the court to take into account the actual underwriter and thus the law will not provide as effective a shield to the nodding donkey. In practice the change in the law is likely to expose insurers to having to give greater discovery of documents than previously (insureds and reinsureds will want to look at other similar risks underwritten by that insurer or reinsurer), and it will be more difficult (but not impossible) to run a non-disclosure case without calling the underwriter."

The fact that London is a broker's market as well as that the quality of those intermediaries varies to a considerable degree might serve as explanation for the frequency of the problem. There are numerous hints in the literature on how the quality of brokers may vary and in which position of conflicts of interests they sometimes find themselves.[150] The lawyers interviewed expressed a strong view that some brokers are more concerned with the volume of business, the turnover and their premium than anything else. Although the information the brokers give the reinsurer can only be as good as that received from the ceding office, the presentation of the risk lets an area open to dress up a risk more attractively in order to find reinsurance cover for it. It was indicated by the interviewed that in nearly 40 % of the cases which lead to disputes or in which legal advice is sought brokers are involved. This means that a large share of disputes revolve around the problems of misrepresentation and non-disclosure.[151]

The involvement of underwriting agents in disputes is lower. Twelve of the interviewed would not mention the agents in the questionnaire at all. The remaining nineteen interviewed assessed the involvement of agents at 30 % of the cases which lead to disputes or in which legal advice is sought. The question of cover of a reinsurance contract also contributes considerably to reinsurance disputes. In a half of all cases, whether a claim falls within the scope of a reinsurance con-

---

150 J. S. Butler, *Reinsurance Practice and the Law*, London: Lloyd's of London Press Ltd., 1993, looseleaf, Service Issue No. 7, 1 September 1996, 2.3, Christoph Pfeiffer, *Einführung in die Rückversicherung*, 4th ed., Wiesbaden: Gabler, 1994, 1.3.3, Dirk Schmidt-Prange, "Katerstimmung in der Rückversicherung und wie es dazu kam", in: *Zeitschrift für das Versicherungswesen*, 21/85, 572 – 574 (574)

151 see *inter alia* : Everett v Hogg, Robinson & Gardner Mountain (Insurance) Ltd., (QB Com Ct) (1973) 2 Lloyd's Rep 217

tract or not is debated.[152] The duties of the parties are also frequently discussed. In 60 % of cases, certain questions give rise to disputes between the reinsurer and the reinsured, for example:

is the reinsurer entitled to inspect the records of the cedant ?

does the reinsurer have to follow the cedant's settlement of the cedant with the insured ?

4.1.3 Liquidation and cross-border insolvency

Liquidation and „run-off" are not subject to disputes but frequently initiate disputes. Run-off is a situation in which an insurance or reinsurance company has ceased underwriting. Nevertheless they must deal with the contracts that they are running. There are two possibilities to cope with this situation. The former company can carry on working with a small number of staff. This will be done whilst other parts of the company continue to function. The other and very common possibility is to give over the claims handling to a run-off company. Those interviewed made it clear that the suspicion of the other party being close to or in liquidation or run-off might be a reason to start proceedings. As not all companies in the marketplace are registered in England, liquidation is an important legal issue regarding cross-border conflicts. Many companies are trading branches of foreign corporations who may have assets, and perhaps creditors, within the English jurisdiction.[153] The question arises as to how English law deals with the insolvency of the foreign company where a winding-up order is made in its home country. Unfortunately, no universal code governing international insolvency has yet been produced. The European Union has produced a draft of a Bankruptcy Convention, but „insolvency proceedings concerning insurance undertakings" are specifically excluded from its scope. The Convention does not define „insurance undertakings". But it is likely that this expression will be interpreted to include insurance and reinsurance companies. Other schemes, such as the Model International Insolvency Co-operation Agreement (MIICA), designed to take effect by way of a signed international convention, are in a speculative stage only. They are unlikely to become statutory law in any form for some decades.

---

152 Under a treaty contract this question will arise more often than under a facultative contract.

153 J. S. Butler, *Reinsurance Practice and the Law*, London: Lloyd's of London Press, 1993, looseleaf, Service Issue No. 7, 1 September 1996, 23.4.4

The explanation in the introduction regarding unification efforts generally, can once again be proved here concerning the specific matter of insolvency. The immediate effect of the lacking unification regarding cross-border insolvency is, that national rules of the respective jurisdiction must be applied. The insolvency of some London market insurance companies is becoming a major concern for brokers, insureds and reinsureds doing business in the London market.[154] Figures compiled in the Insurance and Reinsurance Solvency Report[155] indicate that approximately fifty-five companies in the London market have ceased writing business since 1986. Of course, there are various reasons for this, in many cases not insolvency related. However a number of these companies are troubled financially or insolvent. Furthermore, there are indications that the number and size of insurance companies entering into insolvency proceedings will continue to rise. Given the number of failed insurance companies, the London market's response to the issue of insolvency is crucial. The shear number of collapses and the size of some of them mean that policyholders and other creditors cannot afford to simply write off insurance recoveries from insolvent insurance companies. It is important to remember that many of these companies have considerable assets. These assets exist as either cash or potential reinsurance recoveries or both. If these assets can be sold off and used to pay the creditors' claims quickly, then the market as a whole will benefit.

Traditionally, insolvent insurance companies were dealt with by way of liquidation. This has worked reasonably well for those companies with a predictable tail of business, for example, personal line business. However since the mid-1980s, it has become apparent that liquidation was not the best way to run off all insolvent insurance companies. This applied especially where the aim was not to ensure the quickest and most efficient return to creditors and pressure thus grew in the London market to find an alternative to liquidation. One of the alternatives developed in the London market is the creditors' scheme of arrangement under section 425 of the Companies Act 1985. In recent years, rather than to go into liquidation, a number of companies in the London market have successfully implemented schemes.

If a company's creditors consist of a large number of policyholders with small claims, an informal arrangement may not be feasible. But, for certain insurance companies, particularly those writing exclusively reinsurance business, there may be a small number of policyholders who account for a very large pro-

---

154 Andrew Wilkinson, „Alternative to liquidation", Paper presented at the Hawksmere seminar, „Insurance and Reinsurance Insolvency", 1-21, (8,9) November 1994, St James' Court, London, 1

155 Issue No. 83, September 1992

portion of actual and contingent liabilities. In such circumstances, it may be possible to reach an agreement with certain creditors, restoring the financial position of the company. This may happen by releasing contingent liabilities or by means of some form of debt equity or related instrument. These creditors may have every incentive to continue outside liquidation, thereby avoiding the uncertainty, expense and delay of liquidation. When looking at cross-border cases, the cross-border insolvency in reinsurance is an important issue, because not all companies in the marketplace London are registered in England. Many are trading branches of foreign corporations, and perhaps creditors, within the English jurisdiction.[156] There is at present no international convention regulating insolvency. In the absence of an international convention, it is necessary to adopt a pragmatic approach to international insolvencies, moulding existing remedies available under national laws to deliver appropriate relief.[157] International co-operation can only be achieved on this basis if the national courts are prepared to be flexible in their approach. The national courts could adopt a generous interpretation of the principles of international comity and not strongly support national patriotic interests.

In the UK, Section 426 of the Insolvency Act 1986 is an attempt to provide a mechanism whereby courts of certain jurisdictions can co-operate with each other in matters relating to international insolvencies.[158] The relevant parts of section 426 are as follows. Subsection (4) provides that:

„The courts having jurisdiction in relation to insolvency law in any part of the United Kingdom shall assist the courts having the corresponding jurisdiction in any other part of the United Kingdom or any relevant country or territory."

Subsection (5) provides that:

„For the purposes of subsection (4) a request made to a court in any part of the United Kingdom or in a relevant country or territory is authority for the court to which the request is made to apply, in relation to any matters specified in the request, the insolvency law which is applicable by either court in relation to comparable matters falling within its jurisdiction. In exercising its discretion under this subsection, a court shall have regard in particular to the rules of private international law."

Subsection (10) provides that:

In this section „insolvency law" means

156 J. S. Butler, *Reinsurance and the Law*, London: Lloyd's of London Press, 1993, looseleaf, Service Issue No. 7, 1 September 1996, 23.4

157 Richard Sheldon and Nick Segal, „Cross-border insolvency", Paper presented at Hawksmere Insurance and Reinsurance Insolvency Seminar, 8-9 November 1994, St James Court, London, 1-23, (1)

158 Richard Sheldon and Nick Segal, ibid, 1-23, (8)

(a) in relation to England and Wales, provision made by or under this Act or sections 6 to 10,12,15, 19 (c) and 20 (with Schedule 1) of the Company Directors Disqualification Act 1986 and extending to England and Wales.

....

(b) in relation to any relevant country or territory, so much of the law of that country or territory as corresponds to provisions falling with any of the foregoing paragraphs; and references in this subsection to any enactment clude, in relation to any time before the coming into force of that enactment the corresponding enactment in force at that time."

Subsection (1) provides that:

In this section „relevant country or territory" means

(a) any of the Channel Islands or the Isle of Man, or

(b) any country or territory designated for the purposes of this section by the Secretary of State by order made by statutory instrument.

The present „relevant countries or territories" are the following colonies or former colonies: Anguilla, Australia, Gibraltar, Hong Kong, The Republic of Ireland, Montserrat, New Zealand, St Helena, the Turks and Caicos Islands, Tuvalu, and the Virgin Islands.[159]

There are few cases illustrating the practical use to which section 426 of the Insolvency Act 1986 can be put.[160] A recent case which has given guidance as to the application and use of the section is Re Bank of Credit and Commerce International SA (1993) BCC 787. [161]

(a) BCCI (Overseas) Limited is a company incorporated in the Cayman Islands and in liquidation there. The liquidators obtained from the Cayman Court Letter of Request addressed to the English Court, pursuant to Section 426, seeking orders under sections 212 (misfeasance), 213 (fraudulent trading), 214 (wrongful trading), and 238 (transactions at an undervalue) of the Insolvency Act 1986 against various respondents who were not domiciled in England. Cayman Islands law did not include provisions comparable with all these sections. Nor did the English court have jurisdiction to make such orders in relation to a

---

159 See section 426 (11)(b) of the Insolvency Act 1986, and see SI 1986 No. 2123 (which came into force on 29/12/86) for the list of the relevant countries or territories.

160 Richard Sheldon and Nick Segal, „Cross-border insolvency", Paper presented at Hawksmere seminar Insurance and Reinsurance Insolvency, 8-9 November 1994, St James Court, London, 1-23, (9)

161 See also Re Dallhold Estates (UK) Pty Ltd. (1992) BCC 394 which was concerned with the making of an administration order in relation to an Australian company. Insurance companies within the scope of the Insurance Companies Act 1982 (i.e. those carrying on business in the UK) cannot be subject to an administration order (See Section 8(4) of the Insolvency Act 1986).

foreign company being wound up abroad unless under Section 426 of the Insolvency Act 426.

(b) The liquidators were therefore asking the English court to apply, in relation to a company incorporated in the Cayman Islands and in liquidation there, provisions which did not exist under Cayman law and which were subject only to Section 426.

3. The respondent submitted that it would be wrong in principle that the English court should be in a position to apply its own substantive law to the liquidation of a foreign jurisdiction. Why for example, should a director of such a company be subjected to liability for acts where there would be no liability under the law of the place of incorporation? Section 426 only applied to procedural provisions of English law to give effect to decisions reached by the requesting court.

4. In refusing to strike out the proceedings, Rattee J. held:

(i) There was no justification for restricting the effect of S. 426 to provisions of English law which were described as procedural rather than substantive. The effect of Section 426 was to give the court discretion as to whether it should apply English law, whether procedural or substantive, or the law of the requesting court, to matters specified in the relevant request from the foreign court.

(ii) Section 426 (4) imposed an obligation on the English court to assist the Grand Court in Cayman, though he considered that the English court did have discretion as to how to give such assistance. The court should exercise its discretion in favour of giving the assistance requested by the Cayman Court unless there was some good reason for not doing so.

There was no good reason in the rules of private international law or elsewhere for the court not giving the assistance requested. On the contrary there were good reasons why the court should give the assistance requested because of the affairs of BCCI (Overseas) and BCCI SA were „hopelessly intertwined“ and similar relief was being sought in the proceedings by the English liquidators of BCCI SA arising from the same facts.

(iii) In response to the argument that it would be unfair to impose burdens on persons under a foreign system of law, Rattee J. stressed that the assistance was requested by a foreign court which had thought fit to exercise its discretion to issue a letter of request to have that effect.

In the countries to which Section 426 applies, it is therefore possible for provisional liquidators (and other offices) to seek to apply whichever law is more favourable, through their respective court. These include:

(i) provisions relating to a stay on actions or proceedings or to protect a company's property (e.g. Section 130 (2) of the Insolvency Act 1986;

(ii) provisions to elicit information in relation to the company's affairs (e.g.) the private examination provisions under Section 236 of the Insolvency Act 1986);

(iii) substantive provisions for clawback of assets or for contributions to the estate (e. g. wrongful trading (section 214), preferences (section 239), transactions at an undervalue (section 238).

The assistance of the English court may be sought under Section 426 without the need for full insolvency proceedings here. For example, in a recent case provisional liquidators were appointed in the UK pursuant to a letter of request from the Bermudan court without having to present a petition to wind up the company in England. The law to be applied is „insolvency law", as defined. This will include injunctions ancillary to relief sought under insolvency law. The extent to which common law remedies equating to provisions in the Insolvency Act 1986 will be considered as falling within the definition of „insolvency law" remains to be decided: this is of particular significance as regards jurisdictions whose insolvency law is based on the law in England prior to the Insolvency Act 1986.

It is also to be doubtful whether schemes of arrangements by themselves fall within the definition of „insolvency law" because the relevant provisions are to be found in the Companies Acts and not in the Insolvency Act 1986: however, where insolvency proceedings are initiated with a view to the promulgation of a scheme (e.g. a provisional liquidation or administration orders) Section 426 would apply. One of the issues under Section 426 involves the question of whether it is appropriate **to apply a foreign system of law** in a given case. In exercising its discretion as to which system of law should apply under Section 426(5), the court is directed to „have regard in particular to the rules of private international law." It is not clear what parliament intended by this phrase.[162] Segal and Sheldon maintain that, it would be surprising if these provisions enabled liquidators to go forum shopping, freely within the relevant countries in question, in order to take advantage of laws in a jurisdiction with which the company had no or little connection. If Section 426 of the Insolvency Act is not applicable in relation to a foreign company, it may be possible to obtain a winding up order in the UK. Such an order would have the effect of making available the relief which is generally available under the Insolvency Act 1986. The winding up order in the UK would generally take effect as ancillary to the winding up in the country of incorporation. In general, the English court will not enforce the winding up laws of foreign countries. Thus it is doubtful whether an English court would restrain a creditor subject to the jurisdiction from bringing proceed-

---

162 Richard Sheldon and Nick Segal, ibid, 12

ings to give effect to an automatic stay imposed under a foreign system of law obtaining a stay in specific proceedings brought in the UK.

If a foreign liquidator seeks to protect assets in this jurisdiction or seeks information from a person subject to the English jurisdiction or seeks information from a person subject to the English jurisdiction in relation to a company's assets it may be possible to style appropriate relief under the court's broad powers to grant injunctions, appoint receivers and make ancillary disclosure orders. In the course of insolvency a new defence is increasingly used, the *pay as paid* defence. In cases where the primary insurer becomes insolvent, it was tried to turn directly to the reinsurers for payment. Reinsurers refused payment on the grounds that a reinsurance contract is one of indemnity. The reinsurer shall only be liable if the reinsured has actually paid the insured.

As a matter of course, the Commercial Court came to decide whether the actual payment of the sum should be a condition precedent to the obligation of the reinsurer to pay.[163] The decision of the Commercial Court was upheld by the Court of Appeal. In the finding of the verdict, the Commercial Court Judge Mance J. argued that the words of the ultimate net clause containing the pay as paid clause were intended to ensure reinsurance recoveries at each stage. That way the judge took account of the general purpose of reinsurance in spreading the risk.[164] Here the quite rare case is to be found that more weight was given to the context of the business than was attached to the actual meaning of the words.

The meaning of the *pay as may be paid clause* was recently reviewed in Charman v. Guardian Royal Exchange Assurance plc[165]. Webster J. confirmed that, on the authorities, the phrase meant „properly paid under a liability to pay" but so long as liability existed the fact of some honest mistake having occurred in fixing the exact amount of it would afford no excuse for not paying.

In Hong Kong Borneo Services Co. Ltd. v. Pilcher[166], Evans J. held that in a reinsurance context the words „pay as may be paid" did not, on the authorities, require actual payment of the original insured's claims as a condition precedent to the reinsurer's liability. On the other hand it would not displace the common law requirement of proof that the reinsured's liability had been ascertained or established. He doubted whether the words really added anything to the position as it would be without them. But he was of the view that they at least confirmed that regarding quantum, the intention was that the reinsurer should be bound by a reasonable settlement. The phrase does, however, leave the reinsured exposed

163 Charter Reinsurance Company Limited v. Fagan (1995) CLC 1345 (ComCt) and CA

164 Davies Arnold Cooper, DAC Bulletin, Reinsurance Group, October 1995

165 (1992) 2 Lloyd's Rep. 607

166 (1992) 2 Lloyd's Rep. 593

in the event of a compromise settlement with the insured, because as against the reinsurer he would still have to prove that there was in fact a liability to the insured.

Communication and flow of information between the actors in the market are not to be underestimated when it comes to liquidation. The reinsurance market was characterised by all those interviewed as a "gossipy market". An insurer or reinsurer is in liquidation or in run- off increases the readiness for disputes since the incentive of an on-going business relationship is no longer there. However the initial assumption was not supported that in a situation where an insurance or reinsurance company leaves or has left the market it is likely that it will alter its dispute behaviour regarding arbitration. This assumption was the basis for the question if a run-off situation would harm the value of arbitration clauses to any extent, namely if the interviewees were of the opinion, based on their experience, that parties tended towards avoiding arbitration in favour of court proceedings. The majority of the interviewed solicitors did not support this assumption. Only 9 out of 31 interviewed answered this question affirmatively.

They substantiated their answers as follows:

- There is no continuity of business relations in the future.
- A greater conflict of interests arises because of the lack of a common goal.
- There is a greater tendency to litigate in order to let third parties know that the one in run-off is serious about its position.
- A party in run-off may benefit from the discovery.
- There is a need to revoke the question at stake in a larger number of contracts.

Another issue that was mentioned by the interviewees was the problem of illegality that might occur. It has to be understood that to carry out reinsurance business in the UK, a company must obtain the authority of the Secretary of State for Trade and Industry (DTI) under Section 2 of the Insurance Company Act 1982. It often occurs that companies unintentionally infringe this section of the Insurance Company Act. The question arises if and how such an infringement of public laws influences the contractual private relationship between the insurer and the insured. If authorised permission is not obtained on either side, this may lead to the illegality of the reinsurance contract. Three Commercial Court cases have dealt with this area.[167] After the Bedford and Stewart cases, it was clear that an insurer or reinsurer would be held by a court to be carrying on

---

167 Bedford Insurance Company v. IRB (1984) 1 Lloyd's Rep. 210; Stewart v. Oriental Fire (1984) 2 Lloyd's Rep. 109; Phoenix General of Greece v. Halvanon Insurance Company (1985) 2 Lloyd's Rep. 599

insurance business in the United Kingdom, and thus require authorisation if one or more of the following activities was carried out here:[168]

The court held that, an innocent insured has a right of action against an insurer even if the insurer had not been authorised to issue the policy concerned. The insurer has no right of action against the innocent insured and the insurer may not rely on his illegality and require from his reinsurer settlement of losses under the insurance of the contracts issued without authorisation. It is obvious that this decision was important for the activities of foreign companies in the London market.[169]

Hall (1989) underwent in his reinsurance law casebook the task of categorising the cases that have come to Court under the general legal problems which occur.[170] The questionnaire presented to the practitioners followed these categories. The interviewees were asked to indicate how frequently legal topics arise in their experience in reinsurance arbitration and litigation. The answers made it clear that often more than one legal issue will be brought up in a case and the parties will try to put forward every legal argument that will suit their case. Although every risk is individual, a further initial expectation was that, as long as the reinsurance risks comply with certain technical requirements concerning the knowledge of the risk and premium distribution of the parties, particular legal problems occur jointly with those technical constructions or forms of reinsurance.

Although a few of those interviewed mentioned a certain range of problems under treaty and facultative contracts, e.g. the inspection of records, a systematic result referring to legal problems accumulating in one or the other kind of contract cannot be offered. Probably this result is to blame on an attempt to structure facts by characteristics that they have in common and then extract legal problems from them. In simple terms, a clash of statute law approach on the interviewer's side with a common law approach on the side of the interviewed practitioners might become evident here.

---

168 Gordon Cornish, "Some Recent Developments in English Reinsurance Law", in: *Zeitschrift für Versicherungswesen*, 21/86, 556-560 (556)

169 H. Edward Gumbel, "Englische Rechtsprechung zur Versicherungstätigkeit und Rückversicherung ausländischer Gesellschaften am Londoner Markt", in: *Zeitschrift für Versicherungswesen*, 21/86, 550-554 (550)

170 Geoffrey M. Hall, *Reinsurance Law Casebook*, Business & Maritime Publications Ltd, 1989

4.2 A need for precedents ?

In the Common Law system, the precedent is the central element in the evolution of the law. The precedent is a judgment or decision of a court, normally used as an authority for reaching the same decision in subsequent cases.[171] A lower court is not bound by all aspects of previous decisions but only by those parts of the judgment that constitute the principles of the decision *(ratio decidendi)* and are not merely passing comments *(obiter dicta)* by the judge. The point of this is to create a legal framework which is completely consistent so that one judgment cannot clash with another. Arbitration awards which prevailed in reinsurance disputes are not published and do not create any form of precedent for any future dispute. The only judgments which form a precedent with respect to arbitration awards for future disputes are those which are made at the Court of Appeal or at the House of Lords. Where parties choose the court proceedings instead of arbitration however, the judgments of the first instance court (in our case the Commercial Court Division of the High Court) will also form precedents.

The courts are bound by the principle of *stare decisis* meaning that they must abide by precedents laid down by judgments made in higher courts. The *ratio decidendi* is the main part of a court judgment setting out the legal principles applicable to the case and forming the binding part of the precedent. However judgments of lower courts can be overruled by a higher court to set a new precedent by deciding a case on a different principle. Although there are indicators that the privacy of arbitration has been undermined by the informal exchange of results[172], which may help to assess the case, the claim of legal precedent can still not be made by those awards.

The completely consistent legal framework created by precedents may be the key point in the attempt to explain the "increasing appetite" for disputes in reinsurance during the last decade. Reinsurance business was not shaken by major existence threatening crises in the past. The majority of the few disputes were conducted in the privacy of arbitration. These circumstances have left the reinsurance business without up-to date precedent properly. To a certain extent market practice developed independently of the law.[173] The lack of precedents became evident when the line of business in reinsurance changed. Precedents were needed to assess the chances of success in trying a case and certain issues needed to be revoked. Certainty of law in business in general – and in reinsurance rela-

---

171 Elizabeth A. Martin, A Dictionary of Law, 3d ed., Oxford University Press, Oxford, 1994, 299

172 see: 6.2 Arbitration

173 J. S. Butler, *Reinsurance Practice and the Law*, London: Lloyd's of London Press Ltd, 1993, looseleaf, Service Issue No. 7, 1 September 1996, 25.1

tionships in particular[174] – is an invaluable asset. Therefore legal uncertainty may have triggered off the increased litigation.

The assumption that there is a connection between legal certainty and dispute behaviour is supported by legal theory. The factor of legal certainty in international legal relations has been recognised in legal theory and sociology as crucial for legally relevant behaviour of parties involved.[175] According to a definition of Geiger[176], legal certainty is based on knowledge of law (Orientierungssicherheit) and probability of sanctions against deviant behaviour (Realisierungsicherheit). There is theoretical explanation for a development as in reinsurance, where dispute resolution has moved away from informal negotiations to court proceedings. According to the Intercultural Communication Theory[177] uncertainty is a cognitive phenomenon. An increase in ... ability to gather appropriate information about strangers will produce an increase in ... ability to accurately predict their behaviour. The sources from which to gain certainty about the way the other party is likely to act may however be manifold. They do not necessarily have to spring from the law. They may even come from differentiated societal processes that lead to negotiations, discourses, flexible contracts or mediation. These processes can then prevail over legal certainty.[178] It seems that in the study presented the whole range of socio-legal theoretical approaches wishing to explain the structure of dispute behaviour can be applied. This is because reinsurance disputes were indeed transformed from highly informal mechanisms like negotiations and flexible contracts, into highly formal stages of disputes. The first question is to ask when and why informal structures are able to substitute rigid legal structures without the parties involved being uncomfortable with it. The clue may be given in a statement made by a reinsurance professional[179]:

„For those of us who started our reinsurance careers in a much more gentlemanly era, the thought that anybody could produce a book of such length as

---

174 Colin Croly and Clive O'Connell, „The case for the Commercial Court", in: *The Review*, March 1988, 43

175 Volkmar Gessner, „The Globalisation of Legal Certainty" in: *Cross- border legal Interactions, Empirical Studies on the Globalization of Law Forthcoming,* 2

176 Theodor Geiger, Vorstudien zu einer Soziologie des Rechts, Neuwied: Luchterhand, 1964, 102

177 William B. Gudykunst, Anxienty/ Uncertainty Management (AUM) Theory Current Status, in: Richard L. Wiseman (ed.), *Intercultural Communication Theory,* Thousand Oaks / London / New Delhi, Sage, 1995, 8-58 (10,41)

178 Volkmar Gessner, Kognitive Elemente sozialer Ordnung, in: Monika Frommel, Volkmar Gessner (eds.), *Normerosion,* Baden-Baden: Nomos 1996, 207-224

179 R. A. G. Jackson, Foreword to *Reinsurance Practice and the Law,* in: J.S. Butler, *Reinsurance Practice and the Law,* Lloyd's of London Press, 1993, looseleaf, Service Issue No. 7, 1 September 1996

this one on the subject of Reinsurance Practice and the Law is horrifying. Twenty-five years ago the number of companies accepting reinsurance was few and the number of disputes between them and their reinsureds could be counted on the fingers of one hand. I am not naive enough to believe that, given the opportunity, reinsureds did not wish to take advantage of reinsurers in those halcyon days, but because of the fewer numbers of players on both sides, it would have been very unwise to break the unwritten rules of the game."

According to this and similar other statements from reinsurance professionals during the interviews, certainty was provided by the obedience of unwritten rules. The obedience of such rules met with the expectation of the members of the group doing reinsurance business. This structure as well has familiar theoretical background. The obedience of such rules can claim to have legal character although they are not forced by statutes or any kind of case law. However they converge with what actors expect in given issue areas.[180] Originally this idea was developed to explain the co-operation among nation states. It replaces in political science more and more the focus on international organisations and describes the networks which in some areas have been established in the international arena.[181] The same idea of imagining cross-border networks could also be adopted by legal sociology that deals with individual behaviour rather than national actors. To distinguish between both levels of action – the individual and the state levels – we prefer to use another more traditional term, namely „third cultures". Nevertheless the idea behind both terms is quite the same.

The court decisions mentioned above indicate that a swing has taken place from those informal negotiations towards more formal dispute resolution mechanisms such as court verdicts. Cornish (1994) states that it is a painful experience for a reinsurer and its reinsured to end up in court. Nevertheless the reinsurance market in general benefits in that the decision is reported and written about and so the principle decided upon becomes widely known.[182] This view is shared by Croly and O'Connel (1988).[183] On the other hand there may be cases, in which the avoidance of precedents is preferred.[184] In those cases, arbitration

---

180 S. D. Krassner (ed.), International Regimes, quoted in John Vogler, Regimes and Global Commons: Space, Atmosphere and Oceans, in: Anthony G. McGrew, Paul G. Lewins et al., *Global Politics,* Cambridge: Polity, Press 1992, 122

181 Volkmar Gessner, „The Globalization of Legal Certainty" in: *Cross- border legal Interactions,Empirical Studies on the Globalisation of Law,* Forthcoming, 4

182 Gordon Cornish, "English Reinsurance Law Developments During 1994", in: *Zeitschrift für Versicherungswesen*, 21/94, 579-580 (579)

183 Colin Croly and Clive O'Connel, ' Trials and tribulations', in: *The Review,* January 1998, 18

184 J. S. Butler, *Reinsurance Practice and the Law*, London: Lloyd's of London Press, 1993, looseleaf, Service Issue No. 7, 1 September 1996, 25.5.5

can be useful if the parties to the contract wish to resolve their dispute without setting a precedent for the future. At least in the past, privacy and confidentiality were guaranteed in the entire proceedings. Increasingly it is rare that such matters can be kept from the general awareness of the reinsurance market. Often an inaccurate version of the dispute circulates in the market. This shows that tactical deliberations are involved when dispute resolution mechanisms are chosen. Regarding litigation,however, the question remains as to how the need for precedents and the change in dispute resolution towards more litigation occurred.

4.3 Factors determining the choice of dispute resolution mechanisms

Felstiner, Abel and Sarat (1980)[185] recognised that disputes should to be viewed as social constructs and not as things. This means disputes are to be perceived as a dynamic process (*transformation*) not as static. These authors maintain that disputes are processes by which unperceived injurious experiences are – or are not – perceived (naming), do or do not become grievances (blaming), and ultimately disputes (claiming), and change subsequently. In my view they correctly point out, that viewing cases as things creates the temptation to count them. The mere counting of cases and analysis of number and litigation rates may not be an appropriate scientific method, since litigation rates can be „produced" and manipulated. Felstiner, Abel and Sarat view each of these stages as subjective, unstable, reactive, complicated, and incomplete. They postulate that transformations between them are caused by, and have consequences for the parties, their attributions of responsibility, the scope of conflict, the mechanism chosen, the objectives sought, the prevailing ideology, reference groups, representatives and officials, and dispute institutions. Formal litigation and even disputing within unofficial fora account for a tiny fraction of the antecedant events that could mature into disputes. Moreover, what happens at earlier stages determines both the quantity and the contents of the caseload of formal and informal legal institutions.

Indeed it appears that the understanding of disputes as a dynamic process is crucial to an explanation of what is happening in reinsurance dispute resolution. Reinsurance disputes in the London market provide a field to examine this scheme of dynamic factors. It is suggested that the use of dispute resolution mechanisms change if the prerequisites of the social group that applies them

185 William L. F. Felstiner, Richard Abel, Austin Sarat, „The Emergence and Transformation of Disputes: Naming, Blaming, Claiming ...", in: *Law & Society Review,* Volume 15, Number 3-4 (1980-81), 631-653 (631)

changes, e. g. the number of actors being involved. Various factors influence the way a business community will go about resolving their disputes and together these factors set out a framework in which a business community is likely to act. It appears that these factors are also applicable in cases containing an international element. Firstly, these factors are the characteristics of the parties involved. Parties can either be corporations or individuals. They may be equipped with the same economic strength or one may be inferior to the other. Their encounter may be repetitive (*repeat players)* or they may only do business or have contractual obligations towards each other on a singular occasion.

The assumption regarding the dispute behaviour of *global players* at the starting point of the thesis was that global players tend to resolve their disputes in a less formal and private manner and not through the courts. That is provided that the probability of them meeting again is quite likely. Where either another meeting is not guaranteed, e.g. one party leaves the market or it is permanently and increasingly faced with financial losses, the dispute behaviour is quite likely to change. Regarding the individuals themselves involved in business activities, all kinds of participants entered the London reinsurance market in the 1970s. Numerous individuals hoped to make money with reinsurance by becoming „Names" in Lloyds syndicates. Also primary insurance companies tried to establish reinsurance department or subsidiaries.[186] The traditional "club" of members was intruded by market participants who later have been described as innocent[187] or uniformed[188] capacity. The volume of reinsurance business expanded rapidly. This view again was expressed during the interviews with reinsurance professionals and brokers. A representative statement was:

„The wholly unnecessary increase in the number of reinsurers in the recent past, particularly in the mid 1970s, produced the well-used and appropriate term of 'naive capacity'. The resultant spreading of talent too thinly among reinsurers, inevitably led to substantial losses being sustained by reinsurers all over the world. This of course in turn led to disputes generally arising from what was disclosed (or not disclosed) when the reinsurances were consummated and then later to disputes on the contractual wording themselves."[189]

186 Dirk Schmidt-Prange, "Katerstimmung in der Rückversicherung und wie es dazu kam", in: *Zeitschrift für Versicherungswesen*, 21/85, 572-574 (572)

187 Dirk Schmidt-Prange, "Katerstimmung in der Rückversicherung und wie es dazu kam", in: *Zeitschrift für Versicherungswesen*, 21/85, 572-574 (573)

188 Klaus Gerathewohl, "The International Reinsurance Markets Today – Developments and Perspectives", in: *Versicherungswirtschaft*, 14/1987, 901-909 (902)

189 R.A.G. Jackson, Foreword, in: J. S. Butler, *Reinsurance Practice and the Law,* London: Lloyd's of London Press, 1993

Lloyds alone doubled in size during the 1980s. Half of the business conducted was in reinsurance.[190] It was self-evident that the number of experienced underwriters could not expand in the same proportions as the market. One consequence of this was that some of the new companies started to employ older, frustrated underwriters. Those underwriters had considerable underwriting experience. However they had no incentive to give much thought to developments after their planned retirement in five to six years.[191] Thatcherism at the time tried to encourage a sort of mini-capitalism. Lloyds went about recruiting new Names at the same time, and lowering the standards and qualification of Names in terms of assets and liabilities. During the boom decade of the 1980s house prices increased artificially and this led to the assets of the new Names being overvalued. Also a number of overseas Names were recruited. The result was that a large number of financially weak Names were recruited which were not able to sustain real losses. Foreign Names such as US Names started to react by bringing proceedings against Lloyds almost immediately after being asked by their syndicates to pay claims.

The Names litigation is deemed to have intensified reinsurance litigation. Litigation was open to the Names right from the start because the Names were not collectively bound to arbitration agreements. If, in earlier days, Names followed the *grievance clause*, according to the principle 'first pay then litigate', the enormous losses sustained broke this threshold. When cash calls for members continued to come in, a group of sample members filed an injunction. That was the first time the rule was reversed. This is an example of a rule which was mutually obeyed in earlier times by members of the old business community. This rule was now put aside by new market participants not comparable in economic strength and endurance. The 'certainty' of a group member's behaviour in a specific situation was no longer there.

As a consequence of the Names litigation public attention was attracted to reinsurance on a broad level for the first time. This was a trend wholly undesired by the professional reinsurers and the company market not only for image reasons. The reinsurance community feared that the courts would look at business practices and usage in detail in the Names litigation. These decisions could have consequences also for the company's market. These disputes had eminent economic and legal consequences for the London insurance and especially reinsurance market. For this reason they cannot be left out when dealing with reinsur-

---

190 Adam Raphael, *The Ultimate Risk: The Inside Story of the Lloyd's Catastrophe*, London: Bantam Press, 1994, 313

191 Dirk Schmidt-Prange, "Katerstimmung in der Rückversicherung und wie es dazu kam", in: *Zeitschrift für Versicherungswesen*, 21/85, 572-574, (573)

ance dispute resolution. Lloyds is currently faced with an extremely difficult economical situation mainly deriving from two main sources of losses:

The exposure of Lloyds syndicates to losses originating from asbestos and pollution. The pollution policies having been underwritten in earlier years were – like asbestos – subject to legal changes in the US. This again demonstrates that a reinsurance policy is not only a product created through a contract and definition by the parties. By release of punitive acts, US communities were enabled to sue manufacturers for enormous sums if their sites were polluted. Lloyds was hit twice: its insurance syndicates had insured the asbestos manufacturers and its reinsurance syndicates had reinsured those claims *inter alia*. The problem the Names as personally liable individuals faced, was as follows:

Lloyds operates with a three year accounting system, the so called 're-insurance to close'. A premium is transferred at a set date from the former to the next Name on the syndicate and liability is passed on to them. The problem of closing an account is to work out a fair premium. For some syndicates receiving the asbestosis claims the good years were wiped out by the bad years in which such liabilities had to be paid. When the asbestos litigation started, it became clear that there was no chance of closing the open accounts; they had to be left open. Former Names were therefore not able to transfer their liabilities to other Names and became stuck with the losses. Settlements reached in the Names litigation against their underwriting members of Lloyds were largely funded by payments from the errors and omissions insurance of underwriters. These underwriters were themselves reinsured.[192]

A series of catastrophes[193] hit the market heavily and contributed further to the economic crisis of reinsurance. The Piper Alpha oil platform, which was operated by Texaco, International Thompson, Union Texas Petroleum and Occidental Petroleum, exploded due to a gas accident. Of the 226 workers, 165 died in the flames. It was the worst human tragedy ever experienced by the off-shore oil industry. Fifteen months later, on 15 September 1989, Hurricane Hugo spiralled out of the West Indies, hitting South Carolina with 140 mph winds before three days' continuous torrential rain bombarded surrounding areas. Hundreds of miles of coastline were devastated and thousands of buildings wrecked.

---

192 DJ Freeman, „Ripples from the Outhwaite settlement reach reinsurers“ in: *Reactions*, May 1992, 12

193 Adam Raphael, The Ultimate Risk: The Inside Story of the Lloyd's Catastrophe, London: Bantam Press, 1994, 173-174: Explosion of Piper Alpha oil platform on 6 July 1988, Hurricane Hugo on 15 September 1989, Hurricane Gilbert, Exxon Valdez Oil Spill, San Fransisco earthquake, the Arco Bake fire, the Philipps petroleum explosion, Typhoon Mireille in Japan and three severe gales which struck Britain and Northern Europe at the beginning of 1990.

The final bill totalled $ 5 billion. Not only those two major disasters, but an unprecedented series of catastrophes rang up more than $ 40 billion in insurance losses between 1987 and 1990. This included Enchova oil platform fire, Hurricane Gilbert, the Exxon Valdez oil spill, the San Francisco earthquake, the Arco Baker fire, the Philips petroleum explosion, the Australian earthquake, Typhoon Mireille in Japan, and three severe gales which struck Britain and northern Europe at the beginning of 1990.

The so called London Excess of Loss Market (LMX) spiral led to severe problems. Raphael (1994) describes that as the size of risks underwritten in the London market grew, these complex reinsurance policies, with their numerous intricate layers, tended to become more and more intertwined. Underwriters, influenced by Lloyds instinct on security, began to reinsure one another's excess of loss risks in what became known as the London Excess of Loss Market or LMX. One of these interbred patterns of trading could be seen in that the tiers of insurance became hopelessly confused.[194] The asbestos and pollution claims reached the reinsurance market. The LMX spiral did not exclusively hit the Lloyds Names and its effects are still working their way through the market. Hurricane Andrew and North European windstorms swept through the balance sheets of the majority of London reinsurers.[195] The struggle for survival started and even reinsurers, having been known for their tendency to pay up rather than dispute, began to a closer look at their claims.[196] As for Lloyds, presently about thirty so called action groups of Lloyds Names currently litigate before the Commercial Court. The Commercial Court decided to manage the litigation, otherwise jurisdiction in the matter would have come to a complete standstill. In 1994 Lord Saville and J. Creswell implemented a series of plans. This plan contained a selection of key points at an early stage and a selection of lead cases. As is to be shown later, not only in the Lloyds litigation the Commercial Court plays a central role and has co-ordinating function.

Not only the characteristics of the actors participating in the actual reinsurance business are decisive for the way in which disputes develop. The contribution of the legal professions and advisors towards a more litigious dispute resolution should not be underestimated. The legal professions have contributed to a more litigious and adversial way of dispute resolution. If one tries to illustrate the options and participants in reinsurance disputes, the following chart may serve the purpose:

---

194 Adam Raphael, The Ultimate Risk: The Inside Story of the Lloyd's Catastrophe, London: Bantam Press, 1994, 176

195 Nick Edwards, 'Just an illusion', in: *Reinsurance*, Vol. 25, No 6, Sept. 1994, 9

196 Klaus Gerathewohl, "The International Reinsurance Markets Today – Developments and Perspectives", in: *Versicherungswirtschaft*, 14/87, 901-910 (903)

Participants in reinsurance disputes

1. Participants in arbitration proceedings:

Solicitor	Solicitor
Arbitrator	Arbitrator
Expert Witness	Expert Witness

Insured------***Dispute***-------Reinsurer-------***Dispute***----Retrocessionaire
(cross-border) (cross-border)

2. Participants in court proceedings:

Solicitors	Solicitors
Barristers	Barristers
Expert Witness	Expert Witness
Judges	Judges
(Broker)	(Broker)
(Underwriter /Agent)	(Underwriter/Agent)

Insured------***Dispute***-------Reinsurer-------***Dispute***----Retrocessionaire
(cross-border) (cross-border)

It is significant that solicitors are involved in arbitration as well as in court proceedings. This indicates that proceedings in both areas increasingly resemble each other through the participation of lawyers. There is no unanimous explanation of how the participation of lawyers in arbitration proceedings came about. The arbitration act does not require any such participation and the original idea of arbitration was a concept of solving a problem without legal expertise, but within the business community and with the assistance of a neutral third party. However, a cynical view of one barrister to the contribution of solicitors and barrister suggested the following:

„The growth of reinsurance disputes significantly coincides with a decline in shipping disputes due to a decline in trade. Also the 1979 Arbitration Act stopped the succession of special cases to the courts. This created a vacuum of work and fees received. Dissatisfied reinsurers were a quite easy target to be talked into litigation by lawyers and in 1983 the CTI Oceanus decision[197] gave this development a dramatic push. ....and once the lawyers become involved, the more they find if the right conscious is there."

197 Container Transport International Inc. v. Oceanus Mutual Underwriting Association (Bermuda) Ltd. (1984) 1 Lloyd's Rep 476 (CA)

According to Thompson, the shift of workload from shipping towards reinsurance is also acknowledged by the solicitors[198]. He maintains that solicitors operating in London now say that the major area of growth for their litigation departments is in the field of reinsurance disputes, where some reinsurers have apparently substituted for the shipping industry. The fact that documentation of reinsurance contracts had been treated as a "stepchild" in the past was an also an invitation at least to try to avoid payments under the policy. English courts interpret contract wording according to "the word means what the word says" – but what happens if there is no wording? When asked to rank factors contributing to disputes in the reinsurance business, the following graph emerged:

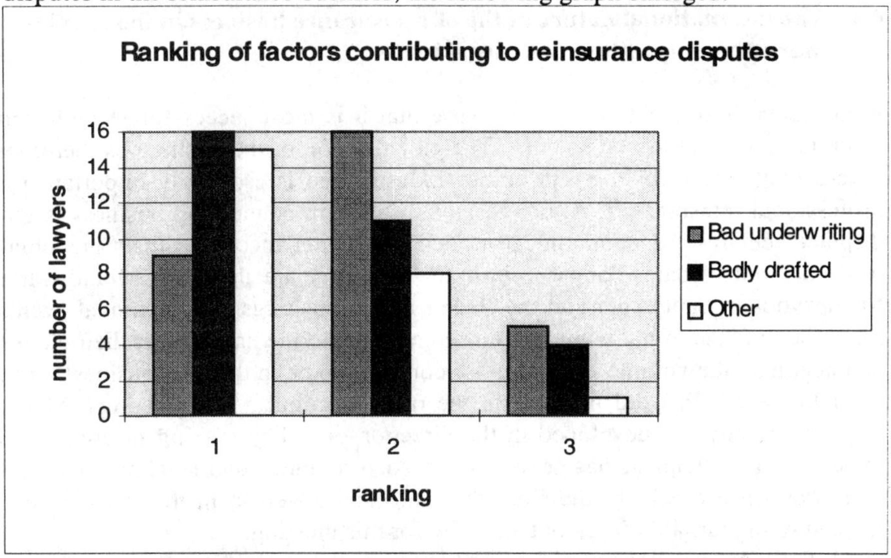

When naming other factors it further emerged that poor economic results coupled with a lack of trust is the breeding ground for creating disputes that harden to become litigious conflicts. Great pressure is now put upon some of the basic insurance principles as a result of narrowing profit margins.[199] This pressure has generated an unrivalled process of concentration on a relatively small number of „global players". Approximately 40 % of the premium volume of $100 billion are earned by the four leading reinsurance companies and their subsidiaries. The following four large companies in this special insurance business- Münchener Rück and Schweizer Rück which are Continental and Employ-

198 Hugh Thompson, „Who shall arbitrate ?", in: *Reinsurance,* September 1991, 69
199 Hugh Thompson, „Reinsurance Dispute Resolution Internationally", in: *Asia Insurance Review*, May-June 1992, 59

ers Re and General Re which are US American enterprises-continue to grow and try to buy other reinsurers in their non domestic market. Münchener Rück has recently bought American Re. According to the interviews, the pressure on results generated an increasing lack of trust. Reinsurers have become increasingly critical of their duty to pay. The attitude as a whole is becoming less professional. This refers not only to the reinsurers and the cedant, but also to the conduct of brokers and intermediaries. Information was inadequately or inaccurately placed.

4.4 The international nature of the of reinsurance business in the London market and its influence on legal issues

Reinsurance is international in the sense that it is most successfully conducted when not confined to one country. The globalisation of the business is therefore an essential feature of the reinsurance industry and is especially important for professional reinsurers.[200] Although globalisation in conducting business is undisputed, centres for communication and traditional meeting rituals are obviously not out of date. For the reinsurance industry are these the Monte Carlo Rendezvous in September and the Baden-Baden meetings. Those annual events serve the purpose of allowing the reinsurers and intermediaries meet their clients and negotiate the volume and terms for contracts to be in the next business term. Over the years, this did not remain the only function of the meetings. Monte Carlo especially has developed in the direction of policy making meetings and the circle of participants has grown larger. Also solicitors and legal advisers find their way once a year to the Cote d' Azure and advertise in the 'Rendezvous Brochure', a journal brought out annually for this meeting.

A fictitious example of risk distribution shall be given to illustrate the dimension of the international nature of reinsurance, particularly in reinsurance business placed in the London market. Let us suppose, a primary insurance company seeks cover for its motor insurance portfolio to the value of £ 50 million. This volume of reinsurance cover will be provided in shares through the London market by reinsurance companies spread all over the globe. The slip, which documents the reinsurance contract in a short form containing the very basic information on the risk covered, will bear stamps of reinsurers from e.g. Switzer-

200 C. E. Golding, *The Law and Practice of Reinsurance*, 5th ed., London: Witherby & Co. Ltd., 1987, 24; Horst K. Jannott, "Rückversicherung – Einige praktische Aspekte der Arbeit im Ausland", in: *Versicherungswirtschaft*, 7/87, 376-386 (386); Alois Alzheimer, "Probleme der internationalen Rückversicherung", in: *Versicherungswirtschaft*, 12/71, 733-736 (733)

land, Japan, Germany and Lloyds reinsurance syndicates showing the share of risks they will carry as percentages.

The volume of business alone does not necessarily lead to the international nature of reinsurance. This idea is promoted even more by the risk spreading idea that contains also an element of geographical risk distribution. This is why nearly all reinsurance transactions of greater volume will include a multitude of international parties on the slip. It has positive aspects for the risk takers regarding the insurers and reinsurers as far as the risk spreading idea is concerned. However, it also means that the sources of definition of risks and the liability attached to them are spread and are likely to increase as a result.

4.4.1 Definition of the underlying risk by Foreign Jurisdictions

It was a harsh experience that a foreign jurisdiction's redefining of liability led to it being extended enormously. This was the case with asbestos and pollution litigation in the US jurisdiction. The problem posed by asbestos for the London reinsurance market, and especially Lloyds reinsurance syndicates, arose from the following situation. Before the early 1960s, product liability in the United States was limited to consumer products designed for human consumption, such as food and cosmetics. A change in jurisdiction of American courts in the mid 1960s significantly extended the doctrine of strict product liability. A claim for compensation was granted whenever 'the defective condition of the product makes it unreasonably dangerous to the user'. Consequently, victims of asbestosis were enabled to bypass the inadequate redress provided by workers' compensation schemes and sued the asbestos manufacturers directly instead.[201]

Three main legal questions arose when a court in the US dealt with claims of workers against the producers of asbestos. When is the correct time to put in a claim? When the claimant came into contact with asbestos? At the point when the asbestosis (the illness) manifested itself? Or at another point?. Between 1980 and the late 1980s, different US court decisions were reached, none of which was seen as carrying any weight and none of these were ever confirmed by the Supreme Court. The District Court of Columbia however, once came up with the so called *„triple trigger theory"*. This theory maintained that the entire period of exposure to manifestation was relevant and sufficient to constitute an asbestosis claim. Although this was not a decision by a superior court, the triple trigger theory was followed by other US courts.

---

201 see: Adam Raphael, *The Ultimate Risk: The Inside Story of the Lloyds Catastrophe*, London: Bantam Press, 1994, 104-105

One alleged reason why the courts willingly accepted this theory without challenging it is that it provides a very wide spectrum for constituting a claim. As one barrister commenting on the reasons for the Lloyds litigation put it:

„ It was felt that the triple trigger theory fitted in the American courts' policy of supporting the workers claims. In the US the system of social welfare is in large parts not as extensively developed as for example in Europe. Insurance in the US courts' understanding was deemed to act like a cushion and close the gaps of the existing system. Asbestos claims originating from the Continent were hardly there. This fact exemplifies the ranking of insurance and reinsurance as well as the understanding of its function by the courts."

During the interviews with City lawyers it became clear that the interviewed practitioners carefully monitor the development in US liability and tort law and the reform it shall undergo. One solicitor expressed his view towards the probability of a change in the American tort law as follows:

„The political influence of American tort lawyers in the Congress has managed to leave the tort law unchanged and probably will do so in the future. It is well recognised in the market that the American jurisdiction in the liability's cases will in the long run ruin the insurance industry."

Further problems arise due to the fact the reinsurance contract parties are international. This refers to cross-border cases with the implied problems of where to initiate a case and which law is applicable if this is not stated in the contract.

4.4.2 Where to proceed – The question of jurisdiction

If one has any experience of pursuing or defending litigation, particularly in the field of reinsurance, one will be fully aware of the fact that, before the dispute in question can be resolved, it may be necessary to resort to lengthy and costly preliminary litigation in order to decide which of several available tribunals should decide upon the dispute.[202] In some disputes, the case can be regarded as lost or won depending upon which tribunal is to decide upon it. Disputes over jurisdiction usually occur because the defendant perceives that he will be at a certain advantage if the plaintiff's choice of tribunal can be overridden. The plaintiff, if he has been properly advised, will have brought proceedings in the tribunal which he perceives will be favourable to him. This is called „forum shopping". Several factors may influence the choice of tribunal. The courts of one country

---

202 Andrew Bandurka, „Problems of Jurisdiction: How and where to proceed", Paper for DYP reinsurance course „ Reinsurance Litigation – 'When to avoid it – How to win it', 13th – 15th April, 1994, London, B6- B7

may have power to award certain relief which is not available in another country: e.g. punitive damage. Similarly, jury trials in civil cases are available in the United States, but they are generally not available in the UK.

There is another category of case. Jurisdiction disputes often occur when a defendant wishes to test the plaintiff's case at a very early stage at the litigation. A bill of lading may change hands several times before the ultimate holder sues for this very reason. The holder must provoke his title to sue on the bill of lading. By provoking a fight on jurisdiction, a foreign defendant may, at an early stage, force the plaintiff to prove that he possesses the title. If the defendant succeeds, the English court will decline jurisdiction and the plaintiff must start fresh proceedings elsewhere. If the defendant is not successful in challenging English jurisdiction, then at the very least he will obtain a full insight into the plaintiff's case and evidence. This is always valuable in litigation. Enforcement of a judgment is also an important consideration. If the defendant is a foreign national who has assets in the UK, an English judgment may be straightforward to enforce, particularly if the assets can be frozen in the meantime,for example by a Mareva injunction. This is obviously far better than pursuing a trial and seeking enforcement in a foreign country.

The principles which guide the English Court in jurisdiction disputes are laid down in conventions entered into with other states, in English statutes, in Rules of Court and English case law. The usual relief granted on a successful challenge to jurisdiction is a stay or a dismissal of the plaintiff's action, by the court in which the action is brought. However, in exceptional circumstances the English court will grant injunction restraining from pursuing foreign legal proceedings. There are two distinct regimes of rules that apply: the so-called „convention", and „non-convention rules", and it is vital to establish which set applies at the very outset of litigation. A plaintiff who brings proceedings in the wrong court will at best waste time and money when his action is struck out or stayed. He will also be at a psychological and perhaps tactical disadvantage in subsequent proceedings. At worst, the situation may be irremediable: the applicable statute of limitations may bar further proceedings in another jurisdiction.

The convention rules are embodied in the Brussels Convention, which came into effect in the UK in 1987, being enacted in the Civil Jurisdiction and Judgments Act of 1982. The Brussels Convention provides an exhaustive code for determining which EC countries have jurisdiction in a particular dispute. Jurisdiction is conferred on the courts of the state in which the defendant is domiciled. The second regime applies to those cases to which the Convention does not extend, and the rules are embodied in English case law and in Order 11 of the Rules of the Supreme Court.

4.4.2.1 Non-convention cases

When an English writ is served on a defendant who is present in England or Wales, the English court will assume jurisdiction[203]. For this purpose a company is deemed to be present if it conducts business from an office in England where the writ may be served, or where it has a registered office in England. It is quite common for insurance and reinsurance agreements to contain a „service of suit" clause under which the parties agree that service of proceedings shall be effective if carried out at the office of an appointed solicitor. The English court will give effect to such an agreement. On the other hand, if service cannot be effected on a defendant who is present in England and Wales, then in non-convention cases, the plaintiff will require the court's leave to serve the defendant out of the jurisdiction. A writ is issued in the normal way, but it is stamped „Not for service out of the jurisdiction". It is then for the plaintiff to make an application to a Master (or Judge of the Commercial Court) for leave to serve the writ overseas. The application is made on paper only – there is no hearing and no opportunity for the defendant to argue his case. The grounds upon which the court will grant such leave are set out in RSC Order 11 Rule 1.

The party applying for leave must show that his case falls within one of the grounds listed in Order 11 Rule 1. For insurance and reinsurance cases only a handful of these grounds are relevant:

„ ... service of a writ out of the jurisdiction is permissible with the leave of the court if .... –

(c) The claim is brought against a person duly served within or out of the jurisdiction and a person out of the jurisdiction and a person out of the jurisdiction is a necessary or proper party thereto; or,

(d) The claim is brought to enforce, rescind, dissolve, annul or otherwise affect *contract* or to recover damages or obtain other relief in respect of the breach of a contract, being ..... a contract which –

(i) was made within the jurisdiction, or

(ii) was made by or through an agent trading or residing within the jurisdiction .... , or

(iii) is .... governed by English law, or

(iv) contains a term to the effect that the High Court shall have jurisdiction ....; or,

203 Andrew Bandurka, „Problems of Jurisdiction: How and where to proceed", Paper for DYP reinsurance course „ Reinsurance Litigation – 'When to avoid it – How to win it', 13th – 15th April, 1994, London, B16 – B 44

(e) The claim is brought in respect of a *breach committed* within the jurisdiction of a contract made within or out of the jurisdiction ... ; or,

(f) The claim is founded on a *tort* and the damage was sustained, or resulted from an act committed, within the jurisdiction. ....„

It is only necessary to bring the case on one of these grounds.

A typical case under Rule 1 (1) (c) occurs when a reinsurer resident outside the jurisdiction avoids the contract for non-disclosure, and the plaintiff brings an action for damages both against the reinsurer, and against the London broker whose fault it may have been that the non-disclosure happened. The court will obviously assert jurisdiction over the London broker on the basis of his presence within the jurisdiction. If it can be demonstrated that the reinsurer is a necessary or proper party to the same action, grounds exist for leave to serve the reinsurer.

A common situation under Rule 1 (1) (d) (ii) is where the reinsurer has participated in a contract through his underwriting agent within the jurisdiction. For the court to grant leave, it is the defendant's agent who must trade or reside with the jurisdiction[204]. It is not sufficient for the plaintiff to assert that the contract was made through his own broker who trades or resides within the jurisdiction.

As for Rule 1 (1) (d) (iii), the existence of an arbitration clause providing for arbitration in London would infer that the contract was governed by English law. Generally with regard to Rule 1 (1) (d), if the claim in the writ is for a declaration that no contract existed between the plaintiff and defendant, it will not be possible to rely on this ground. In Finnish Marine -v- Protective National (1989) 2 LLR 99, the plaintiff made a declaration that a reinsurance contract concluded by its underwriting agent never came into existence and was not binding because the agent exceeded his written underwriting authority in accepting the reinsurance. The plaintiff obtained leave *ex parte* to serve a writ on the US cedant, relying on Rule 1 (1) (d):

„the claim is brought to ... otherwise affect the contract ... „

which was made within the jurisdiction. The cedant then applied to set aside service of the writ and was successful since:

(i) the contract relied on under Rule 1 (1) d had to be a contract between the plaintiffs and the defendants, and the contract between Finnish Marine and the agent (agency agreement) could not be taken into consideration;

and

(ii) the plaintiff's claim denied the existence of a contract with the defendant and this situation was not covered by the Rule.

---

204 see: The Union International Insurance Company Limited -v- Jubilee Insurance Company Limited (1991) 1 All ER 740

According to ground (e) an argument commonly invoked is the rule in Thompson -v- Palmer (1893) 2 QB 80. Where a cedant is owed money under a reinsurance contract he may assert that (unless the contract provides otherwise) it is the duty of the debtor to pay the cedant at his residence or place of business. A failure to pay money therefore constitutes breach of contract within the jurisdiction, if the cedant resides in England. Once the plaintiff establishes a good arguable claim, and this claim falls under one or more of the permissible grounds, he must then show that it is proper for the English court to grant leave to serve the defendant out of the jurisdiction. Whether or not to grant leave is ultimately a matter for the court's discretion, and exercising its discretion, the court makes an assessment of a number of relevant factors, which are thrown into the balance. The test was enunciated by the House of Lords in Spiliada Maritime Corp -v- Consulex (1986) AC 460. In order to obtain leave:

(i) the plaintiff must clearly show that the English court is *the* natural or appropriate forum (or the *forum conveniens*) for resolution of the dispute. In deciding whether the English court or a foreign court is the natural forum, the court will choose the court in which the case can be tried most suitably in the interest of all parties and in the interest of justice.

The court will look for the forum which the action has the most to do with. One factor which will be almost conclusive is a *choice of courts clause* which specifies the English court. Other important factors will be taken into account such how convenient it is to try the action in another court; whether witnesses would be available to travel to the English court; whether the governing law of contract is English or foreign; whether the parties reside or conduct business here or in the foreign country; whether the evidence is predominantly here or abroad, etc.

(ii) If the court is satisfied that substantial justice will be done to all the parties in the natural forum, it will not generally take into account any personal or juridical advantage which would be available in England, but not in the foreign forum, or vice versa. For instance, if the plaintiff presents evidence that the foreign court would award him lower damages, or that the foreign court has no effective mechanism for the discovery of documents, then this is not usually persuasive. In refusing to take such factors into account, the court ignores the very considerations which may have motivated the plaintiff to bring proceedings in England in the first place. This has not always been the case. Lord Denning in MacShannon -v- Rockware Glass (1977) 1 WLR 376 said:

„Previously we were disposed to think too much of our own legal system. It was so superior to all others that, if a plaintiff managed to serve a defendant whilst in this country, we nearly always let him continue with it ... in so laying down the law we were going back in mind to those good old days, the passing of which many may regret, when the inhabitants of this island felt an innate superiority over those unfortunate enough to belong to other races."

The entry of the UK into the Common Market has brought many changes. One of them may be the recognition that the legal systems of other countries have their merits too. If the English court is persuaded *ex parte* to assert jurisdiction, the plaintiff will then serve his writ on the defendant. At that stage it is open to the defendant to re-open the issue and argue that leave should not have been granted. His application will be determined by a judge – this time after full verbal argument. The principles applied by the judge will be very similar to those applied when the plaintiff sought and obtained leave under Order 11. However there are some differences:

(i) Firstly, whereas the burden was previously on the plaintiff to show that the English court was clearly the appropriate forum, now the burden is on the defendant to show that there is another competent forum which is clearly more appropriate than the English courts.

(ii) If the defendant cannot show this, the English proceedings will normally be allowed to proceed. If the defendant can show that there is clearly another more appropriate forum, then the burden of proof shifts to the plaintiff to give reasons why the English proceedings should continue. One of the reasons which the plaintiff may put forward is that he will not obtain justice in foreign proceedings. It is not easy to convince the court of this.

These principles are collectively known as the theory of *forum non conveniens*. A related theory, known as *lis alibi pendens*, is invoked by the English courts where foreign proceedings are already under way. The principles which guide the court are almost identical to those on *forum non conveniens*. The existence of foreign proceedings is not generally relevant, unless the foreign proceedings are extremely advance. Even then, the existence of the foreign proceedings is just another factor to be taken into account. An example of a reinsurance where the defendant was unsuccessful in setting aside a writ had been served pursuant to Order 11 is Islamic Arab Insurance Co -v- Saudi Egyptian American Insurance Co[205]. The plaintiffs (IAIC) were incorporated in the United Arab Emirates and conducted reinsurance business. The defendants (SEARCO) involved in reinsurance business, and were incorporated in Panama with their principal office in Ohio, USA. IAIC insured certain risks in Saudi Arabia and were reinsured through London brokers, by SEARCO. IAIC commenced English proceedings to claim sums due under the reinsurance, and they were granted leave to issue and serve a writ on SEARCO. SEARCO applied to set aside the writ on the grounds that Saudi Arabian courts were the *forum conveniens*.

---

205 (1987) 1 LLR 315

SEARCO were successful at the first instance. In the Court of Appeal, the decision was overturned, and English action was allowed to proceed. One of the factors which the Court of Appeal took into account in applying the Spilida test was that England had a specialist court (the Commercial Court) and specialist lawyers who were well versed in the practices and technicalities of reinsurance practice and law. On the other hand Saudi Arabia had no such claim to specialists, indeed some doubt was expressed as to whether a Saudi Arabian Court would even acknowledge a reinsurance contract.

In exceptional circumstances, the English court will grant an injunction restraining a party from commencing proceedings in a foreign jurisdiction The general principles to be applied by the court have some similarity to those adopted in forum *non conveniens* cases. However they are not the same (CSNI Aerospatiale -v- Lee Kui Jak)[206]: it is more difficult to persuade the court to restrain foreign proceedings since this is really an interference into the procedures of the foreign courts. The principles applied are as follows:

(i) if the only issue is whether an English or a foreign court is the most appropriate forum for the action, the foreign court should be allowed to decide this on its own principles of *forum non conveniens*, and the English court will not interfere;

(ii) if exceptionally, the English court concludes that pursuit of the action in the foreign court would be vexatious and oppressive, and the English court is the natural forum, it can properly grant an injunction preventing the plaintiff pursuing his action overseas;

(iii) in deciding whether the action in the foreign court is vexatious or oppressive, consideration must be given to the possible injustice to the defendant (in the foreign action) if the injunction is not granted, and the possible injustice to the plaintiff (in the foreign action) if it is granted. The English court should therefore try to strike a balance.

It is very difficult to persuade the English court to restrain from foreign proceedings. However, the court will take into account the factors which it refuses on a *forum non conveniens* application. For instance, juridical advantages such as the right to a jury trial in a civil case, or pre-trial discovery in another jurisdiction are relevant. In the Aerospatiale case, attempts in Texas to halt Texan litigation which had been brought under the „minimum contact" theory of jurisdiction were unsuccessful. However, the Privy Council, on appeal from the Brunei Courts, restrained the Texan proceedings which were held to be „oppressive". In Midland Bank Plc -v- Laker Airways Ltd[207], both parties were

---

206 (1987) AC 871
207 (1989) 1 QB 689

English, and the actions were carried out in England. Laker Airways wished to join the bank as a defendant in an anti-trust suit in Washington DC, but the English Court of Appeal granted an injunction to prevent Laker from doing this. The extra-territorial effect of the US anti-trust legislation was held to be oppressive and unscrupulous, and this justified the court in preventing Laker from bringing US proceedings.

Before drawing conclusions on non-convention cases and before considering convention cases, a brief remark shall be made to so called „negative declarations“. A negative declaration is a declaration by the court to the effect that certain rights do not exist. The common declaration is that the contract has been validly avoided for misrepresentation, or non-disclosure of material fact. Negative declarations allow a reinsurer to make a pre-emptive strike before he is sued by the cedant and this may have certain tactical and procedural advantages. Not least is that it allows the reinsurer to indulge in forum shopping. Negative declarations are viewed with suspicion by the courts. Despite this, negative declarations are not disallowed by the court, and they are a valuable part of the reinsurance litigator's weaponry.

4.4.2.2 Convention cases (The Brussels and Lugano Conventions)

The Brussels Convention of 1968 is an attempt to harmonise, codify and simplify the rules on choice of jurisdiction that apply in the EU. It provides a complete code that sweeps aside all the contracting states' different principles of *forum conveniens* and replaces them with a uniform set of rules. In very broad terms the Convention seeks to achieve harmonisation by providing a set of rules which determine which courts within contracting states shall have jurisdiction in a particular dispute. There are different rules for different types of dispute, e.g. insurance contracts have their own special regime. There are cases where the Convention confers jurisdiction on the courts of more than one country. Then the Convention provides that the court where an action was first started shall determine the dispute, and any subsequent actions in other courts shall be dismissed.

The Convention was given the force of law in England by the Civil Jurisdiction and Judgments Act 1982. It has been in force since 1st October 1987. The Convention principles have been extended by the Lugano Convention to cover members of the European Free Trade Area (EFTA). This Convention is designed to apply Brussels Convention principles as between EFTA members *inter se*, and between EFTA members and EC countries. The EFTA countries are Finland, Austria, Iceland, Norway, Sweden and Switzerland. The Lugano Convention was brought into effect in the UK by the Civil Jurisdiction and Judgments Act 1991 (CJJA) which came into force on 1st May 1992. The Brussels Convention only applies to certain civil and commercial matters. It does not cover arbitration. Arbitration was thought to be adequately catered for in the 1958 New York Convention on the Recognition and Enforcement of Foreign Arbitral Awards, and it is not applicable in matters relating to insolvency. The Convention does not determine the proper law that governs a particular contract – it simply determines which court shall have jurisdiction on a particular dispute. The Convention applies to most cases of insurance and reinsurance litigation. However, as shall be discussed below, the precise manner of its application to reinsurance litigation is still the subject of some dispute.

The primary rule of the Convention is contained in Article 2:

„Persons domiciled in a contracting state shall, whatever their nationality, be sued in the country of that state."

Consequently, if the defendant is domiciled in England, then *prima facie*, unless Article 2 is displaced by another rule contained in the Convention, the defendant must be sued in England. Moreover, the English court will not be entitled to deny jurisdiction. It will have no discretion to consider whether a foreign court is the *forum conveniens* – it must accept jurisdiction. It is therefore important to establish the domicile of a prospective defendant before starting litigation, to establish firstly whether the Convention applies, and secondly to determine which court or courts have jurisdiction. 'Domicile' is not defined in the Convention. For Convention purposes „the seat of a company ... shall be treated as its domicile" and to determine the seat, the court concerned with the matter must apply its own domestic private international law regulations (Article 53). The English definition of „seat" is contained in CJJA 1982: a company will have seat in the UK if it was incorporated in the UK and has its registered office or official address in the UK, or if its central management and control are exercised in the UK. A company may be domiciled in more than one country.

In contrast to RSC Order 11 Rule 1, the plaintiff does not require leave to issue and serve a writ on a defendant when the English court has jurisdiction by virtue or the Convention. The writ is issued in the normal way, but the plaintiff's solicitor endorses the writ with a statement that, by virtue of the CJJA, the English court has jurisdiction. This is sufficient in the first instance for the English court to allow service of the writ abroad. Of course, this will not prevent the defendant, once served, from contesting English jurisdiction, if he so chooses.

4.4.2.3 Insurance matters according to the Convention

The Convention contains a number of exceptions to Article 2. Section 3 of the Conventions applies to insurance contracts and includes Articles 7 – 12. As a mandatory regime it excludes the other rules in the Convention, in all matters relating to insurance. It is not clear if Section 3 of the Convention applies to re-insurance to the same extent as it does to insurance.

The overall effect of Section 3 of the Convention is two-fold:

(i) It restricts the insurer, with very few exceptions, to commencing actions against the policyholder in the courts of the contracting state where the policy-holder is domiciled;

(ii) Alternatively, it gives the policyholder a wide choice as to the courts in which he is able to sue his insurer.

In other words, it provides the insured with considerable scope for forum shopping, whilst it denies the insurer the same rights. This is a brand of consumer protection, and this consumer protection principle underpins many of the provisions of the Convention. Article 11 restates the basic principle in Article 2, so that an insurer may bring proceedings only in the courts of the contracting state where the defendant is domiciled (irrespective of whether he is the policy-holder, the insured, or a beneficiary). However, if an original claim is pending in a different court, the insurer may bring a counterclaim in that court. This may be contrasted with the position of the insured, (or the policyholder or beneficiary of the policy), who has a much wider choice. The insured may sue his insurer:

(i) in the courts of the contracting state where the insurer is domiciled (Article 8), or

(ii) in the courts of the contracting state where the insured is domiciled (Article 8), or

(iii) if the insurer is a co-insurer, in the courts or the contracting state in which proceedings are brought against the leading insurer (Article 8), or

(iv) in the courts of the place where the harmful event occurred (Article 9) in cases of liability insurance, or insurance of immovable property, or

(v) in the case of liability insurance once again , (if allowed by local law) by joining in proceedings brought by the injured party against the insured (Article 10).

Article 8 applies for the purposes of establishing whether an insurer is domiciled in a contracting state, and therefore deciding whether he may be sued in that contracting state. This Article provides that an insurer shall be deemed to be domiciled in a contracting state where it has a branch, agency or other establishment, where the dispute is a result of the operations of the branch, agency or establishment. An example of the application of this Article is seen in S&W Berisford PLC -v- New Hampshire Insurance Company[208]. The two plaintiffs were an English company and its New York subsidiary. The defendant was a US corporation. The defendant applied to stay proceedings that had been served on

208 (1990) 1 LLR 454

him at his UK office. The dispute derived from the operation of his branch, agency or establishment in London although the defendant was in fact domiciled in the USA. Therefore the defendant was deemed to be domiciled in England. The Convention was held to apply so that the English court had to assume jurisdiction over the dispute. The defendant had requested a stay of the English action under the *forum non conveniens* principles, but this was held to be inconsistent with the Convention and had no relevance in the case.

Article 12 of the Convention allows the mandatory rules in insurance matters to be departed from by agreement between the parties. Such an agreement will be recognised under the Convention where the parties have agreed that the courts of a particular country shall have jurisdiction only if:

(i) the agreement is entered into after the dispute has arisen, or

(ii) the agreement confers upon the policyholder a greater choice of courts that are embodied in Section 3 itself, or

(iii) the policyholder is not domiciled in a contracting state (except in as far as the insurance is compulsory or relates to immovable property in a contracting state); or

(iv) the agreement relates to a contract of insurance covering one or more certain marine or aviation risk relating to:

(a) loss or damage to sea-going ships or aircraft or off-shore installations or goods in transit (other than passenger baggage) during carriage by ship or aircraft; or

(b) liability arising from the use of such ships or aircraft, or loss or damage caused by goods in transit on such a ship or aircraft (Article 12A).

In summary, the mandatory provisions of the Section may be departed from only by agreement in very limited circumstances. An agreement on jurisdiction in an insurance contract will be of little benefit to an insurer unless the policyholder is domiciled outside the contracting states, or the contract relates to the marine aviation risks listed in Article 12A. This is consistent with the consumer protection principle which I mentioned earlier. A very recent case applies Article 12 with results that undermine one of the aims of the Convention: to avoid duplicity of proceedings in different jurisdictions. In Charman & Brockbank -v- W.O.C. Offshore BV[209], the plaintiffs were Lloyds Underwriters, and the defendants were a Dutch firm of civil engineers. Lloyds insured the engineers concerning contingency risks relating to sea-going and land based equipment which was being used for the reconstruction of a breakwater in Algeria. The insured contingency occurred and the engineers claimed for the equipment under the in-

---

209 1993 1 Lloyd's Rep 378 (QB), affirmed (1993) 2 Lloyd's Rep 551 (CA)

surance contract. The engineers applied in England to set aside the writ on the grounds that the English court had no jurisdiction.

The basic rule for the action brought by the insurer is in Article 11. He should proceed only in the courts where the defendant is domiciled, i.e. in this case Holland. However under Article 12, this could be overridden by the English jurisdiction clause in as far as the contract covered the risks outlined in Article 12A. Lloyds underwriters argued that the whole of the dispute (which encompassed both sea-going and land-based risks under the one insurance contract) should be resolved in accordance with Article 12A by the English court. The engineers argued that Article 12A had a more restricted meaning such that only that element of the dispute which related to the sea-going equipment listed in Article 12A should be litigated in England.

The judge preferred to apply a narrow interpretation to Article 12A. He limited the effect of the English jurisdiction clause to that element of the dispute which referred solely to sea-going risks. Consequently, that part of the dispute which referred to sea-going risks was properly heard by the English court, but the engineers were successful in establishing that the Dutch courts had jurisdiction regarding land-based risks.

4.4.2.4 Reinsurance: To be equated with insurance or not ?

Despite several occasions when the English courts and the European Court of Justice have had to determine whether reinsurance contracts are governed by Section 3 of the Lugano Convention, there has been no definite ruling. In Arkwright Mutual Insurance Company -v- Bryanstone Insurance Company Limited[210], which was a reinsurance case, there was agreement between the parties that insurance rules did not apply to reinsurance. There is some authority for this view since the report of Professor Schlosser, which is a recognised official guide to the interpretation of the Convention, states that „reinsurance contracts cannot be equated with insurance contracts. Accordingly, Articles 7 to 12 do not apply to reinsurance contracts". In a departure from the normal principles governing English statutory interpretation, the English courts are expressly allowed to refer to Professor Schlosser's report in construing any provision of the 1982 Civil Jurisdiction and Judgments Act (by virtue of Section 3). As mentioned supra, this view is consistent with the consumer protection principle, since purchasers of reinsurance are usually substantial corporations who are not in need of consumer protection.

---

210 (1990) 2 All ER 335

However, it is not safe to assume that reinsurance is not governed by the insurance rules since doubt has been cast on this. In Overseas Union -v- New Hampshire[211], the European Court of Justice was asked to decide upon a number of questions including the question as to whether the insurance regime in Section 3 of the Convention applied to a reinsurance contract. Action in the case was started in England[212] and France simultaneously. Hirst J held that French proceedings, seeking payment under contracts of reinsurance brought by an American reinsured against various reinsurers (who challenged the jurisdiction of the French court) and an English action brought by the same reinsurers against the reinsured for a declaration of non-liability, involved the same „cause of action". Because the French court was first occupied with the matter, the English court stayed the action against it pending the French court's decision regarding the validity of its jurisdiction.

The case was then referred to the ECJ. In the event, as a result of its findings on the other questions, the ECJ did not make a ruling as to whether the insurance regime in Section 3 of the Convention applied to a reinsurance contract. Nevertheless, the case was fully argued before the ECJ in the following manner:

(i) The German government said that Section 3 did not apply to reinsurance, basing its arguments on social policy grounds;

(ii) The UK government expressed no view whatsoever;

(iii) The European Commission asserted that reinsurance contracts are covered by Section 3. The Commission felt that there is no fundamental difference between insurance and reinsurance which

would justify the exclusion of reinsurance in the absence of clear exclusionary words in Section 3.

It is immaterial to consider the parties' arguments towards the case, since they argue their own interests, but in some respect the views of the governments and the European Commission could be said to be impartial and of some weight. This issue is a very important one in convention cases. If the cedant is an EC domiciliary and if the insurance regime does apply to reinsurance contracts, then the reinsurer's hands will be tied in terms of where he may commence the action:

(i) If the insurance regime does apply to reinsurance contracts, then a reinsurer who seeks a negative declaration against his EC cedant or who sues for an unpaid premium will be bound in most circumstances to sue in the courts of that contracting state where the cedant is domiciled.

---

211 (Case 351/89, ECJ 27th June 1991)

212 (1992) 1 Lloyd's Rep 218

(ii) moreover, a jurisdiction clause conferring jurisdiction on, say, the courts of the reinsurer's domicile, will be of no help to the reinsurer unless and only in as far as the claim relates to certain marine and aviation risks.

4.4.3 Choice of Law

It was the outcome of the interviews that in fact more than two thirds of the files opened by the lawyers were cross-border in terms of the parties or the facts of the case. Hence the assumption made at the beginning of the study was affirmed that reinsurance disputes are highly international. According to the lawyers interviewed, a dispute arises over the law to be applied in every fourth cross-border case. This result might come as a surprise if one considers that there should be choice of law clauses in the wording of reinsurance contracts. The choice of law clause is one of the most important clauses in any reinsurance contract. Without such a clause, the parties ask a court to indulge in informed guesswork as to the intention of the parties, or if that is not possible, the law most closely connected to the contract.[213] A choice of English law in a contract is one of the grounds under RSC Order 11 for the English court to assert jurisdiction over an overseas party.[214] RSC Order 11 Rule 1 provides that

„ ... service of a writ out of the jurisdiction is permissible with the leave of the court if ..... -

(c) The claim is brought against a person duly served within or out of the jurisdiction and a person out of the jurisdiction is a necessary and proper part thereto; or

(d) The claim is brought to enforce, rescind, dissolve, annul or otherwise affect a contract or to recover damages or obtain other relief in respect of the breach of a contract, being .... a contract which -

(i) was made within the jurisdiction, or

(ii) was made by or through an agent trading or residing within the jurisdiction ..... , or

(iii) is ... governed by English law, or

(iv) contains a term to the effect that the High Court shall have jurisdiction ..... , or

---

213 J. S. Butler, *Reinsurance Practice and the Law,* London: Lloyd's of London Press Ltd, 1993, Service Issue No. 7, 1 September 1997, 11.1.

214 Andrew Bandurka, „The Problems of Jurisdiction: How and where to proceed ", Paper presented at the DYP seminar 'Reinsurance Litigation – When to avoid it – How to win it, 13th – 15th April, 1994, London, B44

(e) The claim is brought in respect of a breach committed within the jurisdiction of a contract made within or out of the jurisdiction .... ; or

(f) The claim is founded on a tort and the damage was sustained, or resulted from an act committed, within the jurisdiction .... „

Choice of law is also important in its own right. It is quite possible for the courts of one country **to decide a dispute in accordance with the laws of another country**.[215] Some reinsurance disputes provide expressly for this, for example a clause providing for arbitration in London, in accordance with New York law. It is also quite possible for the courts of one country to apply its own laws in relation to one aspect of a reinsurance contract, and apply the laws of another country in relation to a different aspect of the same contract, e.g. in the case of Forsikringsaktieselkapet Vesta -v- Butcher[216]. Vesta -v- Butcher involved a Norwegian fish farm which was insured by a Norwegian insurance policy and wholly reinsured on the same terms to London reinsurers. The reinsurance was subject to a „follow the settlements“ clause as well as a „claims control“ clause. Under these clauses, no offer, payment or compromise of a claim would be made without the consent of the reinsurers.[217] These clauses would have been void under Norwegian law. The question arose whether the contract of reinsurance ought to be interpreted according to English or Norwegian law. Thus, although the proper law of the reinsurance was English, the construction and effect of the clauses were to be determined according to Norwegian law, in the same way as they were in the original contract.

A question of particular interest to the London reinsurance market is whether governing law of the underlying cover can be incorporated into a reinsurance contract by means of an incorporation clause.[218] This is important because as already mentioned reinsurers often fail to select a proper law and it is then assumed that the reinsurance transaction is to be governed by English law. Besides Vesta -v- Butcher, a second decision deals with this question. In Citadel Insurance Co. v. Atlantic Union Insurance Co.[219], London brokers placed a facultative obligatory open cover facility with a Greek reinsurer on behalf of a New York broker for its insurer client. The reinsurance contract contained an „as original“

---

215 Andrew Bandurka, „The Problems of Jurisdiction: How and where to proceed “, Paper presented at the DYP seminar 'Reinsurance Litigation – When to avoid it – How to win it', 13th – 15th April, 1994 London, B44 – B46

216 (1989) All ER 402 (HL)

217 C.E. Golding, *The Law and Practice of Reinsurance*, 5th ed., London: Witherby & Co.Ltd., 1987, 71

218 J. S. Butler, *Reinsurance Practice and the Law*, London: Lloyd's of London Press, 1993, looseleaf, Service Issue No. 7, 1 September 1996, 10.6.4.1

219 (1982) 2 Lloyd's Rep 542 (CA)

clause. The question arose if this clause would have incorporated the proper law of the underlying cover, i.e. the law of New York. The English court could only assume jurisdiction over the Greek reinsurer if the contract was governed by English law. If the governing law of the underlying cover had been incorporated, then the English court would not possess jurisdiction. The reinsurer contended that the reinsurance contract was governed by the law of New York where the American broker conducted business. The Court of Appeal rejected this argument. It stated that the reinsurance agreement provided no basis for concluding that it was to be governed by an ascertainable system of law based upon the underlying policies. The court concluded that London was „the centre of gravity“ for reinsurance transactions. The transaction was most closely connected to London and, as such, the proper law of the reinsurance contract was English.

This decision seems to indicate that general words of incorporation do not necessarily bind reinsurers to the governing law of the underlying cover. The importance of the choice of law cannot be over-emphasised. If, as is usually the case with London market slips, there is no express choice of law and there is room for argument and uncertainty as to the law which governs the principles of non-disclosure of material fact, misrepresentation, proper performance, breach of contract etc. i.e. the fundamental doctrine which determines the relationship between the parties. As with jurisdiction, there are two regimes for deciding the proper law of a contract. The common law principles are embodied in a number of judicial decisions. These have been superseded to a large extent by the 1980 Rome Convention, which took effect in England on July 26th 1990 by virtue of the Contracts (Applicable Law) Act 1990.

Under common law principles, the proper law of a contract is determined by the following:

(i) Express reference in the contract to a particular system of law.

This is quite usual in reinsurance treaties, where a provision such as „the laws of England shall apply“ may be incorporated. In contrast to wordings, such clauses are almost unknown in slips.[220]

(ii) If the parties' choice is not set out, the court will determine that system of law which it infers the parties intended to apply.

(iii) If there is no expressed or inferred intention, the court applies the system of law with which the transaction has the closest and most real connection.

The principles governing (ii) and (iii) often tend to overlap.[221] The court will take into account both the terms of the contract and other extrinsic facts. A ju-

220 Andrew Bandurka, „The Problems of Jurisdiction: How and where to proceed ", Paper presented at the DYP seminar 'Reinsurance Litigation – When to avoid it – How to win it', 13th – 15th April, 1994 London, B45

risdiction clause in favour of the courts of a particular country will indicate that that country's laws are to be applied – in this respect, mandatory clauses carry considerably more weight than permissive jurisdiction clauses. Similarly, an arbitration clause may specify a place for the arbitration, and it can thus be inferred that that country's laws are to be applied. Other factors are less persuasive. The use of a standard Lloyds marine policy may be held to infer that English law should govern the contract. The use of the English language, or a reference in the contract to Pound Sterling may indicate, though not very strongly, that English law is the governing one.

It is often difficult to predict with any certainty the outcome of an application of principles (ii) and (iii) in any particular circumstances. It has always been important, and it is now more important than ever, to stipulate in the contract which system of law should apply. The Contract (Applicable Law) Act 1990 brings into force the provisions of the 1980 Rome Convention with effect from 1st April 1991. Contracts made before that date are governed by the common law rules explained above. The Rome Convention was designed to harmonise the rules governing choice of law, and to ensure certainty and the uniformity of application of those rules across the EEC. It appears that it fails to achieve this spectacularly and shall be suggested as proof for what was assumed on provisions which are deemed to assist in the co-ordination of cross-border legal interaction. The scheme set out in the Convention has superficial similarities to the English rules of proper law discussed above:

(i) The parties may choose a system of law in their contract, which is respected and upheld by the Convention (Article 3),

(ii) The choice of law may be implied, rather than expressly stated, and the Convention will respect this as long as the choice can be demonstrated with reasonable certainty by reference to the terms of the contract or the circumstances of the case (Article 3),

(iii) If there is neither an expressed nor an implied choice of law, the proper law is the law of the country „with which the contract is most closely connected "This is presumed to be the country of habitual residence of the party who is to effect the performance which is characteristic of the contract".

However, this presumption shall not apply if the characteristic performance cannot be determined, or if it appears from those circumstances as a whole that the contract is more closely connected with another country. This takes us round in circles, and thus undermines the certainty and clarity which the Convention

221 Andrew Bandurka, „The Problems of Jurisdiction: How and where to proceed ", Paper presented at the DYP seminar 'Reinsurance Litigation – When to avoid it – How to win it', 13th – 15th April, 1994 London, B46 – B48

seeks to achieve. The rules apply to reinsurance contracts and insurance contracts, except insurance of risks which are situated outside the EEC. The rules are not restricted to contracts between EEC nationals, and an application of the rules may result in a non-EEC state's law imposing. Consequently the rules are very wide in their ambit. In sweeping away the old rules of governing law, the Convention may produce completely absurd results in a reinsurance context, for example, a London market reinsurance slip subscribed by five overseas reinsurers, which has no signed wording. It is relatively rare for London brokers to incorporate a choice of law clause in reinsurance slips.

In these circumstances it would be open to each of the five overseas reinsurers to argue that the „performance which is characteristic of the contract" is the payment of claims by reinsurers, and therefore the law of the country where those reinsurers are resident should apply. If the cedant sued these reinsurers in London, the High Court would *prima facie* have to interpret five identical contracts in accordance with five completely different systems of law. This result would obviously not be sensible. As shown above the inclusion of choice of law clauses is often forgotten in the slip and in the wording which is to follow the slip. The question arises why this is so. In this context it must be stressed that reinsurance contract documentation in the past did not obey any strict rules. As mentioned above the reinsurance contract, business placed in the London market is documented by a piece of paper called a 'slip'. The slip is supposed to be followed by a wording, but the slip has the function of a contract. until this wording is issued.

The solicitors and barristers interviewed stated that in the past the documentation in reinsurance used to be handled quite sloppily. As a consequence, the lawyers find themselves in the position of having to give legal advice on a contract where no documentation of the reinsurance exists other than the slip. The free format interview relating to the quality of drafting revealed a conflict of interest as well as some professional tension between lawyers and brokers. It has to be said that some of the interviewed also work for brokers, sometimes in cases where the latter have to be defended on allegations of misrepresentation or non-disclosure. Because of this conflict of interests, the lawyers might not have expressed their opinion as freely as they might have done without the existence of this conflict. Some of the interviewees came up with clear comments on the quality of drafting in the past. Drafting was left to junior brokers and clerks. Often it consisted of clauses and paragraphs pieced together. This „scissors and paste approach" to the drafting of slips and policies resulted in it being impossible to rely on the primary approach to the construction of contracts, which is to construe words in accordance with their natural and ordinary meaning.[222]

A classic example[223] of this sort of problem is the Alexion Hope case [224] in which Lloyd L. J. stated as follows:

„In this case we are concerned with a new type of insurance. It seems a pity, therefore, that the parties should have incorporated their contract in a form which as long ago as 1792 was described by Mr. Justice Buller as absurd and incoherent ...

Clause 1 consisted of eight numbered paragraphs ... we were not told if there is a Clause 2. If there is, it was not incorporated, for which we should perhaps be grateful. What we were told is that Clause 1 is a translation from the Swedish ... we were urged by both parties to give certain words ... their plain and ordinary meaning. Whether they have a plain and ordinary meaning in Swedish I do not know but they certainly have no plain or ordinary meaning in English. We were also urged to construe the document as a whole against the contractual background but the combination of a medieval English form with the translation from modern Swedish does not make this task any easier.“

A further disadvantage was that the brokers who negotiated and those who did the final drafting were not the same people. Also the dilemma of time and diligence has been mentioned in the sense that reinsurance contracts require a quick decision and therefore the slip at least must be issued quickly. In interviews with two of the major and one of the middle-sized broker houses, it became apparent that the above described attitude towards drafting has changed and the awareness of legal problems which may arise due to poor quality drafting has increased. These statements by brokers are supported by the fact that nowadays nearly all larger than average broker firms have a legal department of varying size, contrary to 10 or 15 years ago at which time legal departments rarely existed. However, according to the interviewees, the assistance of outside counsels in drafting, remains, as one interviewee put it, 'a touchy issue'. Drafting has for a long time been the broker's domain and the idea that an outside counsel shall be of assistance in this matter, a perspective the lawyers would like them to appreciate, has not really caught on.

It so happened that certain phrases in reinsurance contract wording have become „soft targets“.[225] Much of the recent reinsurance litigation has turned on

---

222 Colin Edelman, „Current 'soft targets' in UK Reinsurance contract wording“, Paper presented at the 2nd annual Euroforum Reinsurance Dispute Strategy Conference, 17th November, 1995, The Merchant Centre, London, 2

223 ibid, 2

224 (1988) 1 Lloyd's Rep. 311

the disputed meaning or effect or applicability of phrases and clauses. The courts are confronted with sometimes ambiguous or contradicting reinsurance contracts which they are required to construe[226]. The judicial process of construction is undergone in accordance with a number of rules and presumptions, whereby the primary approach is to construe words in accordance with

(a) their **natural and ordinary meaning;**

(b) the **underlying commercial purpose** of the parties.[227]

The peculiarity of reinsurance terminology also means that judicial precedent is unlikely to be of assistance for the purpose of construction. This may result in the fact that construction according to the contextual meaning is likely to be the most fruitful approach. This involves reading the word or phrase not only in the context of the clause, but also in the context of the policy as a whole, having due regard for any other clauses which may provide information about its intended meaning. With regard to the underlying commercial purpose of the parties, the courts will assume in reinsurance that it was back to back cover. The reinsurer will be liable under the reinsurance (subject to the specified limits of liability) whenever the reinsured is liable under policies covered by the reinsurance. This presumption was put in the following terms by Lord Griffith in Forsikringsaktieselskapet Vesta v. Butcher[228] :

„In the ordinary course of business reinsurance is referred to as „back-to-back" with the insurance, which means that the reinsurer agrees that if the insurer is liable under policy the reinsurer will accept liability to pay whatever percentage of the claim he has agreed to reinsure. A reinsurer could, of course, make a special contract with an insurer to bear the full cost of the other risks. Such a contract would, I believe, be wholly exceptional, a departure from the normal understanding of the back-to-back nature of reinsurance and would require to be spelt out in clear terms. I doubt if there is any market for such reinsurance."

Applying the presumption of back-to-back cover to the facts of the above case, resulted in the House of Lords holding that as a matter of construction in accordance with English law, a warranty incorporated into an English reinsur-

---

225 Colin Edelman, „Current 'soft targets' in UK Reinsurance Contract Wording", Paper presented at the 2nd annual Euroforum Reinsurance Dispute Strategy Conference, 17th November, 1995, The Merchant Centre, London, 1

226 *Construction* is the process of determining the true meaning of a written document. It is interchangeable with the term *interpretation.*

227 Colin Edelman, „Current 'soft targets' in UK Reinsurance Contract Wording", Paper presented at the 2nd annual Euroforum Reinsurance Dispute Strategy Conference, 17th November, 1995, The Merchant Centre, London, 3

228 (1989) 1 Lloyd's Rep. 331 (336)

ance from the original Norwegian insurance policy was to be given the same meaning and effect as it had in the Norwegian policy (to which Norwegian law applied) rather than the meaning and effect that a warranty would have under English law. Consistency of coverage between the insurance and reinsurance was thereby achieved.

In the case of Commercial Union v. Sun Alliance[229], the court was concerned with a slip which provided for the period of reinsurance to be „12 months at 31st December 1985 with 120 days NCAD“.[230] The plaintiffs contended that this had the effect of providing for a fixed term of one year subject to automatic renewal for a further 12 months if 120 days notice of cancellation were not given. The defendants contended that the provision of notice of cancellation was inconsistent with the fixed one year term and was therefore meaningless and should be disregarded. One of the grounds on which Steyn J. favoured the plaintiffs was that all those concerned knew that it was customary in the Dutch and Belgian insurance markets (the original risk being principally located in Holland and Belgium). A fixed annual term subject was subject to automatic renewal in the event that 90 days notice of cancellation was not served. Therefore the original policy covering the risk would in all likelihood include such a provision.

In Axa Reinsurance (UK) v. Field[231], one of the reasons given in the Court of Appeal for construing „event“ in reinsurance as having the same meaning as „originating cause“ in the original insurance for the purpose of the aggregation of losses, was that limiting terms in reinsurance policies should not be readily found to operate more stringently than those of the underlying policy. An example of a decision refusing back-to-back cover is Youell v. Bland Welch (No. 1)[232].The insurers were liable during the estimated 32 months period for the construction of three super-tankers until delivery under a „held covered“ clause (on payment of an additional premium). The reinsurance was in the following terms:

„The reinsured shall cede to the reinsurers and the reinsurers shall accept by way of reinsurance of the reinsured their proportion of liability in respect of risks attaching for periods as original but not exceeding 48 months.“

The argument was whether the provision referred only to the original estimated construction period- so that ship building which exceeded an estimated construction period of 48 months would not be ceded, and that which did not exceed the estimated construction period would be ceded and covered on a back to

229 (1992) 1 Lloyd's Rep. 475
230 NCAD stands for „notice of cancellation at anniversary date“.
231 (1996) 1 Lloyd's Rep 26 (CA)
232 (1990) 2 Lloyd's Rep 423 and (1992) 2 Lloyd's Rep 127

back basis- or if there would be a cut-off regardless of the original estimated period with all vessels being ceded. Philips J. and the Court of Appeal upheld the manner in which the latter point was construed. Beldam L. J. held that this was one of those exceptional contracts which Lord Griffith had referred to in Vesta v. Butcher and the words were construed as they appeared without the application of any presumption as to back to back cover. The fact that the applicable law is not mentioned on the slip explains the relatively high percentage of cases where lawyers have to consider the question of which law is to be applied. Furthermore, in many instances in which there is a choice of law clause, it may be the result of the parties' passive acceptance of a broker standard form rather than a conscious decision on the matter.[233]

Whether or not for some reason the parties fail to choose the applicable law, this situation falls within the scope of the 1980 Rome Convention on the Law of Applicable to Contractual Obligations. The Rome Convention is intended to be of universal or world wide application, i.e. it applies regardless of whether the contract has any connection with a European Union contracting state.[234] The only thing that matters is that the dispute is tried in a contracting state to the Convention. The United Kingdom agreed to it on 1 April 1991. According to Art 1 (4) of the Convention, certain contracts of insurance are excluded from the scope of the Convention. The exclusion does not however apply to reinsurance.[235] The basic principle according to Art. 3 of the Convention is the freedom of choice that 'a contract shall be governed by the law chosen by the parties.'

The Rome Convention is not the only Convention where reinsurance has found no explicit regulation. European Community legislation also falls short in this respect. The European market should have been, according to Article 7a of the Brussels Convention, completed by 31.12.1992. The unification of law is considered one of the most important elements in achieving this goal of eliminating all obstacles to the 'four freedoms'-trade, people, services and capital. For insurance this goal is specified within Art. 61 (2) of the Brussels Convention. There is a close connection between the legal harmonisation of the insurance and capital markets due to the fact that they share a common infrastructure. Also Art. 52 and Art. 59 which regulate the freedom of trade and services apply directly since 31.12.1995, the national insurance markets are still sealed off. The penetration of markets is impeded by the fact that primary insurance is an area traditionally subject to the extensive legislatory activities of the member states. How-

233 J. S. Butler, *Reinsurance Practice and the Law*, London: Lloyd's of London Press Ltd, 1993, Service Issue No. 7, 1 September 1996, 11.1

234 Cheshire and North's, *Private International Law*, 12 ed., Butterworth, 1992

235 see: *The Guiliano and Lagarde Report*, 31; 507

ever it can be said that efforts within the primary (statutory law) and secondary (regulations) sources of community law have either been addressing public law (regulatory aspects) or private law relating to consumer protection. For insurance law this is particularly true regarding the extensive regulations on life insurance and insolvency regulation. Back in 1964, a directive was released on the issue of reinsurance and retrocession (RL 64/225/EWG v. 25.2.1964, Abl. 1964, 878). This regulation/directive concerned freedom of establishment of business and is however not relevant for the cross-border legal interaction of reinsurers with their primaries or retrocessionaires. The Brussels and the Lugano Conventions are however relevant to cross-border legal interaction touching upon the place of jurisdiction, foreign judgments and awards as well as their enforcement.

As shall be later shown, global players are often not dealt with in EU legislation concerning their international activities, and the extent to which regulation applies to them is under dispute. For this reason Lasok and Stone (1987)[236] argue that there should be special rules for reinsurance to avoid such discussions. The question of the applicable law as well as jurisdiction is not at all a theoretical problem. To illustrate this point ,a summary shall be given of the facts of a case which was decided upon by the Commercial Court, division of the High Court, which was handed down on 7th July 1994 – Trade Indemnity Plc v.-Försakringsactiebolaget Njord[237].[238] The dispute between the parties arose from a surplus treaty reinsurance obtained by a Swedish insurer, Försakringsactiebolaget Njord ("Njord") in the London market in respect of the portfolio of European bond and credit risks which included financial guarantees, performance and other forms of bonds, and borrowing liabilities. [239] The reinsurance was placed by London market brokers and exclusively documented by the terms of two reinsurance slips, for the 1990 and 1991 underwriting years, respectively. The slips were led in both years by Trade Indemnity Plc. To lead a slip means to be the first to underwrite a share of the risk. As mentioned before it is quite common that more than just one reinsurer will take a share in a reinsurance cover. Treaty wordings never came into existence. In September 1991, Njord was declared

236 see: Lasok, D. and Stone P. A., *Conflicts of Laws in the European Community,* Professional books ltd., Abingdon, Oxon, (1987)

237 (1995) LRLR 367 (QB)

238 This case serves as classic example for the implication of cross-border structures in reinsurance. It touches upon the choice of law, application of the Brussels and Lugano Conventions to reinsurance and jurisdiction in the absence of a jurisdiction clause. To create an impression of the numerous and international parties involved in such a case, a copy of the writ of Trade Indemnity -v- Njord is to be found under the Exhibit.

239 Stephenson Harwood, *Insurance and Reinsurance Group news letter*, December 1994, 1

bankrupt by the District Court of Stockholm and its affairs were jointly placed into the hands of three liquidators. In the wake of Njord's collapse and the findings of the Swedish Inspection Board, which led to official findings of gross mismanagement, Njord's London reinsurers became concerned that serious misrepresentations might have been made to them which would justify the avoidance of the reinsurance.

In September 1992, the reinsurers obtained an order for the issue and service out of the English jurisdiction of a writ against Njord, seeking declaration that they were entitled to avoid and had validly avoided the 1990 and 1991 reinsurance contracts; and also the return of claims already paid (less premiums received). Njord sought to contest the first action on the basis that the English Commercial Court was not the most appropriate forum for resolving the dispute. The Court held that notwithstanding the fact that cover was governed by English law, it was not appropriate to have the dispute resolved in England because its focus would be the conduct of the reinsured's business in Sweden, in connection with which local and factual witnesses would have to be called.

In the final stages of proceedings, judgments and awards have to be enforced. In an international context as in reinsurance, enforcement may involve asking one country's courts to recognise the validity of a judgment or award elsewhere and permit the attachment of the debtor's assets.[240] The two relevant judicial systems, the one issuing the judgment and the other which is expected to enforce it, may have different legal rules concerning jurisdiction or a court's competence to hear a case. This can result in obstacles to enforcement. Although enforcement is the final step in proceedings, it has to be taken into account right from the start. To increase the chances of enforcing a judgment or award, the action should be brought in the jurisdiction in which the defendant's assets are located. If this is not possible, the plaintiff must find out if the title obtained in one jurisdiction will be recognised and enforced by another.

From the perspective of the defendant in a cross-border action, enforcement also involves tactical decisions. The cross-border element leads to an increase in deliberation in procedural questions. It is however crucial concerning enforcement which is the final goal in putting a claim through. If the defendant is sued in a jurisdiction where he has no assets he may at first instance try to persuade the foreign court that it should not hear the case. If he fails to do so, the trial will proceed. He can further decide to defend proceedings. Alternatively, he can choose to ignore them in the hope that the enforcement of a title will not be successful. If a defendant is sued where he has assets he must defend proceedings.

---

240 J. S. Butler, *Reinsurance Practice and the Law*, London: Lloyd's of London Press, 1993, looseleaf, Service Issue No. 7, 1 September 1996, 28.1

English courts, which will be elaborated on below, allow themselves a rather wide jurisdiction in the hearing of cases. This also applies to reinsurance contracts brokered through the London market. If the contract is brokered through the London market this will constitute the „centre of gravity" necessary to assume jurisdiction for English courts. The rules governing enforcement do not always grant the same leeway to foreign courts.[241] Concerning arbitration awards the methods of enforcement of arbitral awards are similar to judgments. The successful party to an arbitration can either bring an action to enforce an award. This requires a full second hearing. However hardly any decisions could be found which concern the enforcement of arbitral awards. This supports the assumptions made at the beginning. If the parties submit themselves voluntarily to arbitration, they have an interest in coming to mutual a agreement. Once a verdict is reached, the parties will not undermine the efforts involved in reaching it by not obeying the verdict. Where arbitration still takes place there is the common „spirit", which includes obeying the verdict without challenging it. These examples show that conflict of laws and jurisdiction in reinsurance is a common phenomenon. One must bear in mind that the international nature of reinsurance is involved in every possible stage of the relationship of the parties affected by a reinsurance contract. This covers

- risks exposed to interpretation of the foreign jurisdiction
- parties involved originating from different jurisdictions and fighting about the applicable law and jurisdiction
- the enforcement of arbitration awards and court decisions in the various jurisdictions.

The challenging element of this study still remains to conclude whether the globalisation of business is followed by the globalised disputing of legal issues or if cross-border disputes are solved by a national jurisdiction.

241 J. S. Butler, ibid

5. The Institutions of Reinsurance Conflict Resolution in London

5.1. General

Today, London is a venue traditionally appreciated for resolving international disputes – even in cases where neither the parties nor the facts of the case have any dealings with it. This applies to arbitration *and* litigation in the same manner. When the solicitors interviewed were asked to comment on why London is chosen for the arbitration and jurisdiction of reinsurance disputes, the same arguments were repeatedly put forward.

„Clients trust in the expertise and the impartiality of London as a dispute resolution centre. London has a pool of arbitrators and counsels derived of the major reinsurance market because of its long established history in reinsurance. In London more reinsurance disputes are solved than in any other financial centre. The London legal profession likewise is probably the most expert in the resolution of such disputes."

„Concerning arbitration, London has the most sophisticated arbitration laws where the courts have not been able to interfere with the awards. With regard to the Courts, the Commercial Court has the best expertise of all courts to decide reinsurance disputes. English law and procedure are felt to be fair and the law is reasonably certain. With respect to reinsurance it is the best developed body of law with the most predictable outcome."

„The wish for legal guidance and demand for precedents regarding reinsurance has triggered off a run to the Court in the beginning of the 1980ies. Meanwhile there exist sufficient precedents in reinsurance cases although it is to say that the occupation of the English law system with reinsurance was not based on free decision. It was rather based on that the underlying business was brokered through the London market. The choice of English law in reinsurance contracts is made by the brokers who draft the contracts."

„Additional to legal and market expertise the language factor promotes London as a centre for international dispute resolution."

These statements on the whole seem to support London as an international dispute resolution centre, whereas differentiations must be made regarding litigation and arbitration. Whether these comments can be adhered to, or whether they have to be modified or looked at more critically will be discussed below in more detail when the various dispute resolution mechanisms are dealt with. However two major points must be made at this stage regarding litigation:

1. It can be verified that London is increasingly used as a dispute resolution centre for international reinsurance disputes. It can be taken as fact that more and more reinsurance disputes find their way into the court system.[242] The recent issue of a quarterly Lloyds reinsurance law report[243] which came out in January 1995 emphasises this point :the number of decisions made requires a special publication. Although, according to English law the reinsurance contract is one of utmost good faith *(ueberrima fidei)*, meaning a kind of contract which is supposed to require a special bond of trust between the parties, it is a fact that this principle is not adhered to anymore.[244] Whereas imminent disputes were resolved amicably 25 years ago, today the lawyers get involved immediately leading to a true explosion of arbitration and court proceedings. It is actually *this surprising discovery of numerous and expensive disputes and proceedings* which lead the study to change direction in a way expected at the beginning. During the initial search for informal dispute resolution structures in the reinsurance industry it soon became apparent that at least in the last decade a litigious pattern of dispute resolution prevailed. According to the information given by the lawyers, the rise in the number of reinsurance disputes can be traced back to the end of the 1980s.The situation then peaked and a comparatively greater share of those disputes went to court.

2. The use of the Commercial Court by the international reinsurance business seems to contradict what was stated supra in the introduction, where it was proven that especially in commercial cross-border disputes, a national court is not well-suited to cope with the international elements of a cross-border case. It is rarely found that national judges are able to deal with international cases due to their complexity and therefore international parties try to avoid them. The Commercial Court is obviously the exception to this rule because international reinsurance parties also come to London to litigate. They resort to the Commercial Court as a national court. A court and its judges alone are not the only factors in dispute resolution. The use of the forum chosen depends on the appropriate skills of the legal professions surrounding it. Their quality and contribution – whether it be in arbitration or litigation – become essential factors when determining the suitability of a venue.

---

242 J. S. Butler, Reinsurance Practice and the Law, London: Lloyd's of London Press Ltd., 1993, looseleaf, Service Issue No. 7, 1 September 1996, 25.5.1

243 *Lloyds Reinsurance Law Reports,* Lloyd's of London Press, First issue Part (1) 1995, January 1995

244 Gordon Cornish, „Neuere Entwicklungen im englischen Rückversicherungsrecht", in: *Zeitschrift für Versicherungswesen,* 21/96, 618-620 (618)

5.2 The Commercial Court

As far as reinsurance litigation is concerned, one must appreciate that reinsurance cases involve large sums of money and cases with claims over £100 000 will generally be heard before the High Court.[245] Reinsurance cases will almost always be heard before the Commercial Court in the first instance due to the sums involved, although it has no exclusive jurisdiction over them. The Commercial Court as a subdivision of the High Court is a specialist court within the Queen's Bench Division and deals with large commercial cases. One remarkable feature of the work of the Commercial Court is the extent to which it is used by overseas litigants. In 1995, in over 50 per cent. of the cases heard, none of the parties were British and in over 80 per cent. at least one party was from overseas.[246] This fact suggests that the Commercial Court in London has a significantly different capacity in handling cross-border disputes than other, continental courts ,for example. The special role of the Commercial Court was observed not only in this work. In Dezalay/Garth's[247] publication, they acknowledge the Commercial Court as having a status that cannot be compared to other national courts regarding its international flair in supporting the general view of the Commercial Court as *„curia franca of the international commerce"*. It is an international Commercial Court the overwhelming majority of whose judgments are concerned with the rights and obligations of foreign nationals. As will be shown below, its role with regard to arbitration is also significant. Dezalay/ Garth[248] maintain that the Commercial Court in London is actually competing with private international justice and handles cases which would go to arbitration elsewhere.

The position of the Commercial Court regarding commercial litigation was not always as dominant as today. This also applies for its predecessors. However, today its role is outstanding regarding cross-border litigation in general and reinsurance litigation in particular. The reasons for this are manifold:

– Historically, English mercantile law has a special pragmatic approach to solve commercial legal problems according to customs and usage.

---

245 See High Court & County Courts Jurisdiction Order SI 1991, No. 724 (L5)

246 Antony D. Colman and Victor Lyon, *The Practice and Procedure of the Commercial Court*, 4th ed., Lloyd's of London Press, 1995, 12

247 Yves Dezalay and Bryant Garth, *„Dealing in Virtue": International Commercial Arbitration and the Construction of a transnational order*, University of Chicago Press, 1996, Chapter 9, 29

248 Yves Dezalay and Bryant Garth, *„Dealing in Virtue": International Commercial Arbitration and the Construction of a transnational order*, ibid, Chapter 9, 23

- In structure and development the English courts have tried to preserve this approach.
- The case law system seems generally to produce a more pragmatic attitude contrary to a dogmatic and scholarly attitude that seem to be encouraged by statutory law systems. It can probably better correspond and adjust to legal problems as statutory based jurisdictions. If problems arise in those jurisdictions in a commercial field where no statutes exist on which to base the decision, judges are probably more reluctant to tackle the subject.
- In the UK it appears that dispute resolution is understood and perceived as a service industry.
- A will therefore exists to reform courts and their procedures if necessary, accompanied by – with regard to international cases – a readiness to assume jurisdiction over cases with foreign elements. There appears to be little reluctance to apply foreign law to decisions if necessary.

The accumulation of these reasons may have led to a revival of the Commercial Court. This revival started in the 1960s regarding general commercial litigation. Reinsurance disputes in particular started in the late 1970s. The reasons mentioned shall be elaborated in more detail, since this development towards the use of the Commercial Court has only increased during the last three decades. Before 1962 English courts had for centuries had to fight against the reluctance of merchants to use them. Commercial law in England developed long before the Commercial Court in its present form was established. In the medieval, mercantile law, or *lex mercatoria* as it was then called was based upon mercantile customs and usage and developed separately from the common law.[249] In those times the Royal Courts did not have a monopoly of the administration of justice and certain local courts continued to hear cases long after the Royal Courts were established. A notable area involved mercantile and maritime disputes. Local and foreign disputes between merchants, coming about at the fairs where the most important commercial business was transacted in the fourteenth century, were tried in the courts of the fair or borough, and were known as 'courts of pie powder' (*pieds poudres*) after the dusty feet of the traders who used them. These courts were presided over by the mayor or his deputy or, if the fair was held under a private franchise, a steward appointed by the franchise holder. The rules applied were the European law merchants' the rules developed over the years from the customary practices of merchants and the jury was often made up of merchants. The fair of borough courts were supplement for a time by 'Staple Courts' which sat in the staple towns. These towns, which were designated by Edward III (1327-77) as the exclusive centres of trade for such com-

249 Smith's and Keenan's, *English Law*, 10th Ed. Pitman Publ., London, 1992, 14

modities as wine, wool, leather and tin, were required to hold courts to determine the trading disputes of merchants and again the customary practices of merchants were used. Special statutes were enacted for the benefit of the merchant community generally and traders from overseas in particular.[250] These prescribed speedy justice for foreign merchants[251], the application of the law merchant, and the paramountcy of the merchant courts, in mercantile disputes[252], and a procedure for formal acknowledgement of indebtedness under writings obligatory (promissory notes) by taking and enrolment of statutory recognitions which, upon the debtor's default, gave the creditor a statutory title to his lands and chattels until payment, coupled with a right to have the debtor indefinitely sentenced to prison until the debt was paid.[253]

Maritime disputes were heard by maritime courts sitting in major ports such as Bristol. These, too, applied a special European customary law developed from the customary practices of seamen.[254] Common law courts were slow to show an interest in dealing with commercial matters. That was partly due to the idea that their jurisdiction was limited geographically and was restricted to matters which had arisen in England between English citizens. Foreign matters, and many of these commercial disputes did involve either a foreign merchant or a contract made to be performed abroad, were left to some other body, especially if it could raise questions about the relations between the King and foreign sovereigns where the King's Council might be a more appropriate body. To some extent it was also due to the fact that the common law and its courts had come into existence at a time when land was the most important commodity and the procedures and concerns of the common law courts were adapted to problems arising from disputes over the possession and ownership of land. They were formal, slow and ill-adapted to the needs of merchants who required speedier justice and administered according to rules with which they were familiar. When the Court of Admiralty developed, it took over much of the merchants' courts' work, but from the seventeenth century onwards the common law courts began to acquire the commercial work. Many rules of the law merchant were incorporated into the common law. This was achieved partly by fiction. For example, to overcome the fact that it still technically lacked jurisdiction over matters arising abroad, the court accepted allegations that something that had occurred abroad had in fact

---

250 Roy Goode, *Commercial Law*, 2nd. ed., 1995, Penguin Books, London, 4

251 Carta Mercatoria 1303; Statute of the Staple 1353 c.20

252 Statute of Staple, 27 Edw. III stat. 2 (1353), cc. 5,6,8 and 21

253 Statute of Acton Burnell 1238, as amended by the Statute of Merchants 1285; Statute of the Staple 1353

254 Smith's and Keenan's, *English Law*, 10th Ed. Pitman Publ., London, 1992, 14 et subs.,

happened in England within its jurisdiction, e.g. by basing the case on the fictitious assumption that Bordeaux was in Chepside. The decline of the Staple Courts and the Court of Admiralty was largely due to one man, Sir Edward Coke, who was passionately devoted to the common law and its courts.[255] His fierce hostility to all their competitors resulted in the acquisition by the common law courts of most of the country's commercial litigation. However, to capture the commercial business of the former merchant courts, the common law courts were compelled to modify their own principles and practices (albeit with infinite slowness and caution) in order to accommodate the needs of the mercantile community and ultimately to absorb the law merchant into the common law itself. But the real adaptation of the common law to the requirement of the merchants, and the eventual integration of the lex mercatoria into the common law, occurred later. In the latter half of the eighteenth century, trials of commercial actions were frequently held in the Court of King's Bench in the Guildhall in the heart of the City of London.[256] Between 1756 and 1788 Lord Mansfield was Chief Justice of the Court of King's Bench. He was the outstanding judge who put his stamp on English mercantile law at the time and thereafter. Under his influence related principles of mercantile law were developed, particularly in relation to bills of exchange, insurance and shipping.

As has been mentioned, the *lex mercatoria* was international rather than English[257]. When the courts of common law, under the direction of Coke CJ, began to displace the merchant courts in the early part of the seventeenth century, they did not adopt the *lex mercatoria* as corpus of law for disputes between merchants. Though borrowing certain rules, the courts of common law continued in the main to apply the principles of common law with they were familiar with. They made gradual adjustments designed to satisfy the merchant that he could get as good a service from them as he had previously enjoyed from his own courts. The result of this approach was that the common law courts had painfully to develop principles long ago fashioned by the Staple Courts and the Court of Admiralty all over again. The moulding of the resulting diffuse collections of rules into a coherent body of commercial law was largely the work of Lord Mansfield. He proceeded to reduce the vast mass of case law on commercial disputes into an ordered structure, combining a mastery of the common law with a profound knowledge of foreign legal systems and a deep insight into the meth-

255 Roy Goode, *Commercial Law*, 2nd. ed. Penguin Books, London, 1995, 6
256 Antony D. Colman and Victor Lyon, *'The Practice and Procedure of the Commercial Court'*, 4th ed., Lloyd's of London Press, 1995, 1 subs.
257 Roy Goode, *Commercial Law,* 2nd. ed., Penguin Books, London, 1995, 6 subs.

ods and usage of the mercantile world. This was done with respect to the material, but also to the procedural law and the constitution of tribunals:

With regard to the bill of exchange the important custom recognised was that a bill of exchange was negotiable and that mere agreements should be binding as contracts.[258] In this way the custom of merchants relating to negotiable instruments and contracts including the sale of goods became part of the common law, and later, by codification, of statute law in the Bills of Exchange Act 1882, and the Sale of Goods Act, 1979.

The incorporation into English law of mercantile usage and the consequent consistent application of those usages to the cases which came before the Court was brought about by Lord Mansfield's practice of selecting a body of jurymen who were experienced merchants from the City conversant with mercantile usage.[259] Specific questions as to mercantile usage were left to the jury. Their verdict on such questions was then incorporated into the judgment. The same jurymen served over a number of years and Lord Mansfield was thus able to conduct the trials at the Guildhall in such a way as to encourage City merchants to feel that their disputes would be decided by a tribunal closely conversant with trade practice and mercantile law. After Lord Mansfield's era came to an end, commercial cases continued to be tried at the Guildhall but the popularity of the forum with the City merchants seemed to diminish during the nineteenth century. In 1865 the Guildhall sittings were discontinued. The City business houses were obliged to litigate their disputes in the Common Law Courts. This was not an attractive forum. Judges tended to disappear from the circuit, dates for trial were uncertain and often not kept to. More often than not the cases came before judges who knew little or nothing about mercantile law or commercial disputes.

Already at this early stage in the development of commercial law, cyclical movements towards and against the use of courts become visible. If the courts are not considered to be an appropriate and competent forum – which mainly depends on the qualification and availability of judges – another solution has been developed by the business community. In this respect earlier periods in mercantile law and the merchants do not deviate from today's commercial law and business communities. So in the latter half of the nineteenth century there was a strong feeling amongst those trading in the City that the courts were not a satisfactory forum for the resolution of commercial disputes.[260] Litigation was regarded as too slow and too expensive. The common view was that the judges

---

258 Smith's and Keenan's, *English Law*, 10th Ed. Pitman Publ., London, 1992, 15

259 Antony D. Colman and Victor Lyon, *The Practice and Procedure of the Commercial Court*, 4th ed., Lloyd's of London Press, 1995, 1 subs.

260 Antony D. Colman and Victor Lyon , *The Practice and Procedure of the Commercial Court*, 4th ed., Lloyd's of London Press, 1995, 1

and the juries before whom most commercial actions were tried were out of touch with the world of international commerce and were unfamiliar with everyday commercial activity.

Subsequently there was a considerable increase in the popularity of commercial arbitration. When the Judicature Commission was in sitting from 1869 to 1874, the City made great efforts to persuade it to recommend the establishment of commerce tribunals or a system of judicial arbitration. The Judicature Commission rejected the suggestion that there should be commerce tribunals or judicial arbitration. Its report dated 21st January 1874 dealt with the subject of special tribunals for the trial of commercial disputes in detail. The first question addressed in the report refers to the nature of the tribunal. Regarding the constitution of the tribunal, the Commission was unanimous as to whether the judges should be wholly or partly commercial, or partly commercial and partly legal. Also there was disagreement between the members of the Commission as to commercial members of the tribunals being judges having an equal voice in the decision, or assessors or advisers only to a legal judge, in that case presiding over the Court.[261]

The report from the Commissioners revealed that in trying to find a solution, the Commission looked at commerce tribunals in other countries at the time:

„We find moreover that, even in the countries in which tribunals of commerce are established, great diversity exists with regard to the constitution of these Courts. Thus, in France, in Belgium, and in some other countries, all the members of the Court are merchants, except the greffier or registrar, and he has technically no voice in the decision. On the other hand, in many of the German states, the court is presided over by a lawyer. In Dantzig, the tribunal consists of a legal president, four other legal judges, and four merchants, but the merchants do not attend unless required. In Konigsberg, the commercial members have no vote, only a deliberative voice. The decision rests entirely with the legal members of the Court. In Prussia, generally, it is in no contemplation to substitute a paid lawyer for an unpaid merchant as president. There is, in fact, no uniformity in the constitution of these tribunals. In some countries the mercantile, in others the legal element prevails, sometimes in the latter case to the exclusion of the commercial altogether.“

The readiness and openness to deal with foreign legal systems and foreign law is a feature which distinguishes English commissions, judiciary and counsels. The perception of conflict resolution mechanisms as a determining factor in

---

261 Report of the Judicature Commission dated 21st January 1874, Parly Papers, 1874, Vol. 24, Reports from Commissioners, cited in:
Antony D. Colman, *The Practice and Procedure of the Commercial Court*, ibid, 2

a business environment, and thus as a service industry factor that finds itself in competition with other systems, obviously dates far back into the last century. There was and is no reluctance to have a look at „how the other legal systems do it". In today's Commercial Court we encounter the idea that as part of this service industry 'international dispute resolution' is strongly developed and likely to be one key to its current demand. The general perception of London as dispute resolution centre is to be observed in many respects as will be expanded upon below, *inter alia* in the discussion on the recent arbitration bill. However, the Commission of 1874 gave special emphasis to the uniformity of the decisions when looking for the appropriate solution to the constitution of the panel:

„ *Now we think that it is of the utmost importance to the commercial community that the decisions of the Courts of Law should on all questions of principle be, as far as possible, uniform, thus affording* precedents *for the conduct of those engaged in the ordinary transaction of trade. With this view it is essential that the judges by whom commercial cases are determined, should be guided by the recognised rules of the law and by decisions of the Superior Courts in analogous cases. Only judges who have been trained in the principles and practice of the law can be expected to be so guided. We fear that merchants would be too apt to decide questions that might come before them according to their own views of what was just and proper in the particular case. A course which, from the uncertainty attending their decisions, would inevitably multiply litigation, and with the vast and intricate commercial business of this country would sooner or later lead to great confusion. Commercial questions, we think, ought not to be determined without law, or by men without special legal training.* "

The Report recognised the disadvantages of the frequent lack of technical knowledge of commerce displayed by judges and juries. In the end, the Judicature Commission recommended that commercial actions should be tried by a judge assisted by two business assessors. They would be commercially experienced men and their function would be to sit with the judge and to advise him on technical and practical matters which might arise during the trial. The Commission was not unanimous in its recommendation and the City was distinctly sceptical as to its usefulness. The Government did not adopt the Commission's recommendation. The Judicature Acts 1873 and 1875 hindered rather than helped towards a speedy, efficient and informal resolution of commercial disputes. The fusion of common law and equity made certain features of the procedure of the old Court of Chancery in commercial actions available, such as interrogatories and discovery of documents, which tended to lengthen the interlocutory stages of litigation and thereby greatly increase the cost of having disputes resolved in the courts. By 1894 the decline in the volume of commercial litigation was so pronounced that one of the judges published an article in *The Times* of 10th August 1892 commenting on this decline:

„The bulk of the disputes of the commercial world seldom, in these modern days, finds its way into the Courts. Merchants are shy of litigation. No solicitor can tell his client beforehand, even with a moderate degree of certainty, what is the limit of cost to which a man can be put, either in prosecuting or in defending his just rights. ....Two considerations are important to men of business when contemplating the possibilities of litigation. The first is – money. 'How much is it likely at most to cost?' The second is – time. 'How soon at latest will the thing be over?' They want to close their books at the end of the current year, to write off bad and hopeless debts, to know upon what lines next year to deal with similar questions should they arise. For such and other reasons of their own, the mercantile public is not fond of law, if law can be avoided. ... They prefer even the hazardous and mysterious chances of arbitration, in which some arbitrator, who knows about as much of law as he does of theology, by the application of a rough and ready moral consciousness, or upon the affable principle of dividing the victory equally between both sides, decides intricate questions of law and fact with equal ease."

It was generally acknowledged that commercial arbitration at the time was adventurous. The parties could not disturb an award in the courts however obvious the arbitrator's error of law. The only exception was if a special case had been requested or ordered under the Common Law Procedure Act 1854, sections 4 or 5 or, latterly, under Arbitration Act 1889, section 7. A certain disenchantment with commercial arbitration began to emerge. However, several attempts to increase or re-establish the City's confidence in the courts failed, including change of time and venue of sittings. Suggestions were made in 1892 and 1894 that a list for commercial actions should be started and operated separately from the Queen's Bench Division's other work. There were however, still considerable difficulties in founding the Commercial Court as such. This was because the view was held, that it required special legislation. Eventually, subsequent to a „Notice as to Commercial Causes" in February 1895, a separate list came into operation as part of the administration of actions tried by the Queen's Bench Division not conflicting with the existing Rules of the Supreme Court (RSOC). However, there was no new Court at all. During the time from its existence up until 1960 the list enjoyed varying approval. Although the business-like atmosphere of the beginning survived for many years, the original momentum seemed to have been largely lost by the time of the break out of the second world war. There was a loss of speed, a loss of informality of procedure and a loss of efficiency. Orders for trial without pleadings became infrequent. The pleadings which were extremely brief in the Court's early days became long and elaborate.

The commercial judges took a much less positive line on the summons for transfer to the Commercial List than the one they had adopted in the early days of the Court. Parties who set out to prolong commercial litigation by taking up technical points were successful in doing so. By 1960 the Commercial Court had lost popularity with the commercial community. In 1958 only 27 actions were set down for trial and only 21 actions were actually tried in the court. In response to this great decline in the business of the Commercial Court the Lord Chancellor set up a Commercial Court Users' Conference in 1960. The aim was to look into the decline and to report on the views of the commercial community upon any reforms of the constitution, practice and procedure of the Commercial Court which might improve its service. The results of the conference were published in a report in 1962.[262] The Conference attributed the decline in the Court's to the fact that,

- trading organisations had increased in size and become fewer in number,
- only those disputes involving large sums would be litigated,
- foreign trading organisations preferred arbitration to a decision by an English court,
- the accumulation of case law contained in past decisions of the Court had removed doubts as to the law and thereby discouraged litigation,
- the commercial community had an „inherent dislike of publicity and especially of the system of oral examination and cross-examination",
- costs and delays had increased,
- it was more difficult to enforce a judgment of the Court abroad than it was with an arbitral award The reason for this was the result of the Geneva Convention of 1927 on the Reciprocal Enforcement of Awards. This Convention had been signed by more states than states which allowed the enforcement of Commercial Court verdicts within this territory.

However, the remarkable result of the Users' Conference was that in spite of the decline in the business of the Commercial Court, the Conference considered that its importance to the commercial community had not diminished and that the Court should continue to exist, but subject to certain reforms. This consideration later proved to be true and after reform efforts the volume of the Commercial Court's work increased. The reform started with the issue of a new Practice Direction[263] which stressed the importance of not treating the summons for transfer as a mere formality and emphasised the need to draw up a full order for directions. It also underlined the need to shorten and simplify pleadings if they could not be dispensed of altogether. Secondly, 1964 saw the introduction of

262 The Report of the Commercial Court Users' Conference 1962 Cmnd. 1616
263 (1962) 1 W.L.R. 1216

Order 72, rule 4, of the Rules of the Supreme Court. Thus it was made possible for a plaintiff to enter his action in the Commercial List without the need to apply to the commercial judge for an order of transfer. In practice, it was now the plaintiffs' legal advisers who decided whether an action should be entered in the Commercial List. Once the new procedure for automatic entry had been used it was rare for any other party to apply to have the action removed from the List. In the years following the introduction of automatic entry, there was a steady overall increase in the number of actions in the Commercial List. It was not until 1970, under Section 3 of the Administration of Justice Act 1970, that the Commercial Court was formally established as such.[264] During the period from 1975 to 1982 there was an enormous increase in the volume of work before the Commercial Court. In 1975 the number of cases listed for trial was 128. This number had increased by 1982 to 431.[265] During the period from August 1988 to July 1989, 332 cases were given trial dates, of which 80 were tried, 190 settled, 57 were adjourned by consent and five were stood out by the Court. In 1975, 659 commercial summonses were issued. Yet in 1989 this figure had risen to 3.607. In the 12 month period from August 1988 to July 1989, no less than 2,204 commercial summonses were heard.

The periods where the workload increased at the Commercial Court were accompanied by empirical measures to assess its strength and weakness. This control of effectiveness is unknown in continental, at least in German courts. As part of the Civil Justice Review a study of the Commercial Court was produced by Coopers & Lybrand Associated. The study was based on statistical material obtained from the records of the Commercial Court and solicitors' files and on information provided by, and interviews conducted with, the commercial judges, barristers and solicitors. In relation to the question whether there should continue to be a separate specialist Commercial Court, the study identified the perceived advantages of a separate court, the expertise of the commercial judges in dealing with commercial litigation, and the relatively streamlined interlocutory procedures which helped to expedite the conduct of commercial litigation as significant. The majority of those interviewed expressed the view that, if the work of the Commercial Court were to be distributed to the Ordinary Queen's Bench, litigants would conduct their litigation in other jurisdictions, New York in particular.

---

264 see: Lord Chancellor's Department, *Civil Justice Review, Consultation Paper No. 3*, The Commercial Court, November 1986, 1-4

265 Antony D. Colman and Victor Lyon, *The Practice and Procedure of the Commercial Court,* 4th ed., Lloyd's of London Press, 1995, 12 subs.

Following the Coopers & Lybrand study, the Lord Chancellor's Department in November 1986 issued a Consultation Paper based upon the contents of the Study, inviting comments on proposals put forward to shortcut proceedings. Litigation before the Commercial Court is strongly influenced by legal professions accompanying these proceedings. Since there is a high share of international cases the legal professions need special skills to cope with this situation. Probably the English (Anglo-American) legal educational system is especially well suited to provide such skills. The Commercial Judges are recruited from Senior Queen's Counsels who have practised at the Commercial Bar. They therefore have significant experience , also in reinsurance matters. A Queens Counsel (QC) is a senior barrister who has received a patent as „one of Her Majesty's counsel learned in the law". QCs are appointed on the recommendation of the Lord Chancellor and a list of new appointees is published annually. [266]

The fact that judges in the English legal system start out as barristers is an important key to the Commercial Court's reputation in general. This applies in particular to a subject like reinsurance where the technical and economical understanding for reinsurance must be there to grasp the legal implications of clauses incorporated in the reinsurance contract. The principal function of the barrister is to appear in court, represent clients and plead their cases, although they also advise on legal problems in general. They cannot take instructions directly from members of the public, and they have all their work referred to them by solicitors (where litigation is involved) or other approved professions. They are generally regarded as the specialist members of the legal profession, although some other solicitors, particularly those in the larger metropolitan centres, have also become extremely specialised.[267]

Here again the contribution and stratification of the legal profession are closely connected to the development of international dispute resolution. The international nature of reinsurance creates a real dilemma for the commercial bar. Litigation and arbitration have come to lose some of their distinctiveness, a factor contributed to by the reduction of barriers between solicitors and barristers as observed by Dezalay /Garth.[268] The rise in the seventies and eighties of „big business" litigation, which gave solicitors a prominent role and facilitated their growth and increase in prestige, also contributed to a relative increase in prestige and ability to recruit among solicitors. These two related factors – the higher

266 see: Elizabeth A. Martin, A Dictionary of Law, 3d ed., Oxford University Press, 1994, 323

267 Martin Edwards, *Careers in the Law*, London, Kogan Page, 7th ed., 1996, 34

268 Yves Dezalay and Bryant Garth, *„Dealing in Virtue": International Commercial Arbitration and the Construction of a transnational order,* University of Chicago Press, 1996, Chapter 9, 26

status of solicitors and the increased importance of international counsel, who can deal directly with barristers – have also, as maintain Dezalay/ Garth from their interviews with practitioners, contributed to a relative decrease in the „autonomy" of barristers. Barristers have traditionally been able to ignore the wishes of solicitors or in-house counsel to make certain arguments in a particular litigation. The „independence of the barrister was in fact a defining characteristic. It is no doubt more difficult for barristers today to resist those pressures.

Dezalay/Garth cite an Essex Court Chambers QC:

„As you know, the art of litigating is not to have a trial at all. Now you can go I think to 10 or so law firms and they are very, very good tacticians. They know how to handle these massive cases. They know how to bring in different experts and consultants and how to manage the team. These are the skills of man management and handling paper and actually moving people around the world. But solicitors have got very, very good at this. Now there is no way the bar has ever had that particular skill or could never ever acquire it, because you can see they do not have the administrative backup."

Nevertheless barristers are involved in the solicitors' work and form a team with them. They have to come to grips with international cases, especially as this type of work increases. Doing work across national boundaries has always been the one key characteristic of lawyers.[269] For reinsurance cases this skill however is essential. One needs to only look at the writs of reinsurance cases with numerous plaintiffs or defendants originating from different countries to see this necessity. The task may consist of bringing the action groups together. In reinsurance cases it is common that the reinsurer leading the slip will also be the person who leads the litigation. As such he will be the one who will give marching orders to his solicitor and the others on the slip will often follow these instructions. The solicitor's task may be to institute the inspection of records of an insured abroad. It will often occur that the lawyers on both sides will find foreign corporations with which they have to communicate. He will have to convey the peculiarities of the English legal and procedural system to the foreign parties which may only be accustomed to their home country's practices. This will include negotiation of the fees. It became evident that clients nowadays are no longer ready to accept uncertainty as to the legal fees they will face. These fees may be considerable and must therefore be at least approximately discussed in advance. This information may influence the decision to sue or not to sue. These practical aspects were given a clear emphasis by the lawyers interviewed when asked which implications a foreign element in a case has on their daily work. It appears

269 Joanna Shapland, „How do lawyers accomplish cross-national lawyering?" Paper given to Law and Society Association conference, Glasgow, 10-13 July 1996

that this supports the assumption of Shapland[270], that high-flying ideas on world-wide business plans for lawyering are a rather artificial concept. It seems that the chances of law offices becoming actors on a global level or rather remaining in regional activity regarding one specific area of commercial law, and the share of foreign clients they can attract depend more on the legal infrastructure of the place where they are situated.

The activities of London law offices being involved in cross-border litigation in the reinsurance business is certainly an accumulation of circumstances that were not initially geared by the lawyers. The contracts made in the London market and dissatisfaction with arbitration however made it possible for the lawyers to join the business and to build upon this basis and expand. But, a crucial point is that the jurisdiction concerned must provide rules that enable the courts to assume jurisdiction over such cases and the judges must feel ready to do so. The given rules set out supra (Choice of Law, 4.4.3) refer to the place where the reinsurance agreement has the closest connection. Prior to 1st April 1991, when the 1980 Rome Convention on the law of applicable law on contractual obligations was in force, common law referred to the 'centre of gravity' of the contract. Subject to some exceptions the Convention did not impose severe alterations to the traditional principles of choice of law. One argument to establish the 'centre of gravity' of reinsurance contracts in London was of a practical nature. The structure of certain forms of insurance transactions will make the location of the market an important factor in determining the proper law of the contract.[271] If coverage must be sought on a world-wide basis, then the brokers in the insurance centre who place such risks will normally use their own methods and documentation. Thereby they make that centre a focus of any legal inquiry as to the nature of the transaction. The important role played by London market brokers result in many policies with an international character being governed by English law. The chain of arguments' is based on documentation as it should be executed. As demonstrated earlier reinsurance documentation can be rather insufficient. But documentation can still serve as a good argument for the assumption of jurisdiction.

Prior to the Convention, the view on London as a „centre of gravity“ was expressed in Citadel Insurance Co. -v- Atlantic Union Insurance Co. SA[272]. The case concerned Canadian insurers who used a New York broker, who, in turn, arranged for an open cover reinsurance facility with Greek reinsurers via London

270 Shapland, ibid

271 J. S. Butler, *Reinsurance Practice and the Law*, Lloyd's of London Press Ltd., 1993, looseleaf, Service Issue No. 7, 1 September 1996, 11.6.

272 (1982) 2 Lloyd's Rep 542 (CA)

brokers. The cover notes were issued in London. In the course of a judgment permitting the Canadian plaintiffs to bring an English action against the Greek defendants, Kerr and Oliver L J stated that the „centre of gravity“ of the business was London where the mechanics of the transaction took place. As the defendant wished to operate in the London market and did not make an express choice of law, their contract was most closely connected to the English legal system. Support that this approach has survived the coming into force of the Rome Convention[273] can be found in Trade Indemnity Plc and others -v- Forsakringsactiebolaget Njord[274], a case mentioned earlier and of which the writ is shown in the Exhibit[275]. The case involved bonds and credits surplus treaty reinsurance placed in the London market in 1990 and 1991 on behalf of a Swedish reinsured. The reinsured argued that, since the majority of its cover was placed on the Continent, it could not have been intended that different laws would apply to its reinsurances and, consequently Rix J held that this did not outweigh the strong presumption that reinsurance written in the London market is governed by English law, due to involvement of London brokers. The case however was not to be decided by an English court because of other reasons.

The readiness of lawyers to take up the new opportunity of business in reinsurance litigation was promoted because – as mentioned before -, shipping litigation was in decline when the first reinsurance cases came before the Commercial Court. Lawyers probably sensed a good occasion to substitute one business for the other if the work could be accomplished well and clients were content with the result. But to adopt an underlying theory that there was a targeted search to export conceptual or legal practice to reinsurance dispute resolution internationally would clearly miss the point. As Shapland rightly maintains, such a perspective ignores the more insidious and probably more prevalent daily cross-national business dealings, which open up national perspectives and national legal practice, without necessarily leading to the dominance of one particular model, e. g. lawyering. As set out before, knowledge of the choice of law, of the conventions applicable, of enforcement and – quite frequently – knowledge of foreign national laws if the definition of the underlying risk is concerned are essential. These special requirements and the additional technical knowledge of reinsurance business and contract lead to only a relatively small group compared to the overall numbers of lawyers dealing with reinsurance cases. This applies to the solicitors and the barristers chambers connected with them. Since reinsurance

---

273 J. S. Butler, *Reinsurance Practice and the Law*, Lloyd's of London Press Ltd., looseleaf, Service Issue No. 7, 1 September 1996, 11.6

274 (1995) LRLR 367 (QB)

275 see: Exhibit

cases are only dealt with before the Commercial Court in London those law firms are concentrated in the City. Generally, commercial business in London is dealt with at the Royal Courts of Justice, and in the provinces at the District Registries in Liverpool and Manchester, but the overwhelming majority of commercial cases are initiated in London. The Rules of the Supreme Court[276] provide a general description of commercial actions as cases arising from the ordinary transactions of merchants and traders. The Rules also give examples of commercial activity. The main types of cases actually dealt with by the Court relate to:

- the carriage of goods by land, sea or air, – contracts relating to ships and shipping;
- insurance and reinsurance; – banking, negotiable instruments and international credit;
- the purchase and sale of commodities;
- the operation of international markets and exchanges;
- the construction and performance of mercantile contracts.

The Commercial Court's work also includes appeals against the decisions of independent arbitrators. In terms of time, arbitration work accounts for a small percentage of the Court's total business, but involves a substantial number of cases and generates significant interlocutory work. All arbitration appeals must be commenced in the Commercial Court and although a Commercial Judge has the discretion to transfer such appeals to be heard by another Judge or the High Court, appeals still account in numerical terms for at least a third of all hearings. According to section 4 (1) of the Administration of Justice Act 1970 a Judge of the Commercial Court may also accept appointment as a sole arbitrator or an umpire in disputes of a commercial character. It shall be noted that this important and convenient change in the law was introduced as a result of the recommendations set out in the Report of the Commercial Court Users' Conference 1962. One of the results of the enquiry into the Commercial Court's decline in business of was that it was more difficult in many countries to enforce a judgment of the Commercial Court than to enforce an arbitral award under the 1958 New York Convention on Recognition and Enforcement of Foreign Arbitration and the Geneva Convention on the Execution of Foreign Arbitral Awards as mentioned supra. Participation in the New York Convention is widespread and signatories include, among others, Australia, Austria, Belgium, Denmark, Finland, Norway, South Africa, Spain, Sweden, Switzerland and the United States. The earlier Geneva Convention is still applicable, however under restricted circumstances, where the award was made following an arbitration between parties

---

276 R.S.C. Ord. 72, r 1

residing or conducting business in two signatory states. The parties to this Convention include, among others, Luxembourg, New Zealand and Portugal.[277]

As result of the Commercial Court User's Conference 1962 it was recommended that the commercial judges should have the power to sit in private cases as an arbitrator in appropriate cases.[278] An appointment may only be accepted if the Lord Chief Justice informs the Judge that the state of business in the High Court allows him to be made available. Such appointments are rare. In practice, the judges of the Commercial Court will accept appointment only where the dispute involves a question of law or substantial importance or difficulty or which is for some other reason out of the run of commercial arbitration.[279] Judicial arbitration differs from conventional arbitration, principally in relation to the mechanisms of judicial control. Such appeals on legal matters as there may be, in the light of the 1979 Arbitration Act, proceed directly to the Court of Appeal.[280] In reaction to the Commercial Court Users' Report, an English understanding of the Court's functions and dispute resolution as a service industry becomes apparent, which will be observed later on when it comes to the changes in English Arbitration law. Since London has been a traditional forum for resolving disputes it was recognised early on that the Courts and arbitration as a service industry shall provide effective and service oriented solutions. This service oriented approach has led to various decisions *inter alia* not to follow the UNCITRAL rules but to create a new Arbitration law. Also the boundaries in which appeals against arbitration awards have been granted have been narrowed down in the light of arbitration as a service industry standing in competition with other continental arbitration centres. When looking at the reasoning behind the 1962 report the „apparent dislike of publicity in commercial disputing" related to the spirit of those days and correlates to what was said earlier to the attitude towards arbitration in reinsurance. However this spirit has changed and the Commercial Court is increasingly challenged.

277 J. S. Butler, *Reinsurance Practice and the Law*, London: Lloyd's of London Press Ltd., 1993, looseleaf, Service Issue No. 7, 1 September 1997, 28.6

278 Antony D. Colman and Victor Lyon, *The practice and procedure of the Commercial Court*, 4th ed., Lloyd's of London Press, 1995, 174

279 Michael J. Mustill and Stewart C. Boyd, Commercial Arbitration, 2nd ed., London and Edinburgh: 1989, 265

280 Michael J. Mustill and Stewart C. Boyd, Commercial Arbitration, 2nd ed., London and Edinburgh: 1989, 266

5.2.1 *Legal-cultural differences faced by international parties when litigating before the Commercial Court*

Foreign parties are faced with English law when they come to the London forum. According to the solicitors and barristers, international parties perceive the substantive law as fair and the institutions as impartial, otherwise they would not agree to have a London forum clause in the contract. Still, there are legal cultural differences that are significant for cross-border disputes. It is interesting is that these legal-cultural differences become most apparent in procedural questions. In order to understand the differences between litigation and arbitration as well the comments on legal-cultural differences made by those legal professionals interviewed, it may be useful at this stage to give a short outline of the main procedural steps that are taken in a commercial case. There are only slight differences between English procedure if the case is domestic or international, but these will be pointed out below.

5.2.1.1 The writ

As with all High Court cases, proceedings are initiated by issue of a writ that is sealed in the court office.[281] An action is automatically commenced in the Commercial Court by marking the left hand corner with the words 'Commercial Court'. The writ formally notifies the defendant of the claim against him and requires him to indicate to the court and the plaintiff whether or not he proposes to defend it. The writ must be served upon the defendant with four months of issue. The most common methods of service are upon the defendant personally, or by agreement, upon his solicitor. If service out of the jurisdiction is required, the solicitor has to enclose an affidavit as to why the dispute shall be subject to English jurisdiction.

5.2.1.2 Originating summons procedure

Originating summons procedure is a form of originating process used in cases where the issues are likely to be ones of law or the interpretation of documents. It should not be used when questions of fact are involved, for which proceedings begun by a writ are more appropriate.[282] The summons must include a statement of the questions on which the plaintiff seeks the determination or direction of the

281 Lord Chancellor's Department, Civil Justice Review, Consultation Paper No. 3, The Commercial Court, November 1986, 3-4

282 Elizabeth A. Martin, *A dictionary of law*, Oxford University Press, 1994, 280

court or the relief that he claims and sufficient particulars to identify the cause of action. Evidence at the hearing of originating summons is usually by affidavit.

5.2.1.3 Service outside of the jurisdiction

Where the plaintiff resides outside the jurisdiction, the Court's leave may first be obtained before service can take place according to the provisions of the Civil Jurisdiction and Judgments Act 1982. If leave is necessary, application *ex parte* for leave to issue and serve the writ or originating summons outside the jurisdiction under RSC Order 11, rules 1 or 2 should be made to the Commercial Judge.[283] The affidavit in support of the application should

(i) identify the paragraphs of RSC Order 11, rule 1(1), relied upon and set out the facts relied upon as bringing the case within those paragraphs,

(ii) state the belief of the deponent that there is a good cause of action and showing where the defendant is or where he may probably be found,

(iii) outline the matters relied upon as justifying, in terms of the Court's general discretion, the subjection of a party outside the jurisdiction to proceedings within it,

(iv) draw attention to matters which might reasonably be thought to weigh against the making of the order sought,

(v) exhibit all significant documents,

(vi) state in addition to those matters specified in RSC Order 11, rule 4(1) that the plaintiff intends to mark the writ or originating summons with the words „Commercial Court" in accordance with RSC Order 72, rule 4(1).

If the Commercial Judge refuses to give leave to serve the proceedings outside the jurisdiction, an appeal will be made to the Court of Appeal, but only with leave of the Commercial Judge (for which an oral hearing would be needed), or failing that, of the Court of Appeal. [284] It often happens that it is necessary to give leave to serve the jurisdiction proceedings which have to be commenced by originating motion, for example, in relation to English arbitration proceedings. An application to remove an arbitrator or umpire for misconduct[285] under section 23(1) of the Arbitration Act 1950 or to set aside or remit an award under sections 22 or 23(2) must be made by originating motion. So also must applications for the determination of questions of law in the course of a refer-

---

283 Antony D. Colman and Victor Lyon, *The practice and procedure of the Commercial Court*, 4th ed., Lloyd's of London Press, 1995, 40

284 Antony D. Colman and Victor Lyon, *The practice and procedure of the Commercial Court*, 4th ed., Lloyd's of London Press, 1995, 41

285 RSC Order 72, rule 2(1)(b)

ence under section 2(1) of the Arbitration Act 1979,[286] as well as appeals from arbitrators under section 1(2)[287] and applications for declarations that awards are not binding due to want of jurisdiction.[288] In all these cases it is necessary to obtain leave to serve notice of the motion outside the jurisdiction.[289] The procedure is the same as that for writs and originating summonses where the action is to be pursued in the Commercial Court.[290]

5.2.1.4 Pleadings

The exchange of pleadings will begin to take place either at the same time as the service of the writ or shortly afterwards. The purpose of pleadings is to define and narrow down the issues between the parties. The plaintiffs point of claims will set out the grounds for the claim but will not give details of the evidence to be used to prove facts. In his points of defence, the defendant is required to admit or deny specifically each element of claim. On occasions the plaintiff will serve a reply to the defence, but it is rare for further pleadings beyond a reply to be exchanged.

5.2.1.5 Discovery

One of the major differences between litigation in England and many other jurisdictions (including most European countries) is that English litigation normally involves a procedure known as 'discovery'.[291] This means that each party is required to serve on the other a list of all documents relevant to the actions which are or have been in its possession. The term "document" includes anything upon which information is recorded, such as letters, memoranda, internal reports (or drafts of any of these), film, tape recordings, or information held on computers. In major commercial cases, it is very common for parties to have to list thousands of relevant documents. Reinsurance as a business seems to generate more documentation than most. Indeed, the management of documents in a sensible and efficient manner by the client and by the lawyer can often be a decisive

---

286 RSC Order 73, rule 2(1)(e)
287 RSC Order 73, rule 2(2)
288 RSC Order 73, rule 2(3)
289 RSC Order 73, rule 7(1)
290 Antony D. Colman and Victor Lyon, *The practice and procedure of the Commercial Court*, Lloyd's of London Press Ltd., 4th ed., 1995, 41
291 John O' Hare and Robert N Hill, *Civil Litigation*, 7th ed., FT Law and Tax, London, 1995, 375

factor for success in any such dispute.[292] The solicitors stated that the discovery may cause the foreign client major difficulties in understanding. Especially the continental clients consider the disclosure of documents – may or may they not be in favour of the client concerned – as „*Ausforschungsbeweis*".[293] It may therefore occur that clients will not follow the solicitor's instructions to collect certain information and send it to the London forum. This may put again the solicitor in a difficult position as he has an obligation towards the court to compile all information required. If information and material are required, but cannot be delivered, the solicitor has to give an affidavit that no such information exists. It is for this reason that many law firms have brochures for their commercial clients to explain the discovery process in detail in the client's mother tongue.[294] This is despite the solicitors stating that communication problems with their foreign clients especially in the reinsurance industry do not exist. It is just that legal-cultural differences in procedural law can be better conveyed in the mother tongue of the client concerned. Seven days after the parties exchange their lists of documents each party can inspect the other's documents. Each party will usually go to his opponent's solicitor's offices to inspect the documents and is entitled (at his own expense) to take photocopies of any documents concerned. Cases are frequently won or lost as a result of what is revealed through discovery. A party must allow inspection of all relevant documents, but with a limited number of exceptions. Certain documents are exempt from the requirement of being made available for inspection if they can be classified as "privileged". Such documents include all communication between a client and his legal adviser for the purpose of seeking or giving legal advice, documents produced with present or future litigation in mind, or correspondence between the parties which was made as part of a genuine attempt to reach a settlement. It was stressed during the interviews that the importance of discovery in preparing a settlement is of the utmost importance. Tactical deliberations are very important, too. Tactical skills in reinsurance litigation are provided in commercial seminars.[295] In most cases, shortly after all the pleadings have been served, the plaintiff will organise a "Summons for Directions". This differs from general practice in the Queen's Bench Division, mainly because so many commercial cases involve foreign par-

292 J. S. Butler, *Reinsurance Practice and the Law*, London: Lloyd's of London Press Ltd, 1993, looseleaf, Service Issue No. 7, 1 September 1996, 25.6.1.1

293 inadmissible inquiry

294 see e.g. Lovell White Durant, La procedure de 'Discovery' en matiere judiciaire devant la High Court, Client broschure, London 1990

295 'Reinsurance Litigation – When to avoid it – How to win it', DYP Seminar, London, 13th – 15th April 1994

ties and witnesses.[296] The purpose of the "Summons for Directions" is to obtain instructions from the court on how the case should proceed. It will do this by serving a formal document – known as a Summons – on the defendant in which the various requirements will be listed. These will include instructions dealing with the following:

- The place of the trial and whether or not a jury will be used;
- The timetable for service of evidence and other procedural steps;
- The number of independent expert witnesses, if any, which either side may rely upon at trial;
- Any disputes between the parties regarding pre-trial matters.

5.2.1.6 Evidence and expert witness

In the area of evidence a legal-cultural difference between the Common law system and other legal systems becomes evident once again. This difference is probably a key factor as to why the Commercial Court is such an accepted forum for foreign parties in cross-border disputes. It has been mentioned that often national courts have difficulties in handling cases which involve foreign aspects- let alone if foreign law has to be applied. The Commercial Court is not shy of doing so and the reason for this is two-fold. For one the Common Law System runs on an adversarial basis – all information relating to the facts of the case has to be brought before the judge by the party. Secondly the question of the applicable law according to English law is a question of fact. In practice, this means that the parties have to prove that foreign law is applicable by the means of evidence and present it to the judge in a way they think applicable to the case. If in an international dispute e.g. the forum clause says London, but no choice of law clause is made, the parties may in certain cases argue which law is applicable. The application of foreign law by the Commercial Court may become especially relevant for the following reason. It is perfectly possible that a reinsurance contract and the insurance which underlies it are governed by different legal systems.[297] Even if the terms of the contracts are identical, they may be interpreted differently by each legal system. Notwithstanding the commercial understanding upon which reinsurance is based – that it indemnifies a reinsured's liabilities in respect to its insured – the operation of the doctrine of the proper law of contract could result in the reinsured being denied recovery.

---

296 Lord Chancellor's Department, *Civil Justice Review*, Consultation Paper No. 3, The Commercial Court, November 1986, 4

297 J. S. Butler, *Reinsurance Practice and the Law*, London: Lloyd's of London Press Ltd, 1993, looseleaf, Service Issue No. 7, 1 September 1996, 11.7

This was the case in Forsikringsacktieselskapet Vesta -v- Butcher and others[298]. The plaintiffs, a Norwegian insurance company, insured the owners of a Norwegian fish farm against the loss of fish and reinsured 90 % of the risk with London underwriters. The insurance and the reinsurance policies each included an identical condition that a 24-hour watch be kept on the farm and further provided that 'failure to comply' with any of the conditions would render the policy null and void. Following the loss of fish stock in a storm, the plaintiffs settled the owners' claim and sought indemnity under the reinsurance policy from the defendant underwriters. They suggested, that a 24-hour watch condition would not have prevented the loss but the underwriters repudiated liability on the ground, *inter alia* that there had been a breach of the 24-hour watch condition. Under English law, which governed the reinsurance policy, the breach of the 24-hour watch condition, whether relevant to the loss or not, rendered the insurance policy null and void. The judge held that, although the reinsurance policy itself was governed by English law, relevant clauses such the 24-hour watch condition were to be construed according to Norwegian law because the reinsurance policy had been made back-to-back with the original policy, which was governed by Norwegian law, and since under Norwegian law a breach of the 24-hour watch condition did not provide a valid defence to the plaintiffs' claim, the plaintiffs were entitled to judgment against the underwriters. The underwriters appealed to the Court of Appeal, which dismissed their appeal. The underwriters appealed to the House of Lords. The House of Lords held, that since on the true construction of the reinsurance policy the underwriters had agreed to indemnify the plaintiffs against the risks covered by the original insurance policy, the risks covered by the reinsurance policy were to be interpreted by reference to Norwegian law. The underwriters were therefore liable to indemnify the Norwegian insurers for 90 % of the loss which was, under Norwegian law, a risk covered by the reinsurance policy, since once the one word 'failure' and the phrase 'failure to comply', were incorporated from the original insurance policy into the reinsurance policy which meant 'relevant' or 'causative' failure in the English contract of reinsurance. It followed that since the breach of the 24-hour watch condition was irrelevant to the loss it did not render the reinsurance policy null and void. The appeal was therefore dismissed.

Generally, the evidence which parties to litigation may use is divided into two categories, namely factual evidence and expert evidence. Factual evidence is given by the witnesses who have personal knowledge of the particular facts from which the case arises and, in most cases, these witnesses must prepare a signed statement giving a chronological narrative of their knowledge of the events that

298 (1989) 1 Lloyd's Law Rep 331

led up to the claim. The parties to the litigation exchange their witness statements on a pre-determined date so that, by the time of the trial, each party will know the substance of what his opponent's witnesses are going to say. This means that a party will be able to make a better assessment on the strengths and weaknesses of his case before the trial begins and the parties are more likely to agree to compromise. Besides factual witnesses, parties are often at liberty to call expert witnesses. Expert witnesses do not normally have direct knowledge of the particular facts surrounding the case. Instead, they are called to give evidence because of their general expertise on one of the issues concerned. For example, concerning a particular type of technology or the way in which a particular market or industry normally works. Reinsurance is a complex and market driven business.[299] Contrary to continental judicial systems, the expert witness does not primarily act as support for the judge, but to support the view of the party who called him. This position of the expert witness leads to certain consequences in providing evidence, requiring special skills from the expert witness beyond his expertise alone. The following are illustrations of the ways in which experts may assist in the reinsurance context:[300]

(1) The court may require assistance from an expert as to the meaning of a particular phrase in a reinsurance wording, which has no obvious or usual meaning but does have a generally accepted meaning in the market place.

(2) It may be also possible to call a broker to provide evidence as to the proper and reasonable practices in the broking industry if such issues are relevant to the particular case.

(3) It is also relevant, in cases of misrepresentation and non-disclosure, to call an expert underwriter to indicate whether particular facts which have been misrepresented or not disclosed are in fact material to a prudent underwriter.

(4) It may, in certain circumstances, be necessary to call an expert accountant perhaps to deal with certain accounting technicalities pertinent to the issues in question.

Usually, the expert witnesses will prepare reports which, like witness statements, are exchanged with the opponent on a specified date before trial.[301] If full exchange of witness statements has been completed and the case proceeds to trial, the expert witness may be cross-examined. Cross-examining refers to the questioning of a witness by a party other than the one who called him to testify. It may be *to the issue*, i.e. designed to elicit information favourable to the party

299 J. S. Butler, *Reinsurance Practice and the Law*, London: Lloyd's of London Press Ltd., 1993, looseleaf, Service Issue No. 7, 1 September 1996, 25.6.2.1

300 J. S. Butler, *Reinsurance Practice and the Law,* ibid, 25.6.2.2

301 Clifford Chance, *Memorandum* on: "Principal Methods of Resolution of Commercial Disputes in England and Wales", London: January 1994, 7 subs.

on whose behalf it is conducted and to cast doubt on the accuracy of evidence given by the opponent; or *to credit*, i.e. designed to cast doubt upon the credibility of the witness.[302] The true test of an advocate is his or her proficiency in the skill or art, of deadly cross-examination, the ability to destroy the evidence of an opposing witness by asking a series of piercing, puncturing, pulverising questions.[303] An experienced advocate will execute a staged campaign which has frequently been tried and tested on other witnesses and which has been thoroughly adapted and prepared so as to undermine this particular witness. The opening shots are aimed at his confidence; then, several barrages of questions will cause the witness to accept a series of facts damaging to his previous testimony; the final round is often the question 'and yet you still say ... ' which requires years of practice even though, because of the exchange of witness statements it is now so much easier to plan almost every question in advance. The way in which evidence is handled suggests that an expert witness has to have some more attributes than expertise alone. Finding the right expert witness is essential for pleading a reinsurance case, at least if questions of market practice are involved. As Jones (1994) concluded, a composite picture of the expert as a member of an adversial team emerges from the a consideration of the lawyers' ideas regarding good and bad experts.[304]

Images of good and bad expert witnesses are cumulatively built up from the comments of the judiciary, as well from the informal observations of other lawyers and other experts. In this fashion, informal reciprocal understanding accumulates. These conventions gradually obviate the need for more rules and guidelines on experts and their evidence. Expert witnesses absorb these conventions. Understanding becomes mutual: ' one becomes an expert witness; 'one isn't born an expert, one becomes an expert witness'. It is 'a trade learnt on the job'. Only those experts who are accepted as good experts will be employed on a regular basis. Those found wanting in skill become *de facto* inexpert and will not be used again. Finding the right expert witness in reinsurance cases is mostly team work. As solicitors and barrister described, the client himself may sometimes recommend an expert witness. Also the solicitors keep lists of people who may act as expert witnesses. When an expert is found he is 'tested' by the barrister, who will plead the case in court to see if the expert witness fulfils the requirements needed to make a good witness. To see through a cross-examination is no easy task and therefore the barrister may want to test the expert witness'

302 Elizabeth A. Martin, A Dictionary of Law, 3d ed., 1994, 107
303 John O' Hare and Robert N Hill, Civil Litigation, FT Law & Tax, London, 7th ed., 1995, 504
304 Carol A. G. Jones, *Expert witnesses*, Clarendon Press, Oxford, 1994, 139

ability to stay calm and convincing. The ability to speak clearly and sincerely in front of an audience is essential for the credibility of an expert witness. If the barrister thinks the person chosen unfit for the task he will tell the solicitor and the search for a new one begins. Like the arbitrators, market experts may also sometimes approach the solicitors to say that they are available for the job.

5.2.1.7 The Commercial Court as decision-maker

In terms of number, one may be surprised that only a few cases which are tried end in a verdict. The vast majority of cases brought in the English courts never go to a full trial. Generally, there are two ways in which a full trial can be avoided. The first is by obtaining a judgment prior to the full trial, e.g. through a "summary judgment". This is a speedy and cheap way based on documents, the "affidavit(s)". The summary judgment is only appropriate in situations where the plaintiffs claim is a strong one. The second option is for the parties to agree on an out of court settlement. The Commercial Court does not keep any statistics which show the number of disputes in reinsurance.[305] Other existing material does not help us any further. The Judicial Statistics, issued by the Lord Chancellor's Department provide information on the Queen's Bench Division.[306] However this data does not suit the purpose of this research since they do not refer to the workload of the Commercial Court as a subdivision. Furthermore the report refers to remedies and the legal nature of the claim and not to any special commercial area which those claims originate from., e.g. insurance or reinsurance.

Another effort to assess the workload of the Commercial Court was made prior to 1986 by the accountancy firm Cooper & Lybrand. It resulted in the Civil Justice Review which was issued in November 1986.[307] However data referring to reinsurance cases is not available in this paper and the relevant time scope of the last ten years is not covered. So far nobody has undertaken the task of assessing the workload the reinsurance disputes create for the courts, for arbitration tribunals and for the lawyers. The attempt made in the interviews with the solicitors to assess the workload remained unsatisfactory in terms of concrete numbers. This may be attributed to the fact that only practitioners in firms with an organised reinsurance department were able to give a survey on the workload of their firm. In smaller law firms only the personal workload of the individual

305 This information was obtained from David Bird, Chief Executive Clerk of the Commercial Court, during a telephone conversation on Tuesday 21st March 1995.

306 *Judicial Statistics* – Annual report – 1993, A publication of the Government Statistical Service, July 1994, 27 – 35

307 Lord Chancellor's Department, *Civil Justice Review*, Consultation Paper No. 3, The Commercial Court, November 1986

practitioner could be given. However it emerged from the interviews with the lawyers that many legal disputes in reinsurance in which the parties seek legal advice are settled before arbitration or court proceedings are initiated. The majority of disputes which reach arbitration or court proceedings are settled during those proceedings. Only a minority ends in a decision, whereby arbitration awards clearly outnumber court decisions. This general litigation feature is also found in reinsurance disputes. One may argue that it was one of the hoped benefits of litigating in reinsurance disputes to create new precedents or guidelines as some of the interviewed solicitors pointed out. But there is no contradiction in the high rate of settlements and the creation of precedents. The creation of precedents is a desired by-product of the legal disputes in the reinsurance industry. As mentioned earlier the solution of disputes is still steered by the maxim of self interest – especially if there is a lot of money involved as is the case in reinsurance claims. The chance of a settlement will not be passed up if the parties feel it to be the sensible solution to their problem. Parties do not litigate for the sake of it and they will not continue to spend money on legal fees if there is no reasonable solution in sight. The significance of the study, the increased participation of global players in formal dispute mechanisms such as litigation, must be upheld – whether they settle their disputes to some extent or not.

5.3 Arbitration

5.3.1 General

In its most general form, arbitration is based on the express agreement of both parties, although there are numerous statutes which lay down compulsory procedures in various circumstances. The current Arbitration Acts 1950-1979 are principally concerned with arbitration arising from the parties' agreement to use this form of ADR (Alternative Dispute Resolution) for existing disputes or for any disputes which may arise between them in the future. English arbitration legislation does not set out a definite code. There is, for example nothing in the legislation which lays down express rules of procedure or which sets out the minimum standard of fairness to be adhered to by arbitrators, although there are a vast number of court cases dealing with these matters. The first purpose of current English arbitration is to facilitate the parties in reaching the agreement which they think fit as to the qualification and appointment of arbitrators and the subsequent conducting of the arbitration proceedings. The second purpose of English arbitration legislation is to assist the parties by providing default procedures for the appointment of arbitrators, by laying down default procedures for the appointment of arbitrators and generally by giving arbitrators powers to ensure that the arbitration is allowed to proceed smoothly. The High Court exercises a general supervisory jurisdiction over arbitration cases conducted in England and Wales. For example the Court may:-

(1) appoint an arbitrator or umpire if the parties cannot agree;
(2) make orders concerning security for costs, discovery and examination of oath;
(3) remove an arbitrator guilty of delay, misconduct or bias;
(4) appoint a replacement arbitrator;
(5) remit an award to the arbitrators at any time for reconsideration if there is a clear error in the law or in a fact on the face of the award;
(6) extend the contractual time allowed for the commencement of arbitration;
(7) stay any court proceedings which have been commenced in defiance of a binding arbitration agreement;
(8) enforce arbitration awards.

The High Court also hears appeals and applications for leave to appeal against the arbitrators' final award. For example, Section 1 of the Arbitration Act 1979 requires the High Court in the case of an appeal from an arbitration award, only to decide whether the arbitrators have been wrong in law. Section (1) and (3) (a) of the Arbitration Act 1979 provide that an appeal may be brought to the High Court 'on a question of law arising out of an arbitration award with the consent of all other parties to the reference'. In such cases of express agreement to appeal, the arbitrators' award may be made before or after the award is published and the High Court has no discretion to refuse to hear the appeal. If the parties have not expressly agreed to an appeal to the High Court on a point of law, an appeal can only be made with the leave of the High Court. There is nothing in the current arbitration legislation to indicate the criteria which the High court must apply to determine whether leave should be given. The current position is contained in two House of Lords decisions.[308] In the „Nema" the Lords drew a distinction between points of law which were „one-off" affecting only the parties to the dispute and those points of law which are of general importance. In „ one-off" points of law the Lords felt that leave to appeal should be exercised in a much stricter fashion and set guidelines for inferior courts to take into consideration. However in relation to both „one-off" points of law and points of law of general importance, the judge hearing the application for leave

308 Pioneer Shipping Ltd -v- B.T.P. Tioxide Ltd, „The Nema" (1981) 2 ALL ER 1030; Antaios Naviera S.A. -v- Salen Rederierana A.B. The Antaios, (1984) 3 ALL ER 229

must be persuaded that the arbitrators were either probably, (or as the case may be) almost certainly wrong, before leave to appeal would be granted.

5.3.2 Arbitration clauses in reinsurance contracts

Arbitration clauses are very common in reinsurance contracts.[309] The following clause is taken from a quota share agreement in the Case of Harbour Assurance Company (UK) Ltd – v – Kansa General International Insurance Company Ltd[310] :

„All disputes or differences arising out of this agreement shall be submitted to the decision of two arbitrators, one to be chosen by each party, and in the event of the arbitrators failing to agree, to the decision of an umpire to be chosen by the arbitrators before entering upon the reference. The arbitrators and umpire shall be executive officials of insurance or reinsurance companies, or Lloyds underwriters. If either of the parties fails to appoint an arbitrator within one month after being required by the other party in writing to do so or if the arbitrators fail to appoint an umpire within one month of their nomination, such arbitrators or umpires as the case may be, shall at the request of either party be appointed by the Chairman of the Reinsurance Offices Association. The arbitration proceedings shall take place in London ....„

As mentioned, arbitration clauses do not deprive the English court of jurisdiction. It is very common for a reinsurer to commence court proceedings in defiance of an arbitration clause and he is at liberty to do so.[311] If the defendant prefers arbitration, then he must ask the court to stay proceedings so that the arbitration may take precedence. It is suggested that the original idea of implementing arbitration clauses into reinsurance contracts was based on the experience that disputes rarely occurred. Even if they did occur there was the wish that the business relationship should be upheld. It may have therefore seemed a sensible idea that – under these conditions – the parties should solve them with the assistance of arbitrators, i.e. people with market experience, "within one's own peers", so to speak.

---

309 Andrew Bandurka, „The Problems of Jurisdiction: How and where to proceed", Paper presented at the DYP seminar 'Reinsurance Litigation – When to avoid it – How to win it', 13th – 15th April, 1994 London, B 8 – B 9

310 (1992) 1 LLR 81

311 Andrew Bandurka, „The Problems of Jurisdiction: How and where to proceed", Paper presented at the DYP seminar 'Reinsurance Litigation – When to avoid it – How to win it', 13th – 15th April, 1994 London, B 9

Looking again at the model of dispute resolution systems, arbitration can be classified as semi-autonomous. It is an autonomous system in that the parties concerned have their disputes determined by one or more independent arbitrators. Its autonomy, however, is restricted in that the award may be subjected to judicial control and that the courts will stay orders and stay actions commenced in breach of an arbitration agreement or constitute or re-constitute the tribunal, or enforce the award.[312] The degree of judicial control varies from jurisdiction to jurisdiction as a matter of national law. The English arbitration law is currently in motion as a new Arbitration Bill has recently passed Parliament. The need for new regulations was there as arbitration has been looked at more critically with reference to duration and costs of proceedings. The law for arbitration was scattered in a diffuse body of cases and the statute law was also spread across three Acts – 1950, 1975 and 1979. This needed improvement. For ten years, there has been a movement to reform arbitration law. These critical views have to be seen in the light of London as a service industry for dispute resolution. It was perceived that other growing business centres – in France, Sweden, Holland and the Far East – were trying to seize a share of the international commercial arbitration business.[313]

There was consensus on the need for reform; but not on how to go about it. In 1985, the United Nations Commission on International Trade Law adopted a model for international arbitration. The Department of Trade and Industry then set up an advisory scheme under Michael (Lord) Mustill, the law lord, on whether the model should be adopted in place of UK laws. In 1989, the committee decided against this but recommended that all existing law be replaced with a new Act, using the language and framework of the model law. This led to a draft which was originally circulated by the DTI in February 1994 and was subsequently widely criticised. In the wake of the February 1994 drafted Bill's poor reception, Lord Saville, who formerly headed the Commercial Court, took over the chairmanship and sought to rectify the perceived defects in the new Bill. Its main features are that it strictly limits the right of appeal to the courts against an arbitration finding. One criticism of arbitration is that if one party appeals, the courts were too ready to overturn the finding. The courts will now be able to intervene in only limited circumstances. Secondly, it seeks to tackle the criticism that arbitrations have become mini-courts. The Bill imposes a statutory duty on arbitrators to adopt procedures suitable to the dispute, makes it clear that hear-

---

312 Michael J. Mustill, Stewart C. Boyd, Commercial Arbitration, 2nd. ed. Butterworth, London, 1989

313 Frances Gibb, „Disputes Bill fights off foreign rivals", in: *The Times*, Tuesday February 6 1996,

ings do not even have to be oral, and that it may sometimes be appropriate to adopt an inquisitorial approach.[314] The increasing costs of arbitration are hoped to be cut by stating that until the parties agree otherwise, the tribunal may set a limit on the legal costs which they can recover, regardless of what they actually spend. This is done in order to prevent inequality in the event that one party with greater financial resources, may spend a lot of money on the case in the hope of forcing the other into settling.

Since this thesis looks at reinsurance dispute resolution only up until 1996, it refers to the Arbitration Law applicable up to 1996, before the New Arbitration Bill was enacted. The new Bill and its coming into effect is however important to mention. It is a result of the disenchantment with arbitration and therefore delivers living proof of what is suggested on the topic of development and the nature of arbitration regarding the fields of business and the players involved. The criticism aimed at commercial arbitration was shared by practitioners who specialise in reinsurance. The popularity, at least historically, of arbitration clauses which amount in effect to express agreements to arbitrate by the contracting parties may be due to certain perceived advantages: Arbitration delivered a definitive decision more quickly than the courts. It was more likely to be accepted by both parties since the decision was made by individuals with mutual respect and most importantly, were private and confidential both as to the proceedings and the final result. The absence of lawyers and judges was declared a favoured factor in arbitration. This point was frequently mentioned during the interviews. The Arbitration Act 1979 does not stipulate any lawyer participation. Despite this fact when cases became more complicated and legal issues more intricate, lawyers found their way into the arbitration proceedings. As one practitioner who conducts reinsurance seminars frankly put it:

"Arbitrations were hijacked by the lawyers long ago and have been turning into mini-trials ever since."

Subsequently arbitration proceedings grew to resemble court proceedings. The idea of conducting arbitration instead of going to court worked in reinsurance for a considerable period of time, up until quite recently. As one director of a major brokerage house stated:

„Disputes between insurers and their reinsurers that related to the strict interpretation of policy conditions used to be relatively unknown. If they ever occurred, such disputes used to centre on adjustment of claims, and repudiation of the claim outright by the insurer due to non-disclosure, suspected fraudulent activity or similar reasons".

314 Frances Gibb, „Disputes Bill fights off foreign rivals", in : *The Times,* Tuesday February 6 1996

In reinsurance, the genuine concept of arbitration as a dispute resolution mechanism has been overtaken by reality that in recent years, as the appetite for litigation increased, the number of disputes has expanded to a considerable rate. Not only in the United Kingdom but also increasingly in many countries around the world, disputes arising from reinsurance contracts are now commonplace, at least in the Anglo-American jurisdictions. This may be partly due to the Names litigation. US courts, for example had to deal with the question of whether cases relating to North American 'Names' should come before the US courts. The American Names involved in the Lloyds litigation tried to have their disputes heard in courts of their own jurisdiction. In the 1990s they sought to test an agreement dated from January 1987 in which all Names subjected their disputes with Lloyds to the exclusive jurisdiction of English courts.[315] To date, however these actions have been dismissed by courts in California, Colorado, New York, Illinois and Ontario. The only exception to this is provided by a United States District Court in Houston where it ruled that a Texas Name may proceed in a US Federal Court with a claim against Lloyds.[316] This was on the grounds that the exclusive jurisdiction clause in the agreement between Lloyds and the Names is unenforceable because the Names accession to the clause in the agreement was procured by fraud. Lloyds has sought to appeal against the District Court's ruling. Still, the concentration of such reinsurance cases which can currently be observed before the Commercial Court is outstanding. There are hardly any reports of continental reinsurance jurisdictions and arbitration. In Germany there is no reported decision which deals with a court verdict relating to reinsurance, not to mention arbitration. This essentially is related to how reinsurance business with foreign clients is done. For one, such a reinsurance centre does not exist in Germany, i.e. there is not one particular city which specialises in reinsurance. Cologne Re, Munich Re, Hanover Re to mention but a few leading reinsurers do the majority of their business with foreign clients by travelling to them; it is therefore direct business not brokered business. In France and Switzerland there are no reported decisions to be found, just as there are no published arbitration awards. This is very different to Anglo-American jurisdictions. An extraordinary transformation has occurred since former decades when any disagreements were quickly and quietly dealt with; when insurers and reinsurers were at pains to maintain goodwill, and when disputing parties were sometimes regarded as adversely affecting the market's reputation summed up in the phrase of „my word is my bond". In an attempt to resolve some of these disputes without the expense

---

315 J. S. Butler, *Reinsurance Practice and the Law*, London : Lloyd's of London Press Ltd. 1993, looseleaf, Service Issue No. 7, 1 September 1996, 25.1.

316 Leslie -v- Lloyd's of London. No. H-90-1907, slip op. (S.D. Rex., 28 August 1995)

of ever entering a courtroom, efforts have been made to make increasing use of arbitration processes. With an increase in the use of arbitration, reinsurance took on a different aspect. The cost and length of proceedings have increased to an alarming degree.[317] It can be stated that arbitration did not turn out to be a satisfying dispute resolution mechanism when used beyond a certain extent. This reflects the lawyers' views at least on arbitration in reinsurance. The solicitors were interviewed asked to rank the factors which are they perceived as advantages of arbitration. The result is represented in the graph below:

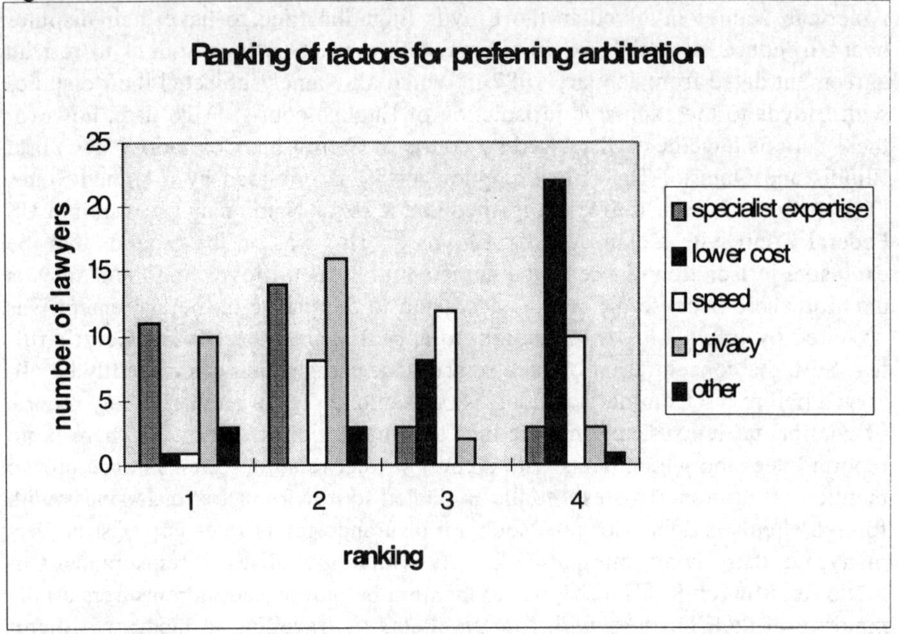

Summarising the opinions given one can conclude that

„ whatever the perceived merits of arbitration are, it can have serious shortcomings. Some arbitrators tend to be nervous about questions of law, and particularly questions of procedural law, and it is sometimes not difficult for a cunning advocate to bully or side-track an arbitration panel. In addition, it is not possible to exclude the jurisdiction of the court completely. Although the court will only overturn an arbitration award in very limited circumstances, nevertheless it is possible to make procedural application to court which can be used as spoiling tactics to 'derail' the arbitration."

317 see: Edward Gumbel, "Auf dem Weg zu einem neuen Schiedsrecht in England", in: *Zeitschrift für Versicherungswesen*, 21/94, 575-578

This opinion given by a solicitor is illustrated by way of example[318]. Involved in the case of Hassneh Insurance Company of Israel -v- Pan Atlantic Group Incorporated and Others[319], which is also mentioned below, he describes what may happen for tactical reasons:

„This reinsurance dispute involved 19 claimants, and one respondent. A few weeks before the arbitration was due to take place, at a time when the parties' solicitors and counsel were involved in heavy preparations for the case, one of the arbitrators retired from his position as executive of a reinsurance company in order to become a consultant at a firm of solicitors. The arbitration clause was drawn in similar terms to the Harbour[320] one and stated that the arbitrators should be insurance or reinsurance executives. Pan Atlantic applied to court to quash this arbitrator's appointment and for the appointment of another arbitrator. At a time when we should have been engaged in the preparations for the substantive hearing, we were suddenly drawn into the High Court, and then into the Court of Appeal, in order to resolve this side issue. In the end common sense prevailed and both the courts of first instance and the Court of Appeal refused to quash the arbitrator' s appointment. The great expenditure which was incurred was cured by an award of costs in Hassneh's favour – the time which had been wasted could never be restored."

In an arbitration involving reinsurance the arbitrators almost invariably choose to closely follow the same procedures as those which are followed in the Commercial Court, i.e. the exchange of formal written pleadings, discovery by Lists of Documents, formal inspection of disclosed material, interlocutory applications for specific discovery, exchange of factual witness statements prior to the trial of the dispute and exchange of expert witness statements, if deemed necessary. Solicitors and barristers are employed to handle and argue the arbitration issues before the arbitrators as in court proceedings, which ensures that the arbitration proceedings are at least as expensive as court proceedings. In many cases the arbitration procedures are more expensive than court proceedings, since the parties to an arbitration are obliged to pay the arbitrators' considerable fees and the hire of the venue in which the arbitration is held. In court proceedings, at least for the time being the Judge, his clerk and the courtroom are free. As far as the speed of an arbitration is concerned, it depends upon the procedure that the arbitrators or the contracting parties choose to adopt. If a strict adherence to

---

318 Andrew Bandurka, „The Problems of Jurisdiction: How and where to proceed", Paper presented at the DYP seminar 'Reinsurance Litigation – When to avoid it – How to win it', 13th – 15th April 1994, London, B 14

319 (1992) LLR 999

320 Harbour Assurance Company (UK) Ltd -v- Kansa General International Insurance Company Ltd (1992) 1 LLR 81

court procedure is chosen, then it is impossible to see how an arbitration is going to be quicker at reaching a final decision than a court. Furthermore, if the express arbitration agreement stipulates that the arbitrator is to be an executive of an insurance company or a practising underwriter, it may be that they do not have the time to devote to their duties as a judge, which can slow down the proceedings. Concerning the alleged better acceptance of the decisions of arbitrators than those of judges it has to be said that no party likes to lose and a losing party in an arbitration is going to be as disappointed as a losing party in a High Court case. In the past, in the reinsurance field, the majority of High Court Judges were unfamiliar with the business and could make uninformed decisions. However nowadays, no doubt as a consequence of the plethora of reinsurance and Lloyds litigation, the majority of Commercial Court Judges are as well informed as many who have worked in the market all their lives. A further perceived advantage is the confidentiality of arbitration proceedings and the arbitrators' award. Although the private nature of an English arbitration was universally accepted, there was and is no reference in the current arbitration legislation to this principle and indeed, until recently, the courts had not been asked to address the nature and scope of the privacy and confidentiality obligations in an arbitration. However, in the case of Hassneh Insurance and Others -v- Stuart J. Mew,[321] Mr. Justice Coleman held that

(i) an agreement to arbitrate contained an implied term which imposed a duty of confidentiality regarding details of the award itself, the arbitrators' written reasons for the award and all other documentary materials relating to the arbitration.

(ii) the implied term further qualified that duty under the exception that the award and the reasons might be disclosed by a party as of right if it was reasonably necessary for one party to disclose them for the purpose of the establishment of that party's legal rights against a third party, either in order to found a defence or as the basis for a cause of action.

Having identified the principle in the Mew case, Mr. Justice Coleman was presented with another case a year or so later which gave him the opportunity to decide on the question of how necessary the award has to be for the protection of the parties' right before he is entitled to disclose. In Insurance Company v. Lloyds syndicate[322] , the defendant took out an excess of loss reinsurance with the plaintiff insurance company and a number of other companies. The plaintiff company was the leading underwriter with a 25 % line. The defendant denied that such losses were covered and avoided the reinsurance policy for non-

321 Hassneh Insurance Company and Others v. Stuart J. Mew (1993) 2 Lloyd's Rep 245
322 Insurance Company v. Lloyds Syndicate (1995) 1 Lloyd's Rep 272 (QB Com Ct)

disclosure of the fact that the syndicate had been writing sports risks. The syndicate instituted arbitration proceedings only against the leader. The arbitrators tried the matter and awarded the defendant interim awards. The defendant sought to send those awards to the following market who was refusing to pay, to obtain their agreement that the losses were covered. The plaintiff claimed that the award and the reasons were confidential, and they sought and were awarded an interlocutory injunction. Coleman J held that the arbitration award and reasons may have had a commercially persuasive impact on third parties with whom the reassured had a contract and does ***not*** make the award an exception to the general rule that it is to be treated by both parties as confidential. For the purposes of complying with the implied term of confidence, disclosing the award must be the ***only*** way of enforcing or protecting the parties' rights.

Nevertheless, virtually all contracts of reinsurance will contain an arbitration clause. There are several different arbitration clauses that have been used. The basic characteristic that all arbitration clauses have in common is that they make a provision that any disputes between the parties to the agreement will be referred to an arbitration tribunal. Usually they will make provision for one single arbitrator, who will be a recognised person with insurance experience.[323] A large section of the London market has used a Standard Arbitration Clause since the 1970s which, as described above, has recently been amended by ARIAS[324]. Some of the arbitration agreements make a provision that each party to the dispute appoints their own arbitrator, and that a chairman is appointed by the two arbitrators. The chairman is again often a respected person within the insurance market. Therefore a panel of three will sit to hear the case presented by both parties. Such an arbitration panel set up by the appointment of the parties is called an "ad-hoc" arbitration. Many arbitrations are conducted on an "ad-hoc basis" with the parties and arbitrators agreeing on the procedures and administration. The alternative is an arbitration institution, for example ICC or ARIAS as referred to below. The Arbitration Act, 1979, gives arbitrators a certain amount of liberty regarding procedural questions. In arbitration it is quite common that no full discovery will be conducted, which might for the reasons described above allow the foreign parties to feel more at ease. According to the practitioners interviewed, the arbitrators are reluctant to look at a large amount of papers especially with a panel of market men.

---

323 For capacity, qualification and impartiality of the arbitrators in general see: Michael J. Mustill and Stewart C. Boyd, *Commercial Arbitration*, 2nd ed., London and Edinburgh: 1989, Chapter 18, 247-256

324 Appendix III, A.R.I.A.S Recommended Arbitration Clause,

The personal qualification the panel must have is relevant experience in the matter that is being arbitrated. Another essential requirement for an arbitrator is of course impartiality. To comment on the number of people in the London market it must be said that reinsurance is a "closed society". Therefore it became increasingly difficult to find people meeting these requirements. The practitioners stated that there has been an increase in the volume and intensity of disputes. This resulted in arbitrators and expert witnesses being in high demand. To overcome these difficulties A.R.I.A.S (UK), Reinsurance and Insurance Arbitration Society, was established in July 1991 under the aegis of AIDA, Association Internationale de Droit des Assurances, to promote and assist in the development of arbitration as a reliable means to dispute resolution for the insurance and reinsurance markets.[325] Other bodies such as the Chartered Institute of Arbitrators, London Court of International Arbitrators also help with the recommendation of arbitrators. However their work comprises the whole range of commercial disputes and does not focus on reinsurance. Based in the London insurance and reinsurance market, the Society draws its membership from organisations worldwide, and aims to serve and assist the international community, not just the domestic market. Many of the big law firms with reinsurance departments were founder members of the society and were known „professional advisers". A.R.I.A.S (UK) provides services such as recommending names of people suitable to serve as party appointed arbitrators. It serves as an appointing authority and encourages uniform arbitration procedures. In order to perform those services A.R.I.A.S keeps a register of persons who are capable of assuming the role of an arbitrator, and are willing to do so. According to A.R.I.A.S, the Society now has approximately 40 to 50 people on its panel list.

As mentioned earlier, a standardisation of contract wording and arbitration clauses in reinsurance contract has not been achieved so far. When founded, A.R.I.A.S considered the drafting of standard wording. In order to uniform arbitration procedures A.R.I.A.S produced a recommended arbitration clause for reinsurance and the ARIAS arbitration rules which were issued in first edition in January 1994. In terms of the volume of work, the Society may assist in 12 to 15 cases per year. For the rest of the cases, the arbitrators are approached directly by the parties or their solicitors. But this is representative of the number of the cases being arbitrated in reinsurance per year. As well as in Alternative Dispute Resolution (A.D.R.) where the mediator can be approached directly by the party and not through a dispute resolution centre, the market man or reinsurance professional known as acting as an arbitrator can be directly approached and not through an organisation like A.R.I.A.S. During the interview with solicitors it

---

325 see: A.R.I.A.S leaflet 1991

became evident that they also carry their own list of reinsurance professionals who serve as arbitrators and expert witnesses. Sometimes they are even approached by reinsurance professionals who want to serve as arbitrators or expert witnesses. The arbitrators will charge a professional fee based upon the number of hours which they take to carry out the arbitration. Some arbitration clauses are silent as to the allocation of these costs. Other clauses allow for the fact that the losing party will pay the costs of the winning party. Other arbitration clauses allow for the fact that all the costs of the arbitration shall be determined by the arbitrators who will take the law and practice of the place of arbitration into account. In practice this means that they usually award the costs of the arbitration against the losing party, although they have the flexibility to apportion it between both sides according to the merits of the two submissions which have been heard. The arbitration clause also usually determines where the arbitration is to be held.

5.4 "Lex Mercatoria" in reinsurance?

The arbitrators are bound to apply the law, if the arbitration is silent as to the manner in which the decision is to be made. Support for this comment is rather difficult to find.[326] For about 175 years, before the 1979 legislation, the English courts had worked out a balance between the interests of finality in the arbitral process, and the desire to ensure that there were no jurisdictions which claimed to draw strength from the law, and still did not manage to meet its requirements. Nevertheless, one can find several isolated statements scattered over the decades to the effect that the arbitrator is bound.[327] In many cases it is necessary to look no further than English law in order to ascertain the nature of the relationships which arise from an arbitration agreement, or to decide the merits of party disputes.[328] But this is not always the case. Commercial arbitration in England has long had an important international element, and in recent years this has been very accentuated. Increasingly it has become necessary to take account of the

326 Michael J. Mustill and Stewart C. Boyd, *Commercial Arbitration*, 2nd. ed., London and Edinburgh: 1989, 69

327 Jaeger v Tolme and Runge and London Produce Clearing House Ltd (1916) 1 KB 939 (953, 957, 961), CA; Re Astley and Tyldesley Coal and Salt Co and Tyldesley Coal Co (1899) 68 LJ QB 252; Cottage Club Estates Ltd. vs. Woodside Estate Co (Amersham) Ltd (1927) 44 TLR 20 (21); Ramdutt Ramkissen Das v ED Sassoon & Co (1929) 98 LJPC 58,

328 Michael J. Mustill and Stewart C. Boyd, *Commercial Arbitration*, 2nd ed., London and Edinburgh: 1989, 59

international character of many commercial arbitrations. This is not simply because so many of the parties to such arbitrations come from the broader international community, but also because commercial arbitration tends more and more to require arbitrators, the courts, and even the legislature to look at the practice of commercial arbitration against the perspective of a broader international horizon. With respect to the application of a national law – English law – it may be necessary to take into account the special aspects of the business concerned. This may be the case particularly where the business is not only international, but highly technical and market driven. Under those circumstances straight forward legal approaches may lead to inequitable results.

This straight forward approach concerns not only the application of law but also the establishment of the arbitration panel and the approach which will be applied in resolving the dispute.[329]Another approach which emphasises market principles is called the "equity" clause. One refers to an "equity clause" in the general sense if the arbitration agreement expressly empowers the arbitrator to apply the law either wholly or in part, by some provision as:[330] „ *the arbitrator shall be entitled to decide according to equity and good conscience and shall not be obliged to follow the strict rules of law*". Or the clause may say: 'The arbitrator shall act as amiable compositeur.' In reinsurance such an equity clause is called an "honourable engagement". In essence, an honourable engagement clause is one which attempts to allow an arbitration panel the right to determine the dispute in accordance with market principles and in good faith.[331] Provisions of this type, raise very difficult theoretical questions.[332] At this point we arrive at the *"lex mercatoria"* discussion. The idea of the *lex mercatoria* derives from the observation that the vast majority of international commercial transactions and business relations are *internationalised.* This *de facto internationalisation* is opposed to the traditional and still dominant theories of the national laws of conflict, which require that the facts of the case be nationalised, that is, evaluated in the light of national law. Those individuals and groups involved in international commerce achieved the *de facto* internationalisation by the development and

---

329 J. S. Butler, *Reinsurance Practice and the Law*, London: Lloyd's of London Press Ltd, 1993, looseleaf, Service Issue No. 7, 1 September 1996, 25.2

330 Michael J. Mustill and Stewart C. Boyd, *Commercial Arbitration*, 2nd ed., London and Edinburgh: 1989, 74

331 J. S. Butler, *Reinsurance Practice and the Law*, London: Lloyd's of London Press Ltd, 1993, looseleaf, Service Issue No. 7, 1 September 1996, 25.3.1

332 Michael J. Mustill and Stewart C. Boyd, *Commercial Arbitration*, 2nd ed., London and Edinburgh: 1989, 75

usage of internationally accepted trade practices.[333] The discussion on *lex mercatoria* is led extremely doggedly depending on the legal background of the discussants – be it the Anglo-American case law oriented system or the statutory law oriented continental legal system. The discussion was even labelled a 'war of faith' and the controversy over the existence and character of *lex mercatoria* is believed to have model characteristics.[334]

Lex mercatoria is discussed in close connection with the construction of amiable compositeur and his authorisation to decide according to requirement of the specific trade.[335] Statements on *lex mercatoria* originating on the European continent are numerous.[336] One reason for this might be that 'equity clauses' in continental arbitration agreements are more common and stimulate the discussion. For example the *„amiable compositeur"* is provided for in Article 1475 of the French Civil Procedure which stipulates that an arbitrator must settle the dispute according to the applicable rule of law, unless the parties have given him, by contract, the task of acting as an *'amiable compositeur'*.[337] By stipulating an *„amiable compositeur"* clause, the parties actually waive a right which they freely enjoy and can freely dispose of. Consequently, the arbitrator will not be allowed to violate or set aside public policy rules to the extent that the parties do not freely enjoy the right to waive and dispose of public policy rules. Another consequence of the *„amiable compositeur"* clause according to French law is that it automatically entails waiving the right of recourse or appeal. Indeed, article 1482 of the French Civil Procedure Code stipulates that the arbitration award is not subject to appeal if the arbitrator is having to act as an *„amiable compositeur"*, unless the parties have expressly reserved that right in their arbitration

---

333 Paul-Frank Weise, *Materielles Recht vor der internationalen Handelsschiedsgerichtsbarkeit,* Frankfurt: Lang 1989, 174

334 Gunter Teubner, „Global Bukowina: Legal Pluralism in the World Society", Gunther Teubner (ed.), *Global Law Without a State,* Aldershot: Dartmouth, 1997, 8

335 Michael Mustill, The New Lex Mercatoria: The First Twenty-five Years, in: *Liber Amicorum for Lord Wilberforce*, Oxford: Clarendon Press, 1987, 149-183 (174 subs.)

336 Ole Lando, "The Lex Mercatoria in International Commercial Arbitration", in: *International and Comparative Law Quarterly*, 34 (1985), 747-768; Michael J. Bonell, "Das autonome Recht des Welthandels Rechtsdogmatische und rechtspolitsche Aspekte", in: *RabelsZ* 42 (1978), 485-506; Clive Schmitthoff, "Das autonome Recht des Welthandels", in: *RabelsZ* 28 (1964), 47-77
A selected bibliography is found in Michael J. Mustill's The New Lex Mercatoria: The First Twenty-five Years, in: *Liber Amicorum for Lord Wilberforce*, Oxford: Clarendon Press (1987), (149-183) 150

337 Gerard Honig, „Role of arbitration, Position of French law on severability and *„amiable compositeur"*, Paper presented at the BILA London Colloquium, International and Reinsurance Arbitration, 22-23d of July 1996, p. 5

agreement. It is worth noting that this rule is specific to arbitration, since Article 12 Paragraph 5 of the French Civil Procedure Code stipulates the contrary, i.e. that in a case where a court orders *„amiable composition"*, the parties have a right to appeal unless they have expressly waived that right. The French Civil Procedure Code does not impose any other formality on the legal enforcement of the *„amiable composition"* clause other than the fact that it must be expressly stated by the parties. French courts uphold the *„amiable compositeur's"* power to soften the consequences of a strict application of contractual clauses on the basis of equity without modifying the economic character of the contract. For instance, an *„amiable compositeur"* may reduce the amount of penalties stipulated in the contract. The *„amiable compositeur"* may also reverse the effects of a clause stipulating a manifestly excessive or excessively low price by adjusting such a price as stipulated in the contract in accordance with equity rules. In English law few cases touch on the problem, and there has been little academic discussion of the matter in the context of English law and practice.[338] In the reinsurance context, several cases relating to the *„honourable engagement clause"* have been decided by the courts and shall be discussed below.[339]

Since dealing with the *lex mercatoria*, its extensive literature and its application in different fields may easily get out of hand in terms of scope, it seems appropriate to narrow down the present focus. The question is: are reinsurance disputes resolved on a *lex mercatoria* basis and are some authors, allegedly referring to the ruling opinion, therefore justified in saying that reinsurance is a loopwhole of lex mercatoria ?[340] The contemporary answer to this question suggests that this is not the case. A view contrary to the alleged ruling opinion must be supported by good arguments. Reference to a prominent comrade-on-arms[341]

338 Michael J. Mustill and Stewart C. Boyd, *Commercial Arbitration*, 2nd ed., London and Edinburgh: 1989, 75

339 Orion Compagnia Espanola de Seguros v. Belfort Maatschappif Voor Algemene Verzekgringen (1962) 2 Lloyd's Rep 257; Eagle Star Insurance Co. v. Yuval Insurance Company Limited (1978) 1 Lloyd's Rep 357; Home Insurance Co. v. ADAS 2 Lloyd's Rep 674; Overseas Union Insurance Ltd. v. A. A. Mutual International Insurance Co. Ltd. (1988) 2 Lloyd's Rep 63, Home and Overseas Insurance Co. Ltd. v. Mentor Insurance Co. Ltd. (1989) 1 Lloyd's Rep 473

340 Andreas Kappus, *"Lex mercatoria" in Europa und Wiener UN- Kaufrechtskonvention 1980*, Frankfurt: Lang, 1990, 182; Fritz Reichert- Facilides, Rechtvereinheitlichung oder Rechtsvielfalt? in: *Europarecht, Internationales Privatrecht, Rechtsvergleichung*, Veröffentlichung der Kommission für Europarecht Nr. 7, Wien 1988, 155-170 (162) with refe rence to Klaus Gerathewohl, *Rückversicherung – Grundlagen und Praxis*, Vol. I, Karlsruhe: Verlag Versicherungswirtschaft e. V., 1976, 541

341 Michael J. Mustill, The New Lex Mercatoria: The First Twenty-five Years, in: *Liber Amicorum for Lord Wilberforce*, Oxford: Clarendon Press, 1987, 149-183 (182)

cannot be considered sufficient. To start the chain of arguments, a definition of *"lex mercatoria"* in its modern context is initially required. The modern discussion of *lex mercatoria* started in the 1960s[342] and various attempts have been made at defining it since.[343] Within this scope various attempts have been made to structure the sources of lex mercatoria. Ehricke (1990)[344] gives a classification as to:

- International law
- Uniform laws
- Procedural) rules of International Organisations
- Standardised contracts
- Arbitration awards
- Decisions of National Courts
- General legal principles
- Custom and market practice
- Public policy (ordre public)
- Code of conduct.

However, Cremades and Plehn[345] also attempt a systematic approach however by stressing the harmonisation aspect of *lex mercatoria*. They present the national and the non-national approach of legal harmonisation which is the goal of *lex mercatoria*. In the national approach, similar or identical national commercial laws such as international treaties, international organisations, and international business practices are established as common substantive guidelines and implemented in the commercial laws of the countries concerned.[346] The non-national approach is characterised by a single commercial law which is autonomous from national laws. As a prerequisite, nations must permit businessmen to avoid the application of national law and a coherent body of law (the New Lex Mercatoria) must be established as an alternative. Cremades and Plehn correctly

---

342 Clive Schmitthoff, "Das autonome Recht des Welthandels – Rechtsdogmatische und rechtspolitische Aspekte", in RabelsZ 28 (1964), 47-77

343 Michael J. Mustill, The New Lex Mercatoria: The First Twenty-five Years, in: *Liber Amicorum for Lord Wilberforce*, Oxford: Clarendon Press, 1987, 149-183 (151); Ulrich Ehricke, "Zur Einführung: Grundstrukturen und Problem der lex mercatoria", *Juristische Schulung*, 1990, 967-969 (967)

344 Ulrich Ehricke, "Zur Einführung: Grundstrukturen und Probleme der lex mercatoria", *Juristische Schulung* 1990, 967-969 (969)

345 Bernardo Cremades and Steven Plehn, "The New Lex Mercatoria and the Harmonisation of the Laws of International Commercial Transactions", in: *Boston University International Law Journal*, 1984, 317-348 (317)

346 Bernardo Cremades and Steven Plehn, „The New Lex Mercatoria and the Harmonisation of the Laws of International Commercial Transactions“, in: *Boston University International Law Journal*, 317-348 (321)

point out that this non-national approach on lex mercatoria, which exists in arbitration for example, runs into difficulties. Under English law the arbitration award will be subject to the nations' court judicial control by way of appeal or at the time of their enforcement if not willingly honoured at the time of execution. Mustill[347] answers the fundamental questions of the sources and application of lex mercatoria in the sense that lex mercatoria is required to be supranational and he resorts to a list compiled by Lando[348]for its sources.

A. Public International Law
B. Uniform Laws
C. The General Principles of Law
D. The Rules of International Organisations
E. Customs and Usage
F. Standard Form Contracts
G. Reporting of Arbitral Awards

Consensus on the characteristics of *lex mercatoria* has not yet been found. The difficulty of reaching agreement according to my opinion is caused by a lack of differentiation. In wanting to cover the whole range of possible sources of *lex mercatoria*, authors[349] tend to make one „sweeping stroke" through private and international legal relations. The worst result is that both fields become intermingled.[350] Relations between states and individual commercial cross-border transaction are two completely different fields which cannot really be compared. The reason for this is that every rule or law, be it autonomous or created by states, is only as good as the probability of it being enforced. Whereas the enforcement of international rules in legal relation of states may be merely a question of power, the *lex mercatoria* as a transnational law of economic transactions between private enterprises may well need to facilitate the assistance of conventions e.g. the enforcement of arbitration awards based on rules of *lex mercatoria*. This important fact seems to be conveniently ignored when it comes down to the discussion of *lex mercatoria.* Publications containing general statements outnumber publications with empirical evidence looking at the law and verdicts in the specific fields. Consequently it seems important at this point to

347 Michael J. Mustill, The New Lex Mercatoria: The First Twenty-five Years, in: *Liber Amicorum for Lord Wilberforce*, Oxford, Clarendon Press, 1987, 149-183 (172 subs.)

348 Ole Lando, "The Lex Mercatoria in International Commercial Arbitration", in: *International and Comparative Law Quarterly*, 43 (1985), 747-768

349 Gunter Teubner, „"Global Bukowina: Legal Pluralism in the World Society", in: Gunter Teubner (ed.), *Global Law Without a State*, Aldershot: Dartmouth, 1997, 3-30

350 Gunter Teubner, ibid

distinguish explicitly between two fields. If the sources of *lex mercatoria* are discussed relating to private commercial activities, any kind of public law must be excluded as a source from the outset as this would destroy the characteristics of autonomously created law. International law or convention law only comes into play if it refers to the facilitation of enforcement. They are not however a source of the *lex mercatoria.*

„*Lex mercatoria"* is considered a body of rules which have emerged from the international practice of commercial transactions. These rules are not part or result of any kind of state enactment and can claim legal observation as a binding authority within the international business community. To offer a qualified and credible response to the question of the application of *lex mercatoria* in reinsurance dispute resolution it would be appropriate to go through the different possible sources one by one. General principles of law comprising rules such as good faith, *'pacta sunt servanda'*, *'rebus sic stantibus'*, abuse of rights and *'culpa in contrahendo'* are alleged sources of *lex mercatoria.* The application of those principles cannot be qualified as *lex mercatoria* in reinsurance for two reasons. Firstly, the qualification of general legal principles as sources of *lex mercatoria* come up against the objection that general legal principles are embodied in most national legal orders which contain those principles. They resemble each other. The qualification of general legal principles as a source of *lex mercatoria* is therefore under dispute. And even if one does not share those concerns regarding the qualification of general legal principles as *lex mercatoria*, one encounters problems in affirming their application in reinsurance. As shown above, those principles are resorted to a great deal in reinsurance, but within a specific scope, e.g. of which quality the utmost good faith has to be within reinsurance usage. A recourse to general principles of law therefore does not help any further in the solution of specific reinsurance problems. Rules of international organisations do not touch on issues relating to private international relationships in reinsurance.

Weise (1989) finds *"lex mercatoria"* where a field of business has drawn up standardised contracts in a very detailed manner[351] and touches on another alleged source of *lex mercatoria.* As shown above, the creation of standard contracts in reinsurance has come up against obstacles. Standard contracts as a source of *lex mercatoria* in reinsurance can therefore be excluded. Thus within the scope of the definition given, it is obvious that "*lex mercatoria*" must – if at all – be found within commercial arbitration, i.e. the field where commercial disputes are supposed to be resolved within "one's own peers". Arbitration awards, if published, certainly could establish precedents transporting customs

351 Paul-Frank Weise, Materielles Recht vor der internationalen Handelsschiedsgerichtsbarkeit, Frankfurt: Lang, 1989, 174

and usage within conflict resolution exceeding those in courts' decisions. In English arbitration, contrary to continental arbitration, there are two factors which limit or hinder the "*lex mercatoria*" from coming into existence within arbitration. As mentioned above, the arbitrators have a duty to apply the "law", which means the national English law. Secondly, and linked to this point, there is the judicial control over arbitration which makes it possible to appeal against an arbitration award. Although the scope of appeal has been narrowed down by the Arbitration Act 1979, the basic feature of judicial control remains.

Reliable knowledge on the commonness of honourable clauses in reinsurance arbitration agreements up to now is not available due to the fact that they are not published. Like other equity clauses they appear to be the exception rather than the rule. However, according to the interviews with solicitors and barristers they are still found in reinsurance contracts. Each clause is slightly different, and therefore its effect and validity need to be considered on every occasion.[352] The courts considered the general principles of law which apply. Traditionally the courts were reluctant to oust their jurisdiction and accept different rules of construction. In Orion Compania Espanola de Seguros v. Belfort Maats[353], concerning a quota share non-marine reinsurance treaty between a Spanish and Belgian party, the court was required to consider the validity of the following clause: *„The arbitrator and umpire are relieved from all judicial formalities and may abstain from following the strict rules of law. They shall settle any dispute under this Agreement according to an equitable rather than strictly legal interpretation of its terms and their decision shall be final and not subject to appeal."*

In the above-mentioned case Megaw J argued that:[354] *„parties can validly provide for some other system of law to be applied to an arbitration tribunal. Thus, it may be, though perhaps it would be unusual, that the parties could validly agree that a part, or the whole, of their legal relations should be decided by the arbitral tribunal on the basis of a foreign system of law, or perhaps on the basis of principles of international law, for example, in a contract to which a Sovereign State was a party. It may well be that the arbitration tribunal could properly give effect to such an agreement, and the Court in its supervisory jurisdiction would also give effect to such an agreement, just as it would give effect to a contractual provision in the body of the contract that the proper law of the contract should be some system of foreign law.*

352 J. S. Butler, *Reinsurance Practice and the Law*, London: Lloyd's of London Press, 1993, looseleaf, Service Issue No. 7, 1st September 1997, 25.3.1

353 (1962) Lloyd's Rep 257

354 ibid, 257 (264)

He concluded that: „*This is no such case. If the parties choose to provide in their contract that the rights and obligations shall not be decided in accordance with law but in accordance with some other criterion, such as what the arbitrators consider to be fair and reasonable , whether or not in accordance with law, then, if that provision has any effect at all, its effect, as I see it, would be that there would be no contract, because the parties did not intend the contract to have legal effect – to affect their legal relations. If there were no contract, there would be no legally binding arbitration clause, and an „award" would not be an award which the law would recognise. The essence of the matter, as I see it, is that , as long as the Courts of this country have statutory supervisory jurisdiction over arbitrators in England, it must remain a firm principle of the law, shall remain in all respects and for all purposes a question of law; and it cannot be turned into something other than a question of law by any agreement to arbitrate otherwise.*" The judge rejected the clause as invalid, as it sought to oust the jurisdiction of the courts. A change of attitude occurred when Lord Denning, in the Court of Appeal, considered the question 15 years later in the case of Eagle Star Insurance Company v. Yuval Insurance Company limited.[355] The reinsurance treaty contained an arbitration clause which provided *inter alia*: „*If any question or dispute shall arise ... the same shall .... be referred ... to arbitration ... The Arbitrators and Umpire shall not be bound by the strict rules of law but shall settle any difference referred to them according to an equitable rather than a strictly legal interpretation of the provisions in this Agreement ... The obtaining of an award ... shall be a condition precedent to any right of action in respect of any difference falling within the scope thereof.*"

Difficulties arose in the parties' relationship after the contract had allegedly been renegotiated and, ignoring the arbitration clause, Eagle issued a writ on which they endorsed a statement of claim. That endorsement was defective and Yuval applied to strike it out. Eagle reissued the statement of claim and took out a summons under R.S.C., order 14, for summary judgment against Yuval. Yuval resisted the summons and applied to stay the proceeding on the ground of the arbitration clause. Lord Denning considered that the clause was not only valid but was in accordance with public policy.[356] Acknowledging that „*clauses providing that the arbitrators are not bound by the strict rules of law but are enjoined to decide ... according to an equitable rather than a strictly legal interpretation of the provisions of the agreement*" are quite common in reinsurance treaties, he refers to the reasoning of Megaw J in Orion Compania Espanola de Se-

355 (1978) 1 Lloyd's Rep 357

356 J. S. Butler, *Reinsurance Practice and the Law*, Lloyd's of London Press, London, 1993, looseleaf, Service Issue No. 7, 1st September 1996, 25.3.1.2

guros v. Belfort Maatschaapij Voor Algemene Verzekgringeen[357], where it was held that the honourable engagement clause was invalid. Lord Denning commented: „ *I cannot accept that view. I do not believe that the presence of such a clause makes the whole contract void or a nullity. It is a perfectly good contract. If there is anything wrong with the provision, it can only be on the ground that it is contrary to public policy for parties to agree. I must say that I cannot see anything in public policy to make this clause void. On the contrary the clause seems to me to be entirely reasonable. It does not oust the jurisdiction of the courts. It only ousts technicalities and strict constructions. That is what equity did in the old days. And it is what arbitrators may properly do today under such a clause as this. .... So I am prepared to hold that this arbitration clause, in all its provisions is valid and full of effect, including the requirement that arbitrators shall decide on equitable grounds rather than a strict legal interpretation.* "

He finds support for his arguments in favour of the validity of the honourable engagement clause by looking at the altered relationship between the courts and arbitration: „ *At one time the courts used to be very jealous of arbitrations. They used to find all sorts of reasons for interfering with arbitrators and their awards. But the approach to arbitration has changed in modern days. The courts welcome arbitration in commercial disputes. They encourage references to arbitration by commercial men in the City of London. They do not lightly interfere with their awards. It seems to me that if a defendant who is being sued in the courts asks that a matter should go to arbitration with their agreement, prima facie that agreement ought to be honoured: The action should be stayed and the matter should be allowed to go to arbitration. Subject to this statutory qualification: If the defendant has taken a „step in the proceedings", then he is too late. He can no longer apply for the court proceedings to be stayed.*

Five years later, this decision was followed by Home Insurance Company v. Administratia Asigurarilor de Stat.[358] The plaintiff insurers entered into three reinsurance contracts with the defendant reinsurers. The first contract, containing the arbitration clause set out below, was signed on behalf of the reinsurers, whereas the second and third contracts were signed directly by the reinsurers themselves.[359] Each of the three contracts provided for the reinsureds to cede and for the whole account of the reinsureds' business. The contract contained the following honourable engagement clause: „ *This treaty shall be interpreted as an honourable engagement rather than as a legal obligation and the award shall*

357 (1962) 2 Lloyd's Rep 257
358 (1983) 2 Lloyd's Rep 674
359 J. S. Butler, *Reinsurance Practice and the Law*, ibid, 25.3.1.2

be made with a view to effecting the general purpose of this treaty rather than in accordance with a literal interpretation of its language ....“

A dispute as to the validity of the contracts arose, whereby the reinsureds claimed that reinsurance contracts were valid. The reinsurers contended that the agreement was binding in honour only and not in law, and that the words in the above clause expressly went against any contractual intention. It was held that, on the true construction of the agreement, it was plain that it was the common intention that there should be an enforceable obligation to arbitrate and abide by the awards. In his decision Parker J. maintained that „*it was the common intention that there should be an enforceable obligation to arbitrate and to abide by the award. All that was intended was to free the arbitrators to some extent from strict rules and this on the authority of the Eagle Star, is permissible.*“

In Overseas Union Insurance Ltd. v. AA Mutual International Insurance Co. Ltd[360], the court had to consider an agreement whereby a subsidiary and parent company authorised insurance underwriters to act on their behalf. An agreement was made by the subsidiary and the underwriters on behalf of the parent company. This agreement contained the following honourable engagement clause:

„*The arbitrators and the umpire shall interpret this reinsurance as an honourable engagement and they shall make their award with a view of ... effecting the general purpose of this reinsurance in a reasonable manner, rather than in accordance with a literal interpretation of the language, the true intention of the parties being that the reinsurer shall follow the fortunes of the company ...*“.

The agreement provided that the parent company undertook to pay all the claims against the subsidiary in excess of a fixed specified limit. The subsidiary company had a claim under this agreement which referred to arbitration. The parent company then commenced proceedings, claiming that it was not liable to pay. When considering the clause, Evans J held that „*Although the clause may entitle the arbitrators to view the matter more leniently than a court would do, I am doubtful whether they can embark on any other enquiries than the law requires, namely finding the natural and proper meaning of the words used in the particular context. The clause does however emphasise that commercial arbitrators may draw upon their own experience and knowledge of commercial matters without form of proof.*“

As for today, the most recent judicial consideration of an honourable engagement clause is provided in Home and Overseas Insurance Company Limited v. Mentor Insurance Company UK Limited[361]. There the honourable engagement clause reads as follows:

---

360 (1988) 2 Lloyd s Rep 63
361 (1989) 1 Lloyd's Rep 473

„The arbitrators and the umpire shall interpret this reinsurance as an honourable engagement and they shall make their award with a view to effecting the general purpose of this reinsurance in a reasonable manner rather than in accordance with a literal interpretation of the language."

Hirst J held that the arbitration clause was valid, stating that: *„In my judgment the „honourable engagement" clause in the present case does entitle the arbitrators to view matters of construction more leniently and with regard more generally to commercial considerations than would be permissible in a court of law."* He gave full effect to the requirement that the arbitrators should decide on equitable grounds rather than by strict legal interpretation. He dismissed Home's application for a declaration, and granted the defendants a stay of proceedings. Home appealed to the Court of Appeal, which, on consideration of the clause, upheld the decision reached by Hirst J. Parker LJ, concluded that :

„A clause which purported to free arbitrators to decide without regard to the law and according, for example, to their own notions of what would be fair, would not be a valid arbitration clause. The clause does not any such thing."

Lloyd LJ said on the question of the effect of the honourable engagement clause: *„ I see no reason why the parties should not require the arbitrators to adopt the more lenient view, even if a court would be likely to adopt a stricter view. By way of illustration, the arbitrators might give greater weight to the preamble to the contract, in which it is stated that the reinsurance is to cover the liability of the reassured, as indicating the general purpose of the contract ..... ."*

Both Court of Appeal Judges (Balcombe LJ concurred) held that such an honourable engagement clause would confer wide powers on the arbitrators to enable them to adopt a more lenient view than the courts would take. They stressed, however, that such a clause would not enable the arbitrators to determine a dispute without regard for the law. Any clause purporting to extend or oust the general law would certainly be invalid. To summarise the results of the above-mentioned cases, honourable clauses are valid in nearly all cases [362], allowing arbitrators a flexibility when construing documents, considering hearsay evidence and taking notice of market practice. The clause is, however, invalid if it attempts to alter or to oust substantive law rather than rules of construction or procedure. The inclusion of an honourable engagement clause meets objections due to its *lack of certainty*. This is a drawback which arises form the inclusion of such a clause. All decisions regarding the validity of the honourable engagement clause are rather vague as to how far the arbitrators may go in deviating from the rules of the law. The borderline between *„a more lenient view than the courts and extending or ousting the general law"* might be hard to draw in some cases.

---

362 J. S. Butler, *Reinsurance Practice and Law*, ibid, 25.3.2

And there are suggestions that the honourable engagement clause does not fit anymore in *today's attitude of reinsurance disputes* anymore and for these two reasons one would rather opt against its inclusion.[363]

When A.R.I.A.S started up its efforts to bring about a standard arbitration clause, they conducted research into the arbitration clauses used so far and their contents. With reference to the honourable engagement clause they concluded that „ *no form of clause recommended by any market association that we have found, includes an honourable engagement clause despite the continued widespread use of such clauses by brokers in preparing treaty wordings.* "[364] When a recommendation for a new arbitration clause was drafted, the decision was not made to include an „honourable engagement clause" as was the case in the previous versions of 1975. In response to the A.R.I.AS. consultation document on arbitration clauses[365] the respondents' arguments pro and contra the honourable engagement clause read as follows:

„Of those that responded a few senior and distinguished market leaders thought that the Honourable Engagement Clause should form part of the arbitration clause. However we prefer the majority view that either there should be no such clause at all or if there was to be one, it should be in a separate provision; the clause causes too much uncertainty to form part of a recommended arbitration clause. .... The view was expressed to us that the Honourable Engagement Clause is anachronistic and forms no part of modern business; most lawyers who responded considered that the clause caused problems and gave rise to arguments because no one really understood what it meant. However other market practitioners felt it might be a useful provision, particularly reminding people of their basic obligation."

Despite these arguments, it seems fair to allow market practice some recognition in reinsurance disputes. This recognition must however be restricted, since arbitrators as market men may exempt the parties from naming expert witnesses in order to undermine their view of a certain market practice, as the arbitrators themselves know the market practice which is used in the interpretation of a legal, reinsurance question. A further difficulty in conceding the existence of *"lex mercatoria"* in reinsurance in London as a dispute resolution centre is, that English law has a precise idea as to when a rule becomes law and therefore binding. Market practice in the sense of a "law merchant" has to pass a test that it is notorious, generally exercised and acknowledged as legally binding. To get away from the criteria of general practice it can be sufficient to call on an expert wit-

363 J. S. Butler, ibid
364 A.R.I.A.S, Consultation Document on Arbitration Clauses, News sheet,
365 A.R.I.A.S. , Response to consultation document on arbitration clauses

ness who comments on a different practice. This shall demonstrate that English law is quite serious on what can be understood as established, even with a market practice that could form a legally binding rule. Finally the spontaneous honouring of arbitration awards has been put forward as an argument for "*lex mercatoria*".[366] There are two objections to this, one factual and one systematic. Firstly, experience shows that the spontaneous honouring of arbitration awards in the London reinsurance market cannot be approved of without limitations. Mustill maintains that this was the case in the past, when the market was tight and default could be fatal. In his experience, reinsurance is nowadays the most bitterly litigious of all areas of commercial activity.[367] The interviews conducted with City practitioners support the view that arbitration awards are not honoured as they were in previous times. Furthermore the question must be posed as to how the spontaneous honouring of arbitration awards can nowadays indeed be attributed to the existence of "*lex mercatoria*". If an arbitration award is not honoured, the claimant has to go to court to obtain a title to enforce his claim. In such a case all efforts to keep the dispute private would be destroyed. Hence a more pragmatic approach suggests that the spontaneous honouring of arbitration awards is driven by the intention of the parties involved to preserve the major advantage which arbitration has sustained over litigation: privacy.

5.4. Alternative dispute resolution

A paper referring to dispute resolution in a Common Law country would not be complete without mentioning Alternative Dispute Resolution (ADR). In the UK the expression ADR covers any of a variety of techniques for resolving civil disputes without the need for conventional litigation. It may include *mini-trial* (a shortened and simplified form of a court hearing), informal methods of arbitration and (especially) structured forms of conciliation using a special trained mediator who acts as a go-between.[368] It is a process by which a third party, at the invitation of the contestant, is brought in with a view to the dispute being resolved amicably and without a legally binding award. However, where the mediation process results in an agreement, it will be binding if so intended by the

366 Bernardo Cremades and Steven Plehn, „The New Lex Mercatoria and the Harmonisation of the Laws of International Commercial Transactions“, in: *Boston Univ. ILJ 1984*, 317-348 (317)

367 Michael J. Mustill, The New Lex Mercatoria: „The First Twenty-five Years“, in: *Liber Amicorum for Lord Wilberforce*, Oxford: Clarendon Press, 1987, 149-183 (182)

368 Elizabeth A. Martin, *A Dictionary of Law*, Oxford University Press, 3d. ed., 1994, 20

parties.[369] In the UK it covers any process other than litigation, arbitration or direct negotiation which is used to resolve a dispute. This differs from the US terminology where ADR includes arbitration. Typically, ADR processes involve a neutral third party who assists the parties in arriving at a settlement to the dispute. This may be done either before or during the conventional litigation or arbitration processes[370]. Commercial Judges are anxious to encourage the settlement of commercial disputes, particularly those which would be unduly costly or cumbersome to litigate before the court. To this end the parties involved in such disputes are encouraged to investigate the possibility of utilising ADR techniques, such as conciliation and mediation, as a means of reaching a settlement. The Commercial Court Registry maintains a list of individuals and organisations which offer ADR services.

By interviewing a representative of one of the numerous organisations[371] which provide such services, it became clear that certain prerequisites have to be fulfilled if ADR is to have a chance to succeed. ADR may succeed if enough information is available to the parties to make a real assessment of the case and direct negotiations have not proven effective. On the other hand, ADR is excluded where an emergency injunction is sought, a precedent is needed and where the parties are not willing to meet. The interviewed representative saw a special role for ADR in cross-border disputes because the law to be applied and the jurisdiction are not always clear. A good example for its application in international disputes is in the field of construction. In disputes over large scale construction projects ADR has already established itself as an alternative to litigation. Since 1990, ADR has been implemented during Commercial Court proceedings so that the Commercial Court Standard Direction requires the lawyers to inform their clients to consider ADR. As part of the pre-trial check list[372] questions are intended to direct the attention of the litigants' legal advisers to ADR as a means of avoiding a trial. These questions read:

10. Have you or counsel[373] discussed with your client(s) the possibility of attempting to resolve this dispute (or particular issues) by Alternative Dispute Resolution ?

---

369 Roy Goode, *Commercial Law*, 2nd Ed., Penguin Books, London, 1995, 1138

370 Baker McKenzie, Seminar Materials, Alternative Dispute Resolution 'From Theory into Practice', London, 14 July 1994, 1

371 CEDR-Centre for Dispute Resolution, launched in 1990 by the Confederation of British Industry as a result of dissatisfaction with litigation.

372 This check list is required to be completed by all parties not later than two months before the trial.

373 The standard order of direction is addressed to the solicitor and 'Counsel' means barrister in this context.

11. Might some form of ADR procedure assist to resolve or narrow down the issues of this case ?

12. Have you or your client(s) explored with the other parties the possibility of resolving this dispute (or particular issues) by ADR ?

Due to this directive as well as to the growing scepticism towards arbitration, ADR could also become relevant in reinsurance disputes. The outcome of the free format interview with the solicitors made it clear that its current use in reinsurance is not really worth mentioning. This was a view commonly shared. The evaluation of the use and future prospects of ADR in reinsurance disputes was however quite intensely discussed. While one solicitor maintained that *„A.D.R. can have a role especially where it proves that many parties are involved and the decision or resolution reached shall prevail for all of them,"* another stated that *„ADR is no more than sophisticated negotiations and is not helpful at all."*

Some would see a future for ADR as an alternative to the current adversial based system if the lawyers were still able to be involved to a sufficient degree. Here again the hypothesis set out at the beginning of the thesis proved to be correct: The selection of the dispute resolution mechanisms is very much influenced by factors not at all relating to the law being applied, but by the interests of the actors involved and the legal professions which want to protect their status. There was also an attempt to differentiate under which conditions ADR could prosper -from the solicitors' perspective. ADR could benefit from two aspects: „ *for one that lawyers are fed up with arbitration because of its uncertain outcomes and the clients are dissatisfied with the high costs involved. Secondly the advisory element in English procedure is so strong that chances for settlements are missed even where they were possible.*

Nevertheless a sceptical attitude was voiced towards ADR and its special merits. *„If the dispute can be settled it can be settled just as well by the solicitors. If lawyers do fear to advise a client in a certain direction or lack creativity, ADR might be of assistance. Generally speaking he does not think it a useful instrument, but only a „new dress" for what lawyers have to provide anyway."* In effect this comes down to the fact that ADR can do nothing that a good solicitor with negotiation skills cannot do. The claims managers could also have a sceptical attitude towards ADR because they consider it their task to decide whether a claim is negotiable or not. The executives of insurance and reinsurance companies might think differently. On the different spread of ADR in the UK and the US, the following opinion was given: „ *The success of ADR in the US where ADR comes from might be better because in the US every party bears its own costs in litigation. In the UK and in the continental countries the party who loses bears its own and the other party's costs with the exception of employment disputes. Also maybe ADR is more common in the US because the evil of litigation* *there is even more obvious. The typical situation for ADR. being a successful instrument is where one party is obviously weaker and economically inexperienced (example: worker has asbestosis claim and has not sued within a class action).*

This situation does not usually arise in reinsurance disputes where two equally strong and experienced parties come together. An argument against ADR was that it provides no binding solution such as a judgment or an award which will be imposed on the parties. If ADR. proceedings fail, additional costs and delays are incurred. Some solicitors pointed out that A.D.R. is not catching on because the discovery elements are lacking. The opportunity to give a presentation to a forum is not available. These two points are important in the tactics of litigation and arbitration. In litigation, as shown above, discovery has a central role in obtaining information at a pre-trial stage that may help in assessing the case. Nevertheless some of those interviewed conceded that A.D.R. might be bound to spread even in reinsurance. Essential for ADR was „ *the genuine will to come to a settlement, and the fact that there are not any general questions of law in the dispute. Misrepresentation or non-disclosure might suit for ADR, if factual questions are concerned.*" Regarding possible motives for implementing ADR into the Commercial Court directions, one solicitor stated: „*ADR is very young in the UK. The reasons for it now being implemented into the Commercial Court rules might be that continental law statutes already provide an obligation on the lawyers (and the judges) for a settlement.*" While one interviewee was pessimistic about ADR in the short term, he thinks speed, lower costs and the control of the result by the parties will speak for it in the long term. Contrary to other solicitors who considered the non-binding character of ADR an obstacle, he does not see a problem; even if a solution has been reached under ADR the parties can still sue. If an agreement is written, the enforcement of an agreement under ADR is not a problem. Nevertheless ADR might become increasingly popular as arbitration proceedings not only resemble court proceedings to an ever greater extent, but also prove to be more expensive. The future prospects of ADR are going to be closely connected to the development of litigation and arbitration. If arbitration does not become a less formal kind of dispute resolution as in former times, ADR. may be likely to offer an alternative.

6. Conclusion

This study on reinsurance disputes in the London market presents two main conclusions. On the one hand, it reveals disputes in an area which was traditionally known as „gentlemen's business“ and characterised by the principle of utmost good faith. On the other hand, it refutes approaches that look for results in the facilitation of cross-border legal interaction by means of an alleged globalisation of the law. It has emerged that a national court may, under certain circumstances, be well suited to the requirements of cross-border legal interaction. Findings which evidence the importance of a national court for cross-border dispute resolution may not suit at a time when *globalisation* – at least in recent socio-legal literature – is deemed to have already reached all areas of human activity and therefore seems to be reality. With regard to the globalisation of law this view has recently been fostered by Teubner.[374] As my findings must be seen as a proof to the contrary to what is described there, it would be an ommission not to comment on this very recent publication. As the concept of legal globalisation is promoted in this essay, the question arises on which sources this global law may be grounded. Teubner's essay is named 'Legal Pluralism in the World Society' and this title already hints that he allocates global law in different field legal relations. Aside *lex mercatoria*, which will be tackled explicitly below, the internal legal regimes of multinational entreprises, a combination of globalisation in labour law, technical standardisation and professional self-regulation, discourse of human rights, the field of ecology and a *lex sportiva internationalis* are sources of a global law according to this essay. This list seems questionable to me as it includes fields of private law as well as public law and political interests such as the *'pax americana'*. This selection appears dubious with regard to *the* decisive feature of law, which is – according to the empirical studies on cross-border legal interaction – the possibility of *enforcement* of rights and claims. Here differentiations have to be made as regards private individiduals and the relations between nations. Whereas nation states have the power factor on their side to support their own legal position or influence other states in a certain direction (as e. g. given in the mentioned *'pax americana')*, private individuals and

374 Gunter Teubner, „Global Bukowina“: Legal Pluralism in the World Society, in: Gunter Teubner (ed.), *Global Law without a State,* Dartmouth: Aldershot, 1997, 3-30

corporations are still in the need of institutional support when enforcing their claims.

Alleged global law is not able to take the place of this assistance. The role of this institutional support provided by the state in putting through claims and effecting rights has been evidenced in studies concerning fields as different as maintenance claims and commercial cross-border claims. As regards maintenance claims[375] it became obvious that this area cannot do without state supported agencies. On the example of the German Institute of Guardianship, Grotheer explains that support agencies are set up to help creditors enforce such claims and obtain their money. Regarding the enforcement of cross-border commercial claims[376] it became apparent that indeed autonomous infrastructures are used to collect claims, but the claim collection is still based on titles obtained through courts, which are state provided institutions. As a result there is no field which can do without state provided structures regarding rules or the enforcement of such rules. As private legal relations are different to the above mentioned political forces and discourse it may consequently be doubted that these fields selected by Teubner are at all suitable to be put into one category as forming global law which is derived from legal pluralism.

This point becomes visible as we almost inevitably come across *lex mercatoria* again as a law of economic transactions which Teubner acclaims among others is a central source of global law. According to my view, *lex mercatoria* cannot – at least for the Anglo-American legal system – be rightly named as a source for a law which is universally applied. However contrary to other authors writing in favour of *lex mercatoria,* he at least undergoes the pains of confronting himself with the numerous counter arguments which are against a *lex mercatoria* as universal law. There he highlights two crucial criteria. Firstly he elaborates in the lex mercatoria debate, that the fact that its rules are rather indeterminate has been used as an argument against its independent existence[377]. Secondly the citerion of conflict resolution as a functional analysis has been used against *lex mercatoria* as it provides no such resolution mechanisms.[378] Then, and this seems significant for most of his constructions in the essay, he tries to invalidate these important critera by challenging their appropriateness. Regarding the inde-

375 Kirsten Grotheer, „Structures of the enforcement of cross-border maintenance claims of children", in: Volkmar Gessner, Ali Cem Budak (Eds.), *Cross-border legal interaction*, Empirical studies on the Globalisation of Law, Forthcoming

376 Ali Cem Budak, „The infrastructure of cross-border debt collection: Examples in Turkey and Germany, in: Volkmar Gessner, Ali Cem Budak (Eds.), *Cross-border legal interaction*, Empirical Studies on the Globalisation of Law, Forthcoming

377 Teubner, ibid, 3-30 (13)

378 Teubner, ibid, 3-30 (13)

termination he maintains that what matters is a self-organising process of mutual constitution of legal acts and legal structures.[379] Concerning the conflict resolution aspect he states that a functional analysis of this kind is not suited to providing the criteria of the delineation of the legal and non legal in *lex mercatoria.* This demonstrates the highly theoretical approach which is followed in this essay and its powers of persuasion suffers because of this. As regards results presented in my study, they rather show that legal certainty and the possible application of rules in conflict are the corner stones on which a business community relies when dissent occurs.

To find a global law in the form of *lex mercatoria* in times of consent of the actors who do business, is probably no difficult task, as mutual understanding of handling certain issues could be mistaken for rules in the sense of law which – putted to the test in conflict – are not adhered to. It is to distinguish between sociological phenomena such as networks or mutual consent in the market practice or usage and the *law*. In order not to lead – especially sociologists – in temptation to mix up both fields, one must stick to the classsical definition of law. It appears that Teubner invalidates and disregards these definitions and criteria which run against his theories of the law, so they fit into what he has named 'global law'. Instead he puts sociological phenomenons in socio-legal categories and 'sells' them as law. To succeed in this he contests that a contract needs to be rooted in a pre-existing legal order. According to his view also this acknowledged principle on which consent sociologists and jurists has to be overcome. Instead of this principle that a contract must be connected to one national legal order he promotes the idea of a self-validating contract. Regarding the spread of global law he predicts that his observations concerning the global law in social peripheries may probably apply to a wider horizon. This results in Teubner's main thesis that global law will grow mainly from the social peripheries and not from the political centres of nation-states and international institutions. His observations relate to rather marginal areas. As I researched in one specific field, it is not up to me to refute this theory as a whole since I have not examined the fields of ecology, *lex sportiva internaltionalis* and other fields which Teubner names. From what I can deduct from my study I am however of the opinion that a complete globalisation in law is very speculative. At best there will be areas of law, in which cases will be treated identically and common rules will probably develop through court decisions or arbitration awards. The degree of globalisation of law will depend upon the ability and sheer necessity of the actors to develop a common will to reach a unification. Therefore I should think that states will be more able to produce global international law than individuals and corpo-

379 Teubner, ibid, 3-30 (13)

rations. In the latter area of private law similar ways are to be observed world-wide to go about business in the sense of usage, but the legal quality of such rules must be doubted. In times of distress in a business field as this study proves, even long standing traditional rules are questioned. As reinsurance is a rather marginal area regarding the number of actors but international in nature, the results of this study speak against Teubner's theory. It has become evident that even in such a marginal area with substantial business interests it cannot be managed to develop a sustainable international conflict resolution mechanism. A national court must step in.

As far as the Commercial Court in London with respect to reinsurance disputes is concerned, this study casts doubt on statements that national courts are ill-suited to solve cross-border disputes. Not only is the average number of non-UK parties using the court for all kinds of commercial transactions extremely high, but the reinsurance industry which used to belong to a typical non-court user group can also be found litigating there. The on-going observation of cases has even shown that parties go through all instances of the English court system in matters that appear of fundamental importance and may still be relevant for future contracts. While the Commercial Court as a first instance court and then the Court of Appeal in the second instance used to influence the legal development through their decision, the House of Lords has to deal increasingly with reinsurance decisions. In three major cases a House of Lords appeal was allowed in 1996.[380] The New York courts, the Milano court *(tribunale)* and German district courts *(Landgerichte)* have been subject to empirical research recently.[381] As regards the judicial reasoning in international matters[382], the result was that in Bremen and Hamburg as well as in New York, the application of foreign law to international disputes is comparatively rare. In comparison to those courts the Commmercial Court is not reluctant to apply foreign law if necessary. With reference to quantity, the afore-mentioned study of international disputes entering the civil courts of first instance observes a 2,5 % share and estimates their absolute number in every year in the fifteen member states of the European Union between 100.000 and 200.000. As in 2/3 of all cases before the Commercial Court either one or both parties are foreign I would guess that therefore the Commercial Court must be one of the leading European courts for international

---

380 Charter Re v. Fagan: (1996) 2 Lloyd's Rep 113 (HL); Hill & Others v. Mercantile and General Reinsurance Co. Pls, (1996) 1 WLR 1239 (HL), AXA Reinsurance (UK) Plc. v. Field (1996) 2 Lloyd's Rep 233 (HL)

381 Volkmar Gessner (ed.), *Foreign Courts: Civil Litigation in Foreign Legal Cultures*, Aldershot: Dartmouth, 1996

382 Freyhold, Gessner, Olgiati, in ibid, „The Role of Courts in Global Legal Interaction", 267-281

matters if not the leading one. The courts which were subject to the afore-mentioned study were much more provincial in their dealings with international cases. Commercial Court judges have a far greater experience with international matters which is partly based on the fact that they are recruited from the bar. As barristers they already have argued reinsurance cases and other international matters in front of the court. From this perspective my results support the conclusion[383] that courts are certainly not insignificant institutions in the legal arena. But whereas the contribution of domestic (national) courts to the globalisation of law in the afore-mentioned publication is given very little credit, not to say denied, I cannot subscribe to this as regards reinsurance disputes. Promoted through the mentioned seminars on reinsurance law, there is close oberservation on the part of the lawyers worldwide of how reinsurance issues are decided by the Commercial Court (and its higher instance courts such as the Court of Appeal and the House of Lords). Although there is no obligation for a US court to follow a certain reasoning, arguments are occasionally adopted. Finally as regards the uncertainty of cross-border exchanges, there are findings, that there are no signs that the foreign parties have less chance to win their cases also in Commercial Court cases.[384] It was stated by the interviewed solictors to the contrary that foreign parties feel this forum to be a fair one. Commercial Court decisions in reinsurance have contributed considerably to legal certainty in a field where precedents were lacking.

The interview results indicate that if there is a choice as to the dispute resolution mechanisms, it assumes prerequisites that actually do not differ from those assumed in litigation involving national parties only. Tactical deliberations belong to these prerequisites. Although the scope of such deliberations is widened in the case of a cross-border dispute, e.g. where to sue; which jurisdiction has the power to decide upon the case; which law is applicable; where the assets of the defendant are located and so on, the tactical element is often left out when the legal institutions resolving these disputes are discussed. The discussion on the solution of cross-border disputes and cross- border legal interaction often appears to be limited in this regard. The prevailing idea seems to be that a unified system of law can be slipped over on all problems generating from international commercial transactions. But this approach clearly overestimates the command of such laws. Often neither the situations from which commercial disputes arise, nor the steps taken in resolving them can be anticipated. Too little attention is paid to empirical information. The Commercial Court profits from the long history of commercial jurisdiction in England which always involved foreign par-

383 ibid, 269
384 ibid. 278

tics. On the other hand, the consequent efforts towards reforms prepared by empirical and statistical reports (Commercial Court User's Conference 1962 e. g.) have supported its status as a forum felt fair and competent to foreign parties. The English Procedural Law regarding discovery and evidence are favourable elements too. Discovery reveals important information and reinsurance trials are often settled at the discovery stage. According to English law the applicable law is a question of fact and therefore of evidence if disputed. The lawyers have to demonstrate the relevant sources and automatically relieve the judge from collecting the information on the foreign law.

It shall not be veiled that additional circumstances must accumulate so that parties sue which used not to go to court at all. The Lloyds crisis and the subsequent Names litigation created a pressure to find a forum which could deal with reinsurance law matters. It forced the expertise into the court, so to speak. Other reinsurers which did not have to deal with problems connected with Lloyds gladly took on the expertise to have other reinsurance problems solved. But it was no longer necessary to explain the particularities of the business to the legal community accompanying the proceedings. As shown the reinsurance industry finds itself in a highly litigious and above all dynamic process of disputing. Disputes are not always conducted as stipulated in the agreement. There may be appropriate reasons for this, e.g. if a case comes to court instead of using arbitration, because of the involvement of third parties; these are not bound by the arbitration agreement and one aims at obtaining a binding decision for all parties involved. But the choice of a certain dispute resolution mechanism – may it be the courts or arbitration – is not always influenced by such obvious motives of mutual advantage. Motives vary. Often the parties hope to benefit not so much from reaching a verdict but expect a result from undergoing certain stages of proceedings and hope that the dispute can be settled during these proceedings. This is due to the already mentioned advantage of the Common Law procedural rules. Although this motive was often mentioned during the interviews, it was difficult to assess in real terms how many reinsurance disputes – with reference to the use of arbitration and jurisdiction – circulate, which ones go to arbitration, which ones go to the courts and how many are settled in the market. No such statistics are available. Even efforts by leading law firms with reinsurance departments were unable to get an idea as to how many arbitrations and court proceedings are initiated by reinsurance disputes. As already stated, an effort was made to assess the workload of reinsurance files in City law firms in the first three months of 1995, whereby it was hoped to check the outcome against the results of the file analysis later in 1995. As the permission of this file analysis was not granted, no absolute statistics can be released.

The results of the study show that although it is felt that litigation in the reinsurance industry has increased – a result which is supported by the increased numbers of verdicts – the majority of cases are not decided by a judge but settled earlier within the proceedings. This could suggest that the „old gentlemen's" informal talks to settle disagreements have now been replaced by proceedings accompanied by lawyers who have taken over the co-ordination of disputes. Indeed it appears that the use of a forum depends on the appropriate skills on the legal professions surrounding it. The Anglo-American case law seems to generate a specific „breed" of legal professions which is suited for commercial cross-border disputes. The reason for this may lay in that the case law system seems generally to produce a more pragmatic attitude contrary to a dogmatic and scholarly attitude that seem to be encouraged by statutory law systems. If problems arise in those jurisdictions in a commercial field where no statutes exist on which to base the decision, judges are more reluctant to tackle the subject. It also appears that the Anglo-American perception on dispute resolution is more service oriented. Especially lawyers treat dispute resolution as a service industry. Whereas lawyers had already found their way into the arbitration proceedings, the new involvement was only possible due to the turn in reinsurance to litigation. The orientation towards a special of conflict resolution mechanism seems to be closely intertwined with the state of business. When business is running smoothly and the number of players in the market remains constant readiness for litigation clearly remains the exception rather than the rule. Increasingly difficult business in reinsurance has changed the dispute resolution culture to a considerable degree and a of lack of precedents has additionally contributed to a trend towards litigation. This was indicated in the interviews with the practitioners, who increasingly participate in and shape the dispute resolution in reinsurance. When asked if they could see a connection between the economic health of the reinsurance business and the level of reinsurance disputes and/or the method of dispute resolution selected, a clear majority answered positively. One can observe a flood of litigation with time delay subsequently to the recession in reinsurance in the late 70s. The fact that basic statistics show a settlement rate of 95 %, which also must be assumed for reinsurance disputes according to the interviews with the practitioners, does not lessen the significance of the general trend. A rather more persuasive argument is that the high share of disputes which are settled allow only a peak of an iceberg of disputes to become visible. Dissatisfaction with both the outcomes of arbitration awards, which are sometimes incalculable, as well as with the increasing costs also contributed to that the legal community in reinsurance thought over the long standing alleged favours of arbitration. In the questionnaire, practitioners were asked to rank the alleged advantages of lower costs, speed and specialist expertise. It emerged that these benefits are given very little credit nowadays. On the contrary, it emerged that litigation is cheaper, quicker and the specialist expertise of Commercial Court judges remains undisputed. This is not to say that legal-cultural differences in using a foreign legal system – especially with respect to procedural questions – do not arise. But in weighing up the pros and cons these legal-cultural differences are minor obstacles and do not prevent the foreign parties from opting for the Commercial Court. The selective use of dispute resolution mechanisms is one remarkable aspect in this respect. Whilst on the whole a tendency of retreat from national courts is to be observed, in cases with an international element the reinsurance community participating in the London market appears to use the legal instrument most suitable to enable cross-border legal comparability and interaction. The increasing disputes in the reinsurance business have not only led to litigation, but to a new sensivity for legal problems which may result from the construction of reinsurance agreements. Increasingly broker houses have their own legal department of varying size or occasionally consult outside counsels on the drafting of wordings. Reinsurance companies consult their legal advisers before signing a contract. Business contact have become more formal in nature and the parties are more aware about the legal implications of a deal. The severe and negative impact of disputes in the reinsurance industry in general and the London market may not be veiled. The Lloyds crisis and problems of the past which remain to be tackled, have left their scars on the London reinsurance market. Also insolvencies of numerous other London market participants have led to a decrease in the importance of London. A reverse trend can only be expected when those problems are solved and a more efficient form of commercial conduct is established.[385] The German reinsurers and the French reinsurance market in Paris have profited by the London market's weakness. The former state enterprise Scor and numerous other middle-sized reinsurers have developed with the support of the Government. The long term aim of French policy is to catch up with London as a reinsurance centre. Besides France, other places such as Luxembourg or Dublin have developed new reinsurance locations. The global number of reinsurance companies has decreased after a period of consolidation and mergers.[386]

What future developments can be expected in the international reinsurance business ? The idea of partnership and companionship in distress between cedant

385 Berhard Laetsch, „Rückversicherung auf neuen Wegen", in: *Zeitschrift für Versicherungwesen,* 21/96, 572-577 (573)

386 Elke Laetsch, „Auf Nummer Sicher – Gigantische Schadensfälle beschleunigen die weltweite Konzentration der Rückversicherer", in: *Die Zeit*, 23. August 1996, 24

and reinsurer is more than in question.[387] The principle of utmost good faith which characterised the commercial relations in the reinsurance industry for decades is probably still acclaimed, but is no more living reality. The partners do not trust each other so easily. This resulted in reinsurers making use of their contractual right to inspect cedant's records. One must also reckon with this right being increasingly used in Continental Europe. Disputes in courts and arbitration will increase in Europe as well. Disputes and questions of reinsurance cover will expose business relationships to a tension test and a probable burst. The traditional reinsurance market characterised by personal relationships, emotions and social understanding is dead and will not return.

387 Bernhard Laetsch, „Rückversicherung auf neuen Wegen", in: *Zeitschrift für Versicherungswesen*, 21/96, 572-577 (575)

Bibliography

Statutes

England

Administration of Justice Act 1970
Applicable Law Act 1990
Arbitration Act of 1889
Arbitration Act of 1950
Arbitration Act of 1975
Arbitration Act of 1979
Arbitration Act of 1996
Bills of Exchange Act 1882
Carta Mercatoria 1303
Carriage by Air (Supplementary Provisions) Act 1962
Civil Jurisdiction and Judgments Act 1982
Companies Act of 1985
Contracts (Applicable Law) 1990
High Court & County Courts Jurisdiction Order SI 199,
Insolvency Act 1986
Insurance Brokers (Registration) Act 1977
Insurance Companies Act 1982
Marine Insurance Act 1906
Model International Insolvency Co-operation Agreement (MIICA)
Practice Direction for the Commercial Court (1962) 1 W.L.R. 1216
Rules of the Supreme Court (RSC) (Amendment) 1987
Sale of Goods Act 1979
Statute of Staple, 27 Edw. III (1353)
Statute of Acton Burnell 1238 as amended by the Statute of Merchants 1285
Uniform Laws on International Sales Act 1967

European Community (EC)

EEC Convention on Jurisdiction and the Enforcement of Judgments in Civil and Commercial Matters (Brussels Convention) 1968, effected in the UK 1987

Civil Jurisdiction and Judgments Act of 1982 (CJJA), effected in the UK in 1987
Rome Convention on the law applicable to contractual obligations 1980 (made part of English law by the Contracts (Applicable Law Act 1990) effected on 1 April 1991)
Directive on Reinsurance and Retrocession 1964 (RL 64/225 EWG v. 25.2.1964, 878)
Hague Convention on the Purchase of Goods 1964
EEC-EFTA Convention on Jurisdiction and the Enforcement of Judgments in Civil and Commercial Matters (Lugano Convention) 1988

United Nations

United Nations Convention on Contracts for the International Sales of Good (1980)

Cases

a'

Alexion Hope, The (1988) 1 Lloyd's Rep. 311
Antaios Naviera S. A. -v- Salen Rederierana A.B. The Antaios, (1984) 3 ALL ER 229
Arkwright Mutual Insurance Company -v- Bryanstone Insurance Company Limited (1990) 2 All ER 335
Astley (Re) and Tyldesley Coal and Salt Co and Tyldesley Coal Co (1899) 68 LJ QB 252
Axa Reinsurance (UK) Plc. v. Field (1996) 1 Lloyd's Rep. 26 (CA), (1996) 1 WLR 1239 (HL)

b'

Bank of Credit and Commerce International SA (1993) BCC 787 (in Re)
Bedford Insurance Company v. IRB (1984) 1 Lloyd's Rep. 210

c'

Charman v. Guardian Royal Exchange Assurance (1992) 2 Lloyd's Rep. 607
Charman & Brockbank -v- W.O.C. Offshore BV (1993) 1 Lloyd's Rep 378 (QB), affirmed (1993) 2 Lloyd's Rep 551 (CA)

Charter Reinsurance Company Limited v. Fagan (1995) CLC 1345 (ComCt) and CA, (1996) 2 Lloyd's Rep 113 (HL)
Citadel Insurance Co. V. Atlantic Union Insurance Co. (1982) 2 Lloyd's Rep (542) CA)
Commercial Union -v- Sun Alliance, (1992) 1 Lloyd's Rep. 475
Container Transport International Inc. v Oceanus Mutual Underwriting Association (Bermuda) Ltd. (1984) 1 Lloyd's Rep 476
Cottage Club Estates Ltd. vs. Woodside Estate Co (Amersham) Ltd (1927) 44 TLR 20 (21)
CSNI Aerospatiale -v- Lee Kui Jak (1987) AC 871

d'

Dallhold Estates (UK) Pty Ltd. (1992) BCC 394 (in Re)

e'

Eagle Star Insurance Co. v. Yuval Insurance Company Limited (1978) 1 Lloyd's Rep 357
Everett v Hogg, Robinson & Gardner Mountain (Insurance) Ltd., (QB Com Ct) (1973) 2 Lloyd's Rep 217

f'

Finnish Marine -v- Protective National (1989) 2 LLR 99
Forsikringsaktieselkapet Vesta -v- Butcher (1989) AC 852, (1989) 1 Lloyd's Rep 331 HL

i'

Islamic Arab Insurance Co -v- Saudi Egyptian American Insurance Co (1987) 1 LLR 315

h'

Harbour Assurance Company (UK) Ltd -v- Kansa General International Insurance Company Ltd. (1992) 1 LLR 81
Hassneh Insurance Company of Israel -v- Pan Atlantic Group Incorporated and Others (1992) LLR 999

Hassneh Insurance Company and Others v. Stuart J. Mew (1993) 2 Lloyd's Rep 245

Hill & Others v. Mercantile and General Reinsurance Co. Plc. (1996) 2 Lloyd's Rep 233 (HL)

Home Insurance Co. v ADAS 2 Lloyd's Rep 674

Home Insurance Company v Administratia Asigurarilor de Stat (1983) 2 Lloyd's Rep 674

Home and Overseas Insurance Co. Ltd. v Mentor Insurance Co. Ltd (1989) 1 Lloyd's Rep 473

Hong Kong Borneo Services Co. Ltd. v. Pilcher (1992) 2 Lloyd's Rep. 593

i'

Insurance Company v. Lloyds Syndicate (1995) 1 Lloyd's Rep 272 (QB Com Ct)

j'

Jaeger v. Tolme and Runge and London Produce Clearing House Ltd (1916) 1 KB 939

l'

Leslie v Lloyds of London, No. H-90-1907, slip. op. (S.D. Res., 28 August 1995)

m'

MacShannon -v- Rockware Glass (1977) 1 WLR 376

Midland Bank Plc -v- Laker Airways Ltd (1989 1 QB 689

o'

Orion Compagnia Espanola de Seguros v. Belfort Maatschappif Voor Algemene Verzekringen (1962) 2 Lloyd's Rep 257

Overseas Insurance Company Limited v. Mentor Insurance Company UK Limited (1989) 1 Lloyd's Rep 473

Overseas Union -v- New Hampshire, Case 351/89, ECJ 27th June 1991

Overseas Union -v- New Hampshire, (1992) 1 Lloyd's Rep 218

Overseas Union Insurance Ltd. v A.A. Mutual International Insurance Co. Ltd. (1988) 2 Lloyd's Rep 63

p'

Pan Atlantic Insurance Company Limited v. Pine Top Insurance Company Limited (1992) 1 Lloyd's Rep 101 (QB Com. Court), (1993) 1 Lloyd's Rep 496 (CA)

Phoenix General of Greece v. Halvanon Insurance Company (1985) 2 Lloyd's Rep. 599

Pioneer Shipping Ltd -v- B.T.P. Tioxide Ltd., „The Nema" (1981) 2 ALL ER 1030

r'

Ramdutt Ramkissen Das v ED Sassoon & Co (1929) 98 LJPC 58

s'

Spilada Maritime Corp -v- Consulex (1986) AC 460

Stewart v. Oriental Fire (1984) 2 Lloyd's Rep. 109

S & W Berisford PLC -v- New Hampshire Insurance Company (1990) 1 LLR 454

t'

Thompson -v- Palmer (1893) 2 QB 80

Trade Indemnity Plc. -v- Försakringsaktiebolaget Njord (1995) LRLR 367 (QB)

u'

Union Insurance Company Limited (The) -v- Jubilee Insurance Company Limited (1991) 1 All ER 740

w'

West -v- National Motor and Accident Insurance Union Limited (1955) 1 Lloyd's Rep. 207

y'

Youell -v- Bland Welch (No.1) (1990) 2 Lloyd's Rep 423 and (1992) 2 Lloyd's Rep 127

Rules and Codes of practice

Insurance Brokers Registration Council's („IBRC“) Code of Conduct 1994

Reports and official papers

Civil Justice Review, Consultation Paper No. 3, Lord Chancellor's Department, The Commercial Court, November 1986

Insurance and Reinsurance Solvency Report, Issue No. 83, September 1992

The Giuliano and Lagarde Report, Commentary of the Working Group responsible for drafting the Brussels Convention, O J C 282 of 31 October 1980

The Schlosser Report, Commentary to the Lugano Convention, OJ 1979, C 59

Judicial Statistics – Annual report – 1993, A publication of the Government Statistical Service, July 1994

Report of the Commercial Court User's Conference 1962 Cmnd. 1616

Newspapers

The Times 10 August 1892

The Times 4 August 1994

The Times 6 February 1996

Press releases and briefing notes

A.R.I.A.S, Consultation Document on Arbitration Clauses, News sheet, obtainable on request from A.R.I.A.S. (UK), 7/8 Philpot Lane, London EC3M 8AA

A.R.I.A.S., Response to Consultation Document on Arbitration Clauses, Information sheet, obtainable on request from A.R.I.A.S. (UK), 7/8 Philpot Lane, London EC3M 8AA

A.R.IA.S, leaflet 1991, obtainable on request from A.R.I.A.S. (UK), 7/8 Philpot Lane, London EC3M 8AA

CLIFFORD CHANCE, *Memorandum* on "Principal methods of dispute resolution in England and Wales", London: January 1994

DAVIES ARNOLD COOPER REPORTS, Back to the Basics – Reinsurance Retro Chic, London, 1994

DAVIES ARNOLD COOPER, DAC Bulletin, Reinsurance Group, London, October 1995

LOVELL WHITE DURANT, „La procedure de 'Discovery' en matiere judiciaire devant la High Court", Client broschure, London, 1990
STEPHENSON HARWOOD, *Insurance and Reinsurance Group newsletter*, December 1994

Conference papers

BAKES, Martin, „Misrepresentation, Non-disclosure and the legal length of Pinocchio' nose", Paper presented at the 2nd Euroforum Reinsurance Coverage Dispute Strategy, 17th November 1995, The Merchant Centre, London
BANDURKA, Andrew, „The Problems of Jurisdiction: How and where to proceed", Paper for DYP reinsurance course 'Reinsurance Litigation – When to avoid it – How to win it' , 13th – 15th April 1994, London
BOUKART, Christian, „Autonomy of choice for dispute resolution", Paper presented at the BILA London Colloquium on International Insurance and Reinsurance Arbitration, 22-23 July 1996, London
CHERRY, Thomas R., „Reinsurance in the United States (Legal and Practical Aspects)", DYP Course documentation, London, 1991
EDELMAN, Colin, „Current 'soft targets' in UK Reinsurance contract wording", Paper presented at the 2nd annual Euroforum Reinsurance Dispute Strategy Conference, 17th November, 1995, The Merchant Centre, London
HANSON, John, „Reinsurance, Binding authorities, Brokers, Fronting companies & Premium Stripping", Paper presented at the 2nd annual Reinsurance coverage dispute Strategy, Euroforum Seminar, 17th November 1995, The Merchant Centre, London
HONIG, Gerard, „Role of arbitration, Position of French law on severability and *amiable compositeur*", Paper presented at the BILA London Colloquium, International and Reinsurance Arbitration, 22-23 of July 1996
SHAPLAND, Joanna, University of Sheffield, „How do lawyers accomplish cross-national lawyering?", Paper given to Law and Society Association conference, Glasgow, 10-13 July 1996
SHELDON, Richard and SEGAL, Nick, „Cross-border insolvency", Paper presented at Hawksmere Insurance and Reinsurance Insolvency Seminar, 8-9 November 1994, St James Court, London
WILKINSON, Andrew, „Alternatives to liquidation", Paper presented at the Hawksmere Insurance and Reinsurance Insolvency Seminar, 8-9 November 1994, St James' Court, London

Books

BOECKSTIEGEL, Karl-Heinz (Ed.), *Rechtsfortbildung durch Internationale Schiedsgerichtsbarkeit,* Heymann, 1989

BROWN, Anthony, *Hazard Unlimited*, London: Lloyd's of London Press Ltd, 1987

BUTLER, J.S. and MERKIN, R., *Reinsurance law*, London: Kluwer, 1986

BUTLER, J.S., *Reinsurance Practice and the Law*, London: Lloyd's of London Press Ltd., 1993, looseleaf, Service Issue No.7, 1 September 1996

von CAEMMERER, Ernst; NIKISCH, Arthur; ZWEIGERT, Konrad, (Eds.), Vom Deutschen zum Europäischen Recht, *Festschrift für Hans Dölle*, Band II, Internationales Recht, Kollisionsrecht und Internationales Zivilprozessrecht, Europäische Recht, Tübingen, 1963

CHESHIRE and NORTH, *Private International Law,* 12th edition, Butterworth, London, 1992

COLEMAN, Anthony D. and LYON, Victor, *The practice and procedure of the Commercial Court,* 4th ed., Lloyd's of London Press, 1995

DAVID, Rene, *The international Unification of Private Law, International Encyclopedia of Comparative Law,* Volume II, Chapter 5, Tübingen: Mohr / The Hague – Paris: Mouton / New York: Oceana, 1971

DEZALAY, Yves and GARTH, Bryant, *Dealing in virtue: International Commercial Arbitration and the Construction of a Transnational order,* University of Chicago Press, 1996

DICEY and MORRIS, *Conflict of Laws,* 12 ed., Vol. 1, Sweet and Maxwell, London, 1993

DICEY and MORRIS, *Conflict of Laws,* 12 ed., Vol. 2, Sweet and Maxwell, London, 1993

DICKSON, G.C.A. and STEELE; J.T., *Introduction to Insurance*, 2nd ed., London: Pitman Publishing, 1984

EDWARDS, Martin, *Careers in the Law*, Kogan Page, London, 7th ed., 1996

FRIEDMAN, Lawrence M. and MACAULY, Stewart, *Law and the Behavioural Sciences,* 2nd ed., Madison, Wisconsin, 1976

GEIGER, Theodor, *Vorstudien zu einer Soziologie des Rechts*, Neuwied: Luchterhand, 1964,

GERATHEWOHL, Klaus, *Rückversicherung Grundlagen und Praxis*, Vol. I, Karlsruhe: Verlag Versicherungswirtschaft e. V., 1976

GESSNER, Volkmar (Ed.), *Foreign Courts: Civil Litigation in Foreign Legal Cultures*, Aldershot: Dartmouth, 1996,

GESSNER, Volkmar, CEM BUDAK, Ali, (Eds.), *Cross-border Legal Interactions, Empirical Studies on the Globalisation of Law*, Forthcoming in 1997

GOLDING, C. E., *The Law and Practice of Reinsurance*, 5th ed., London: Witherby & Co. Ltd., 1987

GOODE, Roy, *Commercial Law*, 2nd. Ed., Penguin Books, London, 1995

GROSSMANN, M., *Rückversicherung – eine Einführung*, Bern, Frankfurt a. M., 1977

HALL, Geoffrey M., *Reinsurance Law Casebook*, Business & Maritime Publications Ltd, 1989

O'HARE, John and HILL, Robert N, *Civil Litigation*, 7th ed., FT Law & Tax, London, 1995

HÜBNER, Ulrich, *Rechtliche Rahmenbedingungen des Wettbewerbs in der Versicherungswirtschaft*, Baden-Baden: Nomos, 1988

JONES, Carol A. G., *Expert witnesses*, Clarendon Press, Oxford, 1994

JONES, Samantha J., *Compensating victims of mass accidents, A Socio-Legal Analysis*, Centre for Socio-Legal Studies and Pembroke College, University of Oxford, Dphil Thesis, 1992

KAPPUS, Andreas, *"Lex mercatoria" in Europa und Wiener UN- Kaufrechtskonvention 1980*, Frankfurt: Lang, 1990

KEGEL, Gerhard, *The Crisis of Conflicts of Laws*, Recueil des Cours, Hague Academy of International Law, Vol. 11 (1964)

KEGEL, Gerhard, *Internationales Privatrecht*, München, Beck, 1987

LASOK, D. and STONE, P.A., *Conflicts of Laws in the European Community*, Professional books ltd., Abingdon, Oxon, 1987

MARTIN, Elizabeth A., *A Dictionary of Law*, 3d ed., Oxford University Press, Oxford, 1994

MUSTILL, Michael J. and BOYD, Stewart C., *The Law and Practice of Commercial Arbitration in England*, 2nd ed., London and Edinburgh: Butterworth, 1989

PFEIFFER, Christoph, *Einführung in die Rückversicherung*, 4th ed., Wiesbaden: Gabler, 1994

RAPAHEAL, Adam, *The Ultimate Risk: The Inside Story of the Lloyds Catastrophe*, London: Bantam Press, 1994

SCHULTE, Andrea, *Rückversicherung in Deutschland und England: Unterschiede in Recht und Praxis*, Karlsruhe: Verlag Versicherungswirtschaft e.V., 1990

SMITH' S and KEENAN'S, *English Law*, 10th Ed., Pitman Publ., London, 1992

TEUBNER, Gunter (Ed.), *Global Law without a State*, Aldershot: Dartmouth, 1997

WEISE, Paul-Frank, *Materielles Recht vor der internationalen Handelsschiedsgerichtsbarkeit*, Frankfurt: Lang, 1989

Articles

ALZHEIMER, Alois, "Probleme der internationalen Rückversicherung", in: *Versicherungswirtschaft*, 12/71, 733-736

BAERMANN, Johannes, „Ist internationales Handelsrecht kodifizierbar ?“ in: *International Law and Economic Order*, Essays in Honour of F. Mann, 548 – 573, München, 1977

BERNSTEIN, Ronald, „Arbitration and the Courts“, in: *The Journal of the Chartered Institute of Arbitrators“*, London, February 1993, Vol. 59, No.1, 4-6

BOECKSTIEGEL, Karl-Heinz, „Die neue Schiedsgerichtsordnung der Internationalen Handelskammer“ in: *Neue Juristische Wochenzeitschrift*, 1977, 463-469

BONELL, Michael J., "Das autonome Recht des Welthandels – Rechtsdogmatische und rechtspolitsche Aspekte", in: *RabelsZ* 42 (1978), 485-506

CEM BUDAK, Ali, „The Infrastructure of cross-border debt collection: Examples in Turkey and Germany“ in: Volkmar Gessner (Ed.) *Cross-border legal Interactions*, Empirical Studies on the Globalisation of Law, Forthcoming

CORNISH, Gordon, "Some Recent Developments in English Reinsurance Law", in: *Zeitschrift für Versicherungswesen*, 21/86, 556-560

CORNISH, Gordon, "English Reinsurance Law Developments During 1994", in: *Zeitschrift für Versicherungswesen*, 21/94, 579-580

CORNISH, Gordon, „Neuere Entwickungen im englischen Rückversicherungsrecht“, *Zeitschrift für Versicherungswesen*, 21/96, 618-620

CREMADES, Bernardo and PLEHN, Steven, „The New Lex Mercatoria and the Harmonisation of the Laws of International Commercial Transactions“, in: *Boston Univ. ILJ 1984*, 317-348

CROLY, Colin and O’CONNEL Clive, „The Case for the Commercial Court“, in: *The Review*, March 1988, 40-42

CROLY, Colin and Clive O’Connel, „Trial and tribulations“, in: *The Review*, January 1988, 18-20

DOELLE-HELMS, Elke, Auf Nummer Sicher – Gigantische Schadensfälle beschleunigen die weltweite Konzentration der Rückversicherer, in: *Die Zeit*, 23. August 1996, 24

EHRICKE, Ulrich, „Zur Einführung: Grundstrukturen und Probleme der lex mercatoria“, *Juristische Schulung* 1990, 967-969

EDWARDS, Nick, „Just an illusion“, in: *Reinsurance*, Vol. 25, No. 6, Sept. 1994, 9

FELSTINER William L. F.; ABEL, Richard and SARAT, Austin „The Emergence and Transformation of Disputes: Naming, Blaming, Claiming ...“, in: *Law & Society Review,* Volume 15, Number 3-4 (1980-81), 631-653

FREYHOLD, Hanno von, „Cross-border Legal Interaction in New York Courts“, in: Volkmar Gessner (Ed.), *Foreign Courts: Civil Litigation in Foreign Legal Countries,* Aldershot: Dartmouth, 1996, 42-148

FRICK, Klaus, „The Infrastructure of cross-border payments“ in: Volkmar Gessner, Ali Cem Budak (Eds.), *Cross-border legal interactions,* Empirical Studies on the Globalization of Law, Forthcoming

GERATHEWOHL, Klaus, "The International Reinsurance Markets Today – Developments and Perspectives", in: *Versicherungswirtschaft* 14/1987, 901-910

GERATHEWOHL, Klaus, „Rückversicherung – einige praktische Aspekte der Arbeit im Ausland“, in: *Versicherungswirtschaft,* 7/1982, 376

GESSNER, Volkmar, „Kognitive Elemente sozialer Ordnung“, in: Monika Frommel, Volkmar Gessner (Eds.), *Normerosion,* Baden-Baden: Nomos 1996, 207-224

GESSNER, Volkmar, „International Cases in German First Instance Courts“, in: *Foreign Courts – Civil Litigation in Foreign Legal Countries,* Aldershot: Dartmouth, 1996, 149-208

GESSNER, Volkmar, "Global Approaches in the Sociology of Law, Problems and Challenges", in: *Journal of Law and Society*, Volume 22, No. 1, 1995, 85-96

GESSNER, Volkmar, „The Globalisation of Legal Certainty“ in: Volkmar Gessner, Ali Cem Budak (Eds.), *Cross-border legal Interactions, Empirical Studies on the Globalisation of Law,* Aldershot: Dartmouth, Forthcoming

GESSNER, Volkmar, „The Institutional Framework of Cross-border Interaction, in: Volkmar Gessner (Ed.), *Foreign Courts: Civil Litigation in Foreign Legal Cultures*, Aldershot: Dartmouth, 1996, 15-41

GESSNER, Volkmar and SCHADE, Angelika, „Conflicts of Culture in Cross-border Legal Relations: The Conception of a Research Topic in Sociology of Law“ in : *Theory, Culture & Society,* Vol. 7, 1990, 253-277

GIBB, Frances, „Disputes Bill fights off foreign rivals“, in: *The Times*, Tuesday February 1 1996

GOLDSTAJN, Aleksander, „The New Law Merchant Reconsidered“, in: Festschrift für C. Schmitthoff, München, 1973, 171-185

GOLDSTAJN, Aleksander, „The New Law Merchant“, in: *Journal of Business Law,* London, 1961, pp. 12 et sequ.

GROSSMANN -DOERTH, Hans, „Der Jurist und das autonome Recht des Welthandels“, in: *Juristische Wochenzeitschrift*, 1929, 3447-3449

GROTHEER, Kirsten, „Structures of the enforcement of cross-border maintainance claims of children“ in: Volkmar Gessner, Ali Cem Budak (Eds.) *Cross-border legal Interactions,* Empirical Studies on the Globalisation of Law, Forthcoming

GUDYKUNST William B.,“ Anxiety/ Uncertainty Management (AUM) Theory Current Status“, in: Richard L. Wiseman (Ed.), *Intercultural Communication Theory,* Thousand Oaks / London / New Delhi, Sage, 1995, 8-58

GUMBEL, H. Edward, "Auf dem Weg zu einem neuen Schiedsrecht in England", in: *Zeitschrift für Versicherungswesen*, 21/94, 575-578

GUMBEL, H. Edward, "Neue Vertriebswege und das Beispiel des britischen Versicherungsmaklers", in: *Versicherungsrecht*, 1992, Heft 31, 1293-1300

GUMBEL, H. Edward, "Englische Rechtsprechung zur Versicherungstätigkeit und Rückversicherung ausländischer Gesellschaften am Londoner Markt", in: *Zeitschrift für Versicherungswesen*, 21/86, 550-554

HALL, Stewart, „The Question of Cultural Identity“ in: *Modernity and its futures, Cambridge, 1992, 273-325*

JANNOTT, Horst K., "Rückversicherung – Einige praktische Aspekte der Arbeit im Ausland", in: *Versicherungswirtschaft* 7/1982, 376-386

KENDALL, David, "Auswirkung der neuesten englischen Rechtsprechung zu den Versicherungsnehmern obliegenden vorvertraglichen Aufklärungspflichten", in: *Zeitschrift für Versicherungswesen*, 21/94, 581-588

KRASSNER, S. D. (Ed.), „International Regimes“, quoted in John Vogler, *„Regimes and Global Commons: Space, Atmosphere and Oceans“*, in: Anthony G. McGrew, Paul G. Lewins et al., *Global Politics,* Cambridge: Polity, Press 1992

LAETSCH, Bernhard, „Rückversicherung auf neuen Wegen“, in: *Zeitschrift für Versicherungswesen*, 21/96, 572-577

LANDO, Ole, "The Lex Mercatoria in International Commercial Arbitration", in: *International and Comparative Law Quarterly*, 34 (1985), 747-768

LANGEN, Eugen, „Vom IPR zum Transnationalen Handelsrecht“, in: N*eue Juristische Wochenzeitschrift,* 1969, 358-360

LANGEN, Eugen, „Transnationales Handelsrecht“, in: *Neue Juristische Wochenzeitschrift,* 1969, 2229-2233

MACAULY, Stewart, in: Lawrence M. Friedman and Stewart Macauly, L*aw and the Behavioural Sciences,* 2nd. ed., Madison, Wisconsin, 1976, 160

Mc GREW, Anthony, „A Global Society ?“, in: M*odernity and its futures, Cambridge, 1992, 61-102*

MUSTILL, Michael J., „The New Lex Mercatoria: The First Twenty-five Years“, in: *Liber Amicorum for Lord Wilberforce*, Oxford: Clarendon Press (1987)

OLGIATTI, Vittorio, „Cross-border Litigation in Italy“, in: *Foreign Courts: Civil Litigotiation in Foreign Legal Cultures*, Alderslot: Dartmouth, 1996, 209-247

REICHERT-FACILIDES, Fritz, "Rechtsvereinheitlichung oder Rechtsvielfalt ? – Überlegungen vor dem Modell des Versicherungsvertragsrechts" in: Fritz Schwind (Ed.) *Europarecht, Internationales Privatrecht, Rechtsvergleichung*, Veröffentlichung der Kommission für Europarecht Nr. 6, Wien 1988, 155-170

SCHMIDTCHEN, Dieter, „Territorialität des Rechts, Internationales Privatrecht und die privatautonome Regelung internationaler Sachverhalte“ in: *Rabels Zeitschrift für Ausländisches und Internationales Privatrecht (RabelZ)* 59, 1995, 57-138

SCHMIDT-PRANGE, Dirk, "Katerstimmung in der Rückversicherung und wie es dazu kam", in: *Zeitschrift für Versicherungswesen*, 21/85, 572-574

SCHMITTHOFF, Clive M., "Das autonome Recht des Welthandels", in: *RabelsZ* 28 (1964), 47-77

SCHMITTHOFF, Clive M., „International Trade Law and Private International Law“, in: Festschrift für Hans Dölle, Vol. II, Internationales Recht, Kollisionsrecht und Internationales Zivilprozeßrecht, Tübingen, 1963, 257-272

SHELLEY, Toby, "Maintaining the City's global role," in: The London Underwriting Centre, One year on, *A Lloyds List Special Supplement*, London, October 1994, 9-10

THOMPSON, Hugh, „Who shall arbitrate?“, in: *Reinsurance*, September 1991, 69

THOMPSON, Hugh, „Reinsurance Dispute Resolution Internationally, in: *Asia Insurance Review*, May-June 1992, 59

YEARLEY, Steven, „Environmental Challenges“ in: *Modernity and its futures, Cambridge, 1992, 117-166*

Appendices

REINSURANCE RESEARCH PROJECT

Questionnaire

THE CENTRE FOR SOCIO-LEGAL STUDIES
UNIVERSITY OF OXFORD

ZENTRUM FUER EUROPAEISCHE RECHTSPOLITIK (ZERP)
UNIVERSITY OF BREMEN
Faculty of Law

Statement of confidentiality

All responses are strictly confidential. Replies to this questionnaire will be made anonymous and no respondent will be identified. Individual response data will not be made available to any outside organisation or agency.

Please answer the questions by circling the number of your chosen answer, ticking within the brackets or by writing in your answers in the underlined spaces provided as appropriate. Please write as much or as little as you wish – I will value any comments and information you can give me. If you come to questions that do not apply to you, or if you have no comment, simply skip them.

1. (1) What is your **main current field** ?
   reinsurance law ( ) insurance law ( ) marine insurance law ( )

   (2) For **how many years** have you been working in this field ?
   (______) years

2. On average, how many files do you open per year ?
   (______) files

3. (1) How many of the files that you open per years are cross-border (international), in respect to the parties involved or the fact of the case ?
   (______) files or (______) %

   (2) In how many of the cross-border files do disputes arise about the **applicable law** ?
   (______) files or (______) %

4. How often do the **general legal problems** listed below arise in the cases you deal with ?

   * **disputes over definition** of reinsurance in the contract
   (__) cases or (__) %
   * **disputes relating to formation of reinsurance contract**
   – misrepresentation (__) cases or (__) %
   – non-disclosure (__) cases or (__) %
   – other ______________________ (__) cases or (__) %
   * **disputes arising from the reinsurance contract itself**
   – duties of the parties (general) (__) cases or (__) %
   – cover of the reinsurance contract (__) cases or (__) %
   – other ______________________ (__) cases or (__) %
   * **disputes relating to the duties or functions of intermediaries**
   – brokers (__) cases or (__) %
   – agents (__) cases or (__) %

* **disputes relating to** (__) cases or (__) %
- conflicts of law (__) cases or (__) %
- liquidation (__) cases or (__) %
- run-off (__) cases or (__) %

5. On average, how many files do you open per year in which **Lloyds** is involved ?

(__) files or (__) %

6. Reinsurance contracts are either proportional or non-proportional; or treaty contracts or facultative contracts. Do you associate any particular legal problems with the

proportional treaty contract: ____________________

non-proportional treaty contract: ____________________

proportional facultative contract: ____________________

non-proportional facultative contract: ____________________

7. On average, how many files do you open per year that do not relate to a reinsurance contract but to **agreements covering other fields of service that reinsurers provide to insurers**, e. g. assistance in calculating premiums, making damage statistics available to them etc. ?

(____) cases or (____) %

8. What factors contribute to disputes in the reinsurance business ?
Please rank in order of importance – **1 (very important), 2 (important), 3 (less important), 4 (not important).**

bad underwriting policy **1 2 3 4**

badly drafted contracts **1 2 3 4**

other factors, namely ____________ **1 2 3 4**

9. Who most often **drafts** the reinsurance contracts and the service agreements between reinsurer and the reinsured ?

reinsurer ( ) reinsured ( ) brokers ( ) outside lawyers ( )

10. Could you enumerate the established factors which contribute to **conflict avoidance** in the reinsurance business, e.g. standard contracts ? If you think there are none, can you explain why ?

____

____

11. **Reinsurance conflicts** are solved by **negotiation**, **arbitration** and the **courts**. In your practice how many conflicts on average per year in relation to the numbers of the files you open

are settled by negotiation before proceedings	(__) conflicts or (__) %
are settled during arbitration proceedings	(__) conflicts or (__) %
end with an arbitration award	(__) conflicts or (__) %
are settled during court proceedings	(__) conflicts or (__) %
end with a court decision	(__) conflicts or (__) %

12. Can you say which factors cause a case to move from negotiation to arbitration or legal proceedings ?

____

____

13. What are the main arbitration institutions for the resolution of disputes in the reinsurance business ? If listing more than one, list in the order you consider effective ?

____

14. The following factors are frequently put forward as being the reason for arbitration being the preferred conflict resolution system compared to courts in the reinsurance business. Please rank the reasons which determine your choice, **1 (very important), 2 (important), 3 (less important), 4 (not important).** Add others if you wish.

specialist expertise of the arbitrators	**1 2 3 4**
lower costs of arbitration proceedings compared to court proceedings	**1 2 3 4**
speed of determination, including finality	**1 2 3 4**
privacy	**1 2 3 4**
other, namely ____________________	**1 2 3 4**

15. Are there **any changes** which you would like to see in the arbitration process or outcomes ?

16. London is often chosen as a place of arbitration and of jurisdiction for reinsurance disputes even though neither the parties nor the facts of the case relate to the UK. Can you explain why ?

____

____

17. (1) Do you consider that arbitration relates more to **market practice and equity** than strictly applied law ?
yes ( )   no ( )

(2) Can you name the **market practices** relating to reinsurance law you consider to be **most often cited by arbitrators** in your cases ?

____

____

18. Do you think it is justified to speak of reinsurance law as a law merchant?
yes ( )   no ( )
because _______________

19. The Reinsurance and Insurance Arbitration Society (A.R.I.AS) is trying to decide if the market wants publication of the effect of those arbitration awards which deal with general industry practice.

(1) Is your firm a member of A.R.I.A.S   yes ( )   no ( )

(2) Is your firm a member of any other arbitration institution ?
yes _______   no ( )

(3) Would you favour the publication of awards as intended by A.R.I.A.S
yes, because _______________________
no, because _______________________

20. (1) Do you exchange **arbitration awards** in which you have been involved with colleagues of other firms ?
yes ( )   no, but _______________

(2) Do you cite other arbitration awards at an arbitration hearing ?
yes ( )   no ( )

21.(1) Can you make out a connection between the economic health of the reinsurance business and the level of reinsurance disputes and /or the method of resolution selected ?
yes ( )   no ( )

(2) If so, can you **exemplify this connection** over the last decade ?

____

____

22. Does a **run-off situation** to any extent harm the value of arbitration clauses, namely have you experienced a stronger tendency for parties to avoid arbitration in favour of legal proceedings ?
yes, this can be proven by ______________________________
no ( )

23.(1) Do you consider special economic expertise in the reinsurance business to be a prerequisite in dealing with the legal aspects of it ?
yes ( ) no ( )

(2) If not a prerequisite, is such economic expertise of assistance ?
yes ( ) no ( )

(3) If you have such expertise, how did you acquire it ?

____

Appendix II: Outline of the English Court system[388]

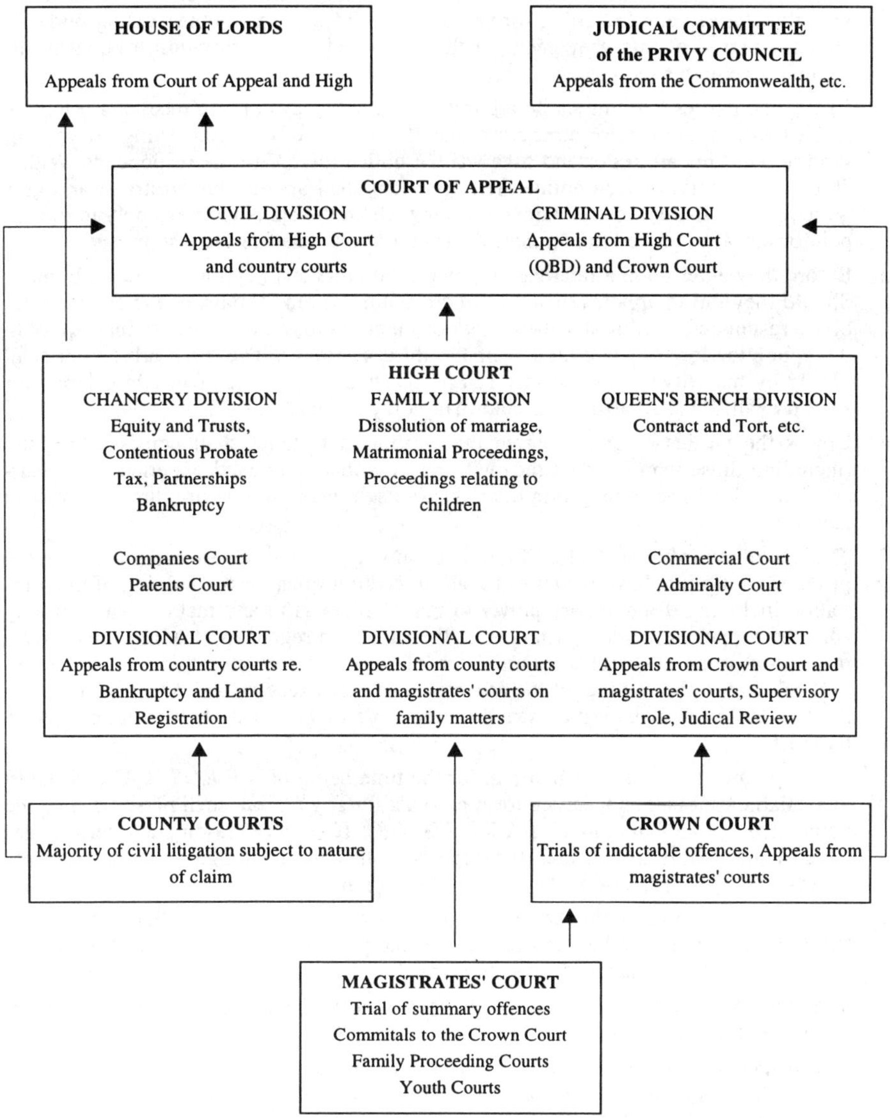

388 This survey is taken from Judicial Statistics – Annual Report – 1993, July 1994, p. 3

Appendix III: Recommended Arbitration Clause

1. All matters in difference between the parties arising under, out of or in connection with this Agreement, including formation and validity, and whether arising under or after the period of this Agreement, shall be referred to an arbitration tribunal in the manner hereinafter set out.
2. Unless the parties appoint a sole arbitrator within 14 days of one receiving a written request from the other for arbitration, the claimant (the party requesting arbitration) shall appoint his arbitrator and give written notice thereof to the respondent. Within 30 days of receiving such notice the respondent shall appoint his arbitrator and give written notice thereof to the claimant, failing which the claimant may apply to the appointor hereafter named to nominate an arbitrator on behalf of the respondent.
3. Before they enter upon a reference the two arbitrators shall appoint a third arbitrator. Should they fail to appoint such a third arbitrator, within 30 days of the appointment of the respondent's arbitrator then either of them or either of the parties may apply to the appointor for the appointment of the third arbitrator. The three arbitrators shall decide by majority. If no majority can be reached the verdict of the third arbitrator shall prevail. He shall also act as chairman of the tribunal.
4. Unless the parties otherwise agree the arbitration tribunal shall consist of person (including those who have retired) with not less than ten years' experience of insurance and reinsurance engaged in the industry itself or as lawyers or other professional advisers.
5. The arbitration tribunal shall, so far as is permissible under the law and practice of the place of arbitration, have power to fix all procedural rules for the holding of the arbitration including discretionary power to make orders as to any matters which it may consider proper in the circumstances of the case with regard to pleadings, discovery, inspection of the documents, examination of witnesses and any other matter whatsoever relating to the conduct of the arbitration and may receive and act upon such evidence whether oral or written strictly admissible or not as it shall in its discretion think fit.
6. The appointor shall be the Chairman for the time being of *A.R.I.A.S (UK)* or if he in unavailable or it is inappropriate for him to act for any reason, such person as may be nominated by the Committee of *A.R.I. A.S.(UK).* If for any reason such persons decline or are unable to act, then the appointor shall be the Judge of the appropriate Courts having jurisdiction at the place of arbitration.
7. All costs of the arbitration shall be determined by the arbitration tribunal who may, taking into account the law and practice of the place of arbitration, direct to and by whom and in which manner they shall be paid.
8. The place of arbitration may be chosen by the parties, but in default of such choice, the place of arbitration shall be London.
9. The proper law of this Agreement shall be the law of .....; in default of an express choice, the proper law of this Agreement shall be the law of the country with which it is most closely connected.
10. The award of the tribunal shall be in writing and binding upon the parties who consent to carry out the same.

EXHIBIT:

Writ of Trade Indemnity Plc. and others v.
Försakringsaktiebolaget Njord (1995) LRL 367

IN THE HIGH COURT OF JUSTICE 1993 FOLIO 267

QUEEN'S BENCH DIVISION

COMMERCIAL COURT

B E T W E E N :

(1) TRADE INDEMNITY P.L.C.
(2) NORWICH WINTERTHUR REINSURANCE CORPORATION LIMITED
(3) ALLSTATE REINSURANCE COMPANY LIMITED
(4) UNIONE ITALIANA (UK) REINSURANCE COMPANY LIMITED
(5) RIVER THAMES INSURANCE COMPANY LIMITED
(6) HANSA GENERAL INSURANCE COMPANY (UK) LIMITED
(7) TOKIO REINSURANCE COMPANY LIMITED
(8) ASSICURAZIONI GENERALI S.p.A.
(9) TIMOTHY JOHN LLEWELYN DAVIES (acting on his own behalf and in a representative capacity on behalf of all members of Lloyds Syndicate No.965)
(10) NIPPON INSURANCE COMPANY OF EUROPE LIMITED
(11) TERRA NOVA INSURANCE COMPANY LIMITED
(12) ENGLISH AND AMERICAN INSURANCE CO. LTD.
(13) FUJI INTERNATIONAL INSURANCE CO. LTD.
(formerly known as Fuji Fire & Marine Insurance Co. Ltd)
(14) METROPOLITAN REINSURANCE COMPANY (UK) LTD
(15) CITY INTERNATIONAL INSURANCE COMPANY LTD
(formerly known as City Insurance Company (UK) Ltd
(16) THE INSURANCE CORPORATION OF SINGAPORE (UK) LTD
(17) ROYAL REINSURANCE CO. LTD

Plaintiffs

– and –

SUPREME COURT OF JUDICATURE 17 FEB 1993 ADMIRALTY & COMMERCIAL REGISTRY

FORSAKRINGSAKTIEBOLAGET NJORD
(in liquidation)

WRIT OF SUMMONS

TO THE DEFENDANTS: Forsakringsaktiebolaget Njord of Box 14240, S-104 40 Stockholm, Strandvagen 5 A, 4tr., Sweden or elsewhere in Sweden.

THIS WRIT OF SUMMONS has been issued against you by the above-named Plaintiffs in respect of the claim set out below.

Within 21 days after the service of this Writ on you, counting the day of service, you must either satisfy the claim or return to the Court Office mentioned below the accompanying ACKNOWLEDGEMENT OF SERVICE stating therein whether you intend to contest these proceedings.

If you fail to satisfy the claim or to return the acknowledgement within the time stated, or if you return the Acknowledgement without the time stated, or if you return the Acknowledgement without stating therein an intention to contest the proceedings, the Plaintiffs may proceed with the action and judgement may be entered against you forthwith without further notice.

Issued from the Admiralty and Commercial Registry this day of February 1993.

NOTE– This Writ may not be served later than 4 calendar months (*or, if leave is required to effect service out of the jurisdiction, 6 months*) beginning with that date unless renewed by order of the Court.

IMPORTANT

Directions for Acknowledgement of Service are given with the accompanying form.

The Plaintiff's claim is for:

(1) A declaration that the First to Sixteenth Plaintiffs are entitled to cancel and avoid a contract of bond and credit surplus treaty reinsurance between themselves as reinsurers and the Defendants as reinsureds for risks attaching on or after 1st January 1990 by reason of the Defendants' failure to disclose and/or non-disclosure and/or misrepresentation of matters material to the First to Sixteenth Plaintiffs and to their effecting of the said contract of treaty reinsurance, which contract was contained in and/or evidenced by a Bond and Credit Surplus Treaty reinsurance slip no. CP 6090.S issued in London by Heath Fielding Reinsurance Broking Limited ("Heath Fielding") and signed down in London by the First to Sixteenth Plaintiffs and/or a Cover Note no CP 6090.S issued by Heath Fielding and dated 12th February 1990.

(2) A declaration that the First to Tenth and Seventeenth Plaintiffs are entitled to cancel and avoid a contract of bond and credit surplus treaty reinsurance between themselves as reinsurers and the Defendants as reinsured for risks attaching on or after 1st January 1991 by reason of the Defendants' failure to disclose and/or non-disclosure and/or misrepresentation of matters material to the First to Tenth and Seventeenth Plaintiffs and their effecting of the said contract of treaty reinsurance, which contract was contained in and/or evidenced by a Bond and Credit Surplus Treaty reinsurance slip no. CP 6090.T issued in London by Heath Fielding and signed in London by the First to Tenth and Seventeenth Plaintiffs and/or by a Cover Note no. CP 6090.T issued by Heath Fielding and dated 14th February 1991. ("the 1991 contract of reinsurance").

(3) A declaration that the First to Sixteenth Plaintiffs' cancellation and avoidance of the 1990 contract of reinsurance and the First to Tenth and Seventeenth Plaintiffs' cancellation and avoidance of the 1991 contract of reinsurance by the letter dated 14th July 1992 of their solicitors, Messrs. Clyde & Co., on their behalf to the Defendants were and are valid and effective cancellations and avoidances of the said contracts and that First to Sixteenth Plaintiffs and First to Tenth and Seventeenth Plaintiffs, accordingly, are not liable to the Defendants thereunder.

(4) An order for the repayment by the Defendants of all claims paid by First to Sixteenth Plaintiffs under the 1990 contract of reinsurance and by the First to Tenth and Seventeenth Plaintiffs under the 1991 contract of reinsurance

less premiums paid thereunder to First to Sixteenth Plaintiffs and the First to Tenth and Seventeenth Plaintiffs by the Defendants.

(5) Further or alternatively, an order for the taking of an account between First to Sixteenth Plaintiffs and the First to Tenth and Seventeenth Plaintiffs and the Defendants in respect of claims paid less premiums paid under the 1990 and 1991 contracts of reinsurance and an order for the repayment by the Defendants to First to Sixteenth Plaintiffs and the First to Tenth and Seventeenth Plaintiffs as aforesaid of the balance of claims paid left after deduction of premiums paid.

(6) Further or other relief.

(7) Costs.

THIS WRIT was issued by Clyde & Co., of Beaufort House, Chertsey Street, Guildford, Surrey GU1 4HA (Ref. RGB/J.296)
Solicitor for the said Plaintiffs whose addresses are

First Plaintiff:	27 Leadenhall Street, London, EC3A 1AA
Second Plaintiff:	40 Lime Street, London, EC3M 5BH
Third Plaintiff:	Fountain House, 130 Fenchurch Street, London, EC3M 5AU
Fourth Plaintiff:	UIR House, 118/119 Fenchurch Street, London, EC3M 5BA
Fifth Plaintiff:	America House, 2 America Square, London, EC3N 2RT
Sixth Plaintiff:	Fountain House, 130 Fenchurch Street, London, EC3M 5DS
Seventh Plaintiff:	120 Fenchurch Street, London, EC3M 5BA
Eight Plaintiff:	117 Fenchurch Street, London, EC3M 5DY
Ninth Plaintiff:	110-2 Fenchurch Street, London, EC3M 5NE
Tenth Plaintiff:	Three Quays, Tower Hill, London, EC3R 6 DS
Eleventh Plaintiff:	Fountain House, 130 Fenchurch Street, London, EC3M 5DJ
Twelfth Plaintiff:	Three Quays, Tower Hill, London, EC3R 6DS
Thirteenth Plaintiff:	Three Quays, Tower Hill, London, EC3R 6DS
Fourteenth Plaintiff:	Three Quays, Tower Hill, London, EC3R 6DS
Fifteenth Plaintiff:	Three Quays, Tower Hill, London, EC3R 6DS
Sixteenth Plaintiff:	Three Quays, Tower Hill, London, EC3R 6DS
Seventeenth Plaintiff:	24b Lime Street, London, EC3M 7ND